EARLY CHILDHOOD EDUCATION SERIES
Leslie R. Williams, Editor

ADVISORY BOARD: Barbara T. Bowman, Harriet K. Cuffaro, Stephanie Feeney, Doris Pronin Fromberg, Celia Genishi, Stacie G. Goffin, Dominic F. Gullo, Alice Sterling Honig, Elizabeth Jones, Gwen Morgan

In the Spirit of the Studio:
Learning from the *Atelier* of Reggio Emilia
LELLA GANDINI, LYNN T. HILL, LOUISE BOYD CADWELL,
& CHARLES SCHWALL, EDS.

Understanding Assessment and Evaluation in Early
Childhood Education, 2nd Edition
DOMINIC F. GULLO

Negotiating Standards in the Primary Classroom:
The Teacher's Dilemma
CAROL ANNE WIEN

Teaching and Learning in a Diverse World:
Multicultural Education for Young Children,
3rd Edition
PATRICIA G. RAMSEY

The Emotional Development of Young Children:
Building an Emotion-Centered Curriculum,
2nd Edition
MARILOU HYSON

Effective Partnering for School Change: Improving
Early Childhood Education in Urban Classrooms
JIE-QI CHEN & PATRICIA HORSCH WITH
KAREN DEMOSS & SUZANNE L. WAGNER

Let's Be Friends: Peer Competence and Social
Inclusion in Early Childhood Programs
KRISTEN MARY KEMPLE

Young Children Continue to Reinvent Arithmetic—
2nd Grade, 2nd Edition
CONSTANCE KAMII

Major Trends and Issues in Early Childhood Education:
Challenges, Controversies, and Insights, 2nd Edition
JOAN PACKER ISENBERG & MARY RENCK JALONGO, EDS.

The Power of Projects: Meeting Contemporary
Challenges in Early Childhood Classrooms—
Strategies and Solutions
JUDY HARRIS HELM & SALLEE BENEKE, EDS.

Bringing Learning to Life: The Reggio Approach to
Early Childhood Education
LOUISE BOYD CADWELL

The Colors of Learning: Integrating the Visual Arts
into the Early Childhood Curriculum
ROSEMARY ALTHOUSE, MARGARET H. JOHNSON,
& SHARON T. MITCHELL

A Matter of Trust: Connecting Teachers and Learners
in the Early Childhood Classroom
CAROLLEE HOWES & SHARON RITCHIE

Widening the Circle: Including Children with
Disabilities in Preschool Programs
SAMUEL L. ODOM, ED.

Children with Special Needs:
Lessons for Early Childhood Professionals
MARJORIE J. KOSTELNIK, ESTHER ETSUKO ONAGA,
BARBARA ROHDE, & ALICE PHIPPS WHIREN

Developing Constructivist Early Childhood
Curriculum: Practical Principles and Activities
RHETA DEVRIES, BETTY ZAN, CAROLYN HILDEBRANDT,
REBECCA EDMIASTON, & CHRISTINA SALES

Outdoor Play: Teaching Strategies with Young Children
JANE PERRY

Embracing Identities in Early Childhood Education:
Diversity and Possibilities
SUSAN GRIESHABER & GAILE S. CANNELLA, EDS.

Bambini:
The Italian Approach to Infant/Toddler Care
LELLA GANDINI & CAROLYN POPE EDWARDS, EDS.

Educating and Caring for Very Young Children:
The Infant/Toddler Curriculum
DORIS BERGEN, REBECCA REID, & LOUIS TORELLI

Young Investigators:
The Project Approach in the Early Years
JUDY HARRIS HELM & LILIAN G. KATZ

Serious Players in the Primary Classroom:
Empowering Children Through Active Learning
Experiences, 2nd Edition
SELMA WASSERMANN

Telling a Different Story:
Teaching and Literacy in an Urban Preschool
CATHERINE WILSON

Young Children Reinvent Arithmetic:
Implications of Piaget's Theory, 2nd Edition
CONSTANCE KAMII

Managing Quality in Young Children's Programs:
The Leader's Role
MARY L. CULKIN, ED.

(continued)

Early Childhood Education Series titles, continued

Supervision in Early Childhood Education:
A Developmental Perspective, 2nd Edition
JOSEPH J. CARUSO & M. TEMPLE FAWCETT

The Early Childhood Curriculum:
A Review of Current Research, 3rd Edition
CAROL SEEFELDT, ED.

Leadership in Early Childhood:
The Pathway to Professionalism, 2nd Edition
JILLIAN RODD

Inside a Head Start Center:
Developing Policies from Practice
DEBORAH CEGLOWSKI

Windows on Learning:
Documenting Young Children's Work
JUDY HARRIS HELM, SALLEE BENEKE, &
KATHY STEINHEIMER

Bringing Reggio Emilia Home: An Innovative
Approach to Early Childhood Education
LOUISE BOYD CADWELL

Master Players: Learning from Children at Play
GRETCHEN REYNOLDS & ELIZABETH JONES

Understanding Young Children's Behavior:
A Guide for Early Childhood Professionals
JILLIAN RODD

Understanding Quantitative and Qualitative Research
in Early Childhood Education
WILLIAM L. GOODWIN & LAURA D. GOODWIN

Diversity in the Classroom: New Approaches to the
Education of Young Children, 2nd Edition
FRANCES E. KENDALL

Developmentally Appropriate Practice in "Real Life"
CAROL ANNE WIEN

Experimenting with the World:
John Dewey and the Early Childhood Classroom
HARRIET K. CUFFARO

Quality in Family Child Care and Relative Care
SUSAN KONTOS, CAROLLEE HOWES,
MARYBETH SHINN, & ELLEN GALINSKY

Using the Supportive Play Model: Individualized
Intervention in Early Childhood Practice
MARGARET K. SHERIDAN, GILBERT M. FOLEY,
& SARA H. RADLINSKI

The Full-Day Kindergarten:
A Dynamic Themes Curriculum, 2nd Edition
DORIS PRONIN FROMBERG

Assessment Methods for Infants and Toddlers:
Transdisciplinary Team Approaches
DORIS BERGEN

Young Children Continue to Reinvent Arithmetic—
3rd Grade: Implications of Piaget's Theory
CONSTANCE KAMII WITH SALLY JONES LIVINGSTON

Moral Classrooms, Moral Children: Creating a
Constructivist Atmosphere in Early Education
RHETA DEVRIES & BETTY ZAN

Diversity and Developmentally Appropriate Practices
BRUCE L. MALLORY & REBECCA S. NEW, EDS.

Changing Teaching, Changing Schools:
Bringing Early Childhood Practice into Public
Education–Case Studies from the Kindergarten
FRANCES O'CONNELL RUST

Physical Knowledge in Preschool Education:
Implications of Piaget's Theory
CONSTANCE KAMII & RHETA DEVRIES

Ways of Assessing Children and Curriculum:
Stories of Early Childhood Practice
CELIA GENISHI, ED.

The Play's the Thing: Teachers' Roles in Children's Play
ELIZABETH JONES & GRETCHEN REYNOLDS

Scenes from Day Care
ELIZABETH BALLIETT PLATT

Making Friends in School:
Promoting Peer Relationships in Early Childhood
PATRICIA G. RAMSEY

The Whole Language Kindergarten
SHIRLEY RAINES & ROBERT CANADY

Multiple Worlds of Child Writers:
Friends Learning to Write
ANNE HAAS DYSON

The Good Preschool Teacher
WILLIAM AYERS

The War Play Dilemma
NANCY CARLSSON-PAIGE & DIANE E. LEVIN

The Piaget Handbook for Teachers and Parents
ROSEMARY PETERSON & VICTORIA FELTON-COLLINS

Visions of Childhood
JOHN CLEVERLEY & D. C. PHILLIPS

Starting School
NANCY BALABAN

Ideas Influencing Early Childhood Education
EVELYN WEBER

The Joy of Movement in Early Childhood
SANDRA R. CURTIS

In the Spirit of the Studio

Learning from the *Atelier* of Reggio Emilia

EDITED BY

Lella Gandini, Lynn Hill, Louise Cadwell,
and Charles Schwall

FOREWORD BY
Vea Vecchi

Teachers College
Columbia University
New York and London

Cover design by Pam Bliss.

Front cover photograph by Charles Schwall.

Back cover photograph by Cathy Topal.

Cover, title page, and chapter heading drawings by children from schools featured in this book in Blacksburg, Virginia; Northampton, Massachusetts; St. Louis, Missouri; and Reggio Emilia, Italy.

Published by Teachers College Press, 1234 Amsterdam Avenue, New York, NY 10027

Library of Congress Cataloging-in-Publication Data

In the spirit of the studio : learning from the atelier of Reggio Emilia / edited by
    Lella Gandini . . . [et al.].
      p.   cm. — (Early childhood education series)
    Includes bibliographical references and index.
    ISBN 0-8077-4591-X (pbk. : alk. paper)
      1. Art—Study and teaching (Early childhood)—United States—Case studies.
    2. Art—Study and teaching (Early childhood)—Italy—Reggio Emilia—Case
    studies. 3. Early childhood education—Curricula—United States—Case studies.
    4. Early childhood education—Curricula—Italy—Reggio Emilia—Case studies.
    5. Educational innovations—United States—Case studies. 6. Educational inno-
    vations—Italy—Reggio Emilia—Case studies. I. Gandini, Lella. II. Early child-
    hood education series (Teachers College Press)
    LB1139.5.A78I52   2005
    372.5—dc22   2004058888

ISBN 0-8077-4591-X   (paper)

Printed on acid-free paper
Manufactured in the United States of America

12 11 10 09 08 07 06 05   8 7 6 5 4 3 2 1

We dedicate our work to you who hold this book in your hands. You are a part of a great collaborative community of educators all over the world who are creating new and vital visions of learning and teaching. May this book both honor your courage and sustain your efforts.

—Lella, Lynn, Louise, and Chuck

Contents

Foreword   ix
Vea Vecchi

Acknowledgments   xi

1   The Context and Inspiration of Our Work   1
Lella Gandini, Lynn Hill, Louise Cadwell, and Charles Schwall

2   From the Beginning of the *Atelier* to Materials as Languages:
Conversations from Reggio Emilia   6
Lella Gandini

3   The *Atelier* Environment and Materials   16
Charles Schwall

4   Experiences from a First *Atelier* in the United States:
Conversations with Amelia Gambetti and Jennifer Azzariti   32
Lella Gandini

5   Melting Geography: Reggio Emilia, Memories, and Place   47
Barbara Burrington

6   The Essential Voices of the Teachers:
Conversations from Reggio Emilia   58
Lella Gandini

7   Border Crossings and Lessons Learned:
The Evolution of an *Atelier*   73
Lynn Hill

8   The Role of the *Atelierista*: Conversations from Reggio Emilia   94
Lella Gandini

9   Voices from the Studio: Stories of Transformation   107
Pauline M. Baker, Patricia Hunter-McGrath, Cathy Weisman Topal,
and Lauren Monaco

10   The Evolution of the *Atelier*: Conversations from Reggio Emilia   133
Lella Gandini

11   The *Atelier*: A System of Physical and Conceptual Spaces   144
Louise Cadwell, Lori Geismar Ryan, and Charles Schwall

12   The Whole School as an *Atelier*: Reflections by Carla Rinaldi   169
Edited by Lella Gandini

13   Pedagogical Patterns   175
Ashley Cadwell

Epilogue   195
The Editors

Glossary   197

About the Editors and Contributors   201

Index   205

Foreword

A book that is intended to reveal the meaning of the *atelier* in the world of schools and learning gives me nothing but joy and receives my warmest support. I am convinced that including an *atelier* within the school curriculum and within a cultural context that considers the expressive languages just as essential as (instead of optional or marginal to) the academic disciplines that are currently privileged can render both the learning experience and the process of education more complete and more whole.

I am further convinced that the specific structure of the languages used in the *atelier* (visual, musical, and others) weaves together emotions and empathy with rationality and cognition in a natural and inseparable way. This weaving together in turn favors the construction of the imagination and a richer approach to reality, and it can contribute to the formation of a wider and more articulate perspective on learning. I think these concepts are an essential part of the foundation for further reflections.

The connections and interweavings among different disciplines with the languages of the *atelier* often produce, in our projects, a shift in established points of view and favor a more complex approach to problems revealing the expressive, empathic, and aesthetic elements that are inherent in any discipline or specific problem. Therefore, it is not surprising that the integration of digital technologies has had a different impact in the preschools of Reggio Emilia from that in most other schools: this experience has been rich in imagination, a stimulus to socialization, and full of merriment.

I am fully aware that it seems ingenuous to suppose that it would be sufficient to introduce an *atelier* and an *atelierista* into a school and expect that everything would automatically be transformed and enriched. Such a transformation can take place, in my view, only if the entire educational program is based on rich and vital bases of learning and teaching. Furthermore, I believe that for the *atelier* to fulfill its role efficaciously today, work needs to be done deliberately in four areas.

First, we have to consider that the art world often has the function of stimulus; it suggests new concepts to explore and to elaborate, offering us poetic, nonconformist views and unconventional interpretations of reality. Therefore, I believe that it must continue to be one of the primary sources of inquiry and inspiration in schools, as long as we make sure that the children and young people remain the protagonists of their personal itineraries. We do not want to place them in a culturally marginal position with regard to very complex artistic events emerging from sophisticated cultures often from distant contexts. It is important not to absorb only the formal part of works of art, as often happens, but instead to work on ideas and concentrate attention on the concepts that generated the work of art.

Second, we have to render evident and visible, through observation and documentation, the vital interweaving of cognitive and imaginative ways of knowing. We must also reveal the personal as well as the social elements that are a part of every representation that is supported by vital teaching and learning. At the same time, it is necessary to render the contribution the *atelier* gives to the development of projects carried out in other disciplines more visible—that is, knowingly carried out and documented.

Third, we have to give closer attention to the processes of learning through the digital media, a subject still little explored with children. The digital experience is much too often exhausted simply in its functional and technical form. However, in addition to its technical aspect, if it is also used in creative and imaginative ways, it reveals a high level of expressive, cognitive, and social potential as well as great possibilities for evolution. It is necessary to reflect on and better comprehend the changes that the digital language introduces in the processes of understanding. We have to be aware of what this adds, takes away, or modifies in today's learning. The presence and the contribution of the *atelier* can be surprisingly innovative in the approach to and exploration of the digital material, as some experiences that have taken place over the last several years in our schools demonstrate.

The fourth and last aspect to consider is the relationship of the schools with the city. It is a relationship that the communicative structure of the *atelier* can greatly support by constructing contexts for dialogue, visibility, and knowledge about the culture of young children and schoolchildren. It is a culture that, if correctly received and recognized, can contribute more than commonly thought to a radical reconsideration of the city and to an improvement in the quality of life.

Above all, the *atelier* brings the strength and joy of the unexpected and the uncommon to the process of learning; it supports a conceptual change that comes from looking through a poetic lens at everyday reality. This is what some define as an "aesthetic project" but in fact is a biological process that evidently belongs to our species. This process, in its apparent levity, is capable of unhinging many commonplace events and banalities, and of giving back relevance and centrality to aspects of life and thought that are often not given enough importance by the greater part of school and social culture. This is because they pertain to unpredictable processes, not easily measurable or easily controllable. However, they reveal themselves to be indispensable for the birth of cultural events that make us grow and move forward, and without which our life would be less full and less interesting.

—Vea Vecchi
Reggio Emilia, Italy

Acknowledgments

First and foremost, we thank the educators in Reggio Emilia for their dedication in realizing and evolving an educational experience that has given teachers all over the world lifelong inspiration and courage to work for something new and bold for children and families in each of our own unique contexts. We thank them for their enormous generosity in contributing such valuable and substantial reflections to this book as well as for providing beautiful visual images of their work. In particular, we thank Loris Malaguzzi, who died in 1994, as well as Carla Rinaldi, Amelia Gambetti, Tiziana Filippini, Vea Vecchi, Giovanni Piazza, Mara Davoli, Laura Rubizzi, Paola Barchi, Lucia Colla, Isabella Mennino, and Barbara Quinti.

We are equally indebted to the contributors from North America who have worked hard to realize the evolution of their work that they write about in the following pages. We thank Pauline Baker, Cathy Weisman Topal, Lauren Monaco, Patricia Hunter-McGrath, Jennifer Azzariti, and Ashley Cadwell for their collaboration and essential contributions to this book. In addition to contributing their own strong chapters, we thank Barbara Burrington and Lori Geismar Ryan for their generous and skilled editorial help with several others. We are all forever grateful to those colleagues with whom we and our contributing authors have worked side by side and day by day in each of our respective settings who share our commitment to this work and who are often central characters in the stories that we tell here. In particular, we thank all the members of the St. Louis–Reggio Collaborative—in particular, teachers Karen Schneider and Melissa Guerra. Other powerful, inspirational teachers from Virginia are remembered for their courage and their ability to continue the journey: Kelly Wells, Kristi Snyder, Gretchen Distler, Christine McCartney, Sara Smidl, Mindy Mottley, Jennifer Brugh, Angi Primavera, Victoria Fu, Andrew Stremmel, and Charles Flickinger.

We thank the *atelieristi* of the first networking group who met in Boulder, Colorado, at the first conference for *atelieristi* hosted by the Boulder Journey School in 2000. As this book was taking shape, a group of us presented at the National Association for Early Childhood Education Conference in 2002 in New York, and then in Chicago in 2003. In fact, the challenge to write this book grew out of lively and constructive conversations in 2002 among a large group of North American *atelieristi* at a glass studio in Brooklyn, New York.

We are enormously grateful to our families for their sustaining support and encouragement. We thank both friends and family for reading parts and whole sections of our manuscript and offering invaluable suggestions, in particular Lester Little; Jill Downen; Ashley Cadwell; Scott, Katie, and Meg Hill; and Ernest Thomas. We thank Judy Kaminsky, who helped us edit Chapter 12 by Carla Rinaldi, and Tina Cancemi, Gulia Ceccacci, and Laura Detti for help with translating and transcribing the Italian interviews. Susan Liddicoat has been a dream editor. We feel as if we have become a team of five as we work on the final stages of preparing the manuscript. We are grateful to all the staff that we have worked with at Teachers College Press for their kindness and skill, and to Pam Bliss for designing our cover. Thank you, as well, to Wyatt Wade of Davis Publishing for his creativity, time, and energy on behalf of this book.

We conclude our acknowledgments with enormous gratitude and admiration for all the children from Italy and North America who live within the words and images of the narrative and landscape of this book.

As we work together on the last phase of putting these chapters together in Lella's home in Northampton, Massachusetts, the sun shines in the bluest of skies on a crisp and perfect New England fall day. So finally, it is with the spirit of collaboration with which we began that we thank each other for the privilege of working together toward such a beautiful result.

The Context and Inspiration of Our Work

Lella Gandini, Lynn Hill,
Louise Cadwell, and
Charles Schwall

I will not hide from you how much hope we invested in the introduction of the *atelier*. We knew it would be impossible to ask for anything more. Yet, if we could have done so we would have gone further still by creating a school made entirely of laboratories similar to the *atelier*. We would have constructed a new type of school made of spaces where the hands of children could be active for messing about. With no possibility of boredom, hands and minds would engage each other with great, liberating merriment in a way ordained by biology and evolution. (Malaguzzi, 1998, pp. 73–74)

In many ways, this book on the development of the ***atelier*** in North America is an exploration into uncharted territory. It is the first book of its kind focused specifically on the values and climate for learning inspired by the Reggio Emilia *atelier* that Loris Malaguzzi invokes in the quote. As such, we see this book as an invitation to look at things as if they could be otherwise. We believe that the act of looking deeply and seeing things in a new way has the potential to restructure and reform our teaching and learning experiences. The *atelier,* or studio (as it is often referred to in North America), is at once an idea and a place that has initiated this kind of transformation.

The transformation in teaching and learning in North America that we and others will describe in this book has its roots in the experience of the municipally funded preschools and early childhood centers of the northern Italian town of Reggio Emilia. These schools were born out of an Italian progressive movement in the 1950s; influenced by the work of Piaget, Dewey, Montessori, Hawkins, and other innovative thinkers in education, psychology, biology, and architecture, as well as other fields; and generously supported from the beginning by the regional and local government. One of the central tenets of the Reggio Approach that has guided and continues to drive the Italian educators' work is the idea that every child is a creative child, full of potential, with the desire and right to make meaning out of life within a context of rich relationships, in many ways, and using many languages. It was from this fundamental premise that the *atelier* was conceived and developed, and still evolves.

We are indeed fortunate that many of the Italian educators have contributed their voices, their experience and ideas, and their most recent thoughts on the development and potential of the *atelier* to this book through their interviews with Lella Gandini. Because our experience grows in relationship to theirs and because the work of each country is in evolution, we have chosen to alternate among Italian and North American voices and stories. With this organization, the book presents a kind of dialogue among cultures, ideas, and continuously deepening theories and practices.

ORGANIZING IDEAS AND QUESTIONS

In many of the chapters, we will consider the practices that are nurtured and developed in an *atelier* that grow from attitudes and dispositions that can develop in a school with or without a physical place that is called an *atelier*. As we think about the way we work with children and one another, we have come to embrace these practices that fit together like a puzzle or prism. We believe in, recognize, and respect the practices of:

- Organizing rich experiences in the world and with materials alongside children.
- Wondering with children about what they see, think, and feel and how they make sense of experiences.
- Observing, noticing, and recording.
- Hypothesizing and posing new questions as adults and with children.
- Looking for and uncovering underlying or overarching ideas.
- Making meaning as adults and children through connecting experiences, ideas, materials, the culture of the school, and the wider community.

Both the Italian and the American authors will also address the more tangible aspects of the *atelier*, including stories about organization and care of the environment and materials, small and large projects explored in many spaces within a school, and the systems of the *atelier* (as both a way of working and a physical place) that foster collaboration, deep thinking, and meaning making among all members of the learning community.

Through dialogue with one another, we have found that many of these practices have become integrated in our style of teaching and working. These attitudes are at the heart of the Reggio philosophy, and we want them to define the spirit of the schools where we work. Our own professional and personal transformations have been shaped by many ideas and questions; for example:

- What promotes the power and pleasure of learning with and through materials?
- How can an *atelier* inspire and sustain creative, innovative thinking and learning throughout the school community?
- What kind of organization and interconnections among materials, spaces, people, and ideas do we need to invent in our North American context for the poetic, expressive languages to flourish and make the teaching and learning experience rich and whole?

These and other questions create the context of this book and will be considered and woven throughout its pages.

AN OVERVIEW OF THE CHAPTERS

Within these pages, we aspire to show the beauty and complexity of working in a way that considers respect for the interests of children, the school environment, the perspective of adults, and the qualities and characteristics of materials. At the end of the book, we have opted to include a glossary of words that are defined in the context of this book. You will find these special words highlighted in boldface the first time they are mentioned in the text, beginning in Chapter 2.

In sum, we want to portray the joy and learning that comes from a commitment to working with the values found in the Reggio Emilia schools while continuing to respect the culture and identification of our own contexts. We have become a collaborative group through the processes of writing and editing and have structured this book in ways that mirror this collaboration. Each author has generously contributed to the knowledge and understanding of all who are interested in learning more about the topic of the *atelier.* We have worked together in a way that we hope other teachers and children would find inspiring and helpful. And so in this collaborative spirit we share our stories.

In Chapter 2, Lella Gandini presents the beginning context, history, and evolution of the *atelier* in Reggio Emilia. Her chapter begins with an interview with the most notable protagonist—Loris Malaguzzi, the pedagogical and philosophical founder of the educational project—and continues with interviews with Mara Davoli and Giovanni Piazza, *atelieristi* who worked with Malaguzzi from the beginning.

Chapters 3, 4, and 5 tell the stories of three different journeys where educators worked to build and develop *ateliers* in the United States during the 1990s. In Chapter 3, Chuck Schwall highlights the experience of overcoming barriers to achieve a purposeful organization of a space; the availability, quality, and range of materials within the space; and children's and teachers' productive use of the preprimary *atelier* at the St. Michael School in St. Louis. In

Chapter 4, Amelia Gambetti, now executive coordinator of Reggio Children, and Jennifer Azzariti, *atelierista,* describe the experience of establishing the first *atelier* in the United States at the Model Early Learning Center, located in the Capitol Children's Museum in the inner city of Washington, DC. In Chapter 5, Barbara Burrington tells the story of 10 teachers who decided to transform their staff room into a studio space for the children at their Campus Children's Center at the University of Vermont.

In Chapter 6, we hear reflections on the philosophical and practical meaning of collaboration in connection with the *atelier* from different perspectives, including those of preschool teachers Laura Rubizzi and Paola Barchi, infant/toddler teacher Lucia Colla, and *pedagogista* Tiziana Filippini. In Chapter 7, Lynn Hill tells the story of a lab school at Virginia Tech where educators chose to visualize and reinvent an *atelier* in a way that embraces their unique context.

In Chapter 8, Mara Davoli and Giovanni Piazza describe ways that the role of the *atelierista* has evolved in Reggio Emilia, and the young *atelieriste* Isabella Meninno and Barbara Quinti reflect on the nature of their roles and their growth. In Chapter 9, we hear studio teachers from different settings in the United Stated speak together in a roundtable of voices that includes Pauline M. Baker (Tucson Public Schools), Patricia Hunter-McGrath (Evergreen Community School), Lauren Monaco (World Bank Children's Center), and Cathy Weisman Topal (Smith College). Together, they consider a collection of questions regarding creating spaces as studios in public schools, private schools, and Head Start settings, the open-endedness of materials, sharing the spirit of the studio, and the possibility for empowering teachers that can occur within an *atelier.*

In Chapter 10, Giovanni Piazza and Vea Vecchi speak about the groundbreaking role of the *atelier* as it affects learning, documenting, and teaching in Reggio Emilia and beyond, and in Chapter 11, Louise Cadwell, Lori Geismar Ryan, and Chuck Schwall, from the St. Louis–Reggio Collaborative, focus on the development of processes and systems, born out of the conceptual *atelier,* that support their work.

In Chapter 12, Carla Rinaldi, pedagogical consultant to Reggio Children, reflects on the nature of creativity and the work of listening and observing, as well as the process of understanding that is embedded in research and documentation. In Chapter 13, Ashley Cadwell, headmaster of the St. Michael School in St. Louis, describes how two *ateliers*—one for preprimary children, and the other for elementary ages—function in the program as well as the pedagogical approach of the school. The idea of the studio within Cadwell's school and any school where educators have embraced it has altered the way that they define "schooling" and "teaching." Finally, in the Epilogue, we return to the thoughts of Loris Malaguzzi as he reflects on the genesis and meaning of creativity. In conclusion, we believe with Carla Rinaldi that "the whole school has to be a large *atelier.*" Rinaldi's words, which echo Malaguzzi's quote at the beginning of this chapter, reveal the Reggio Emilian educators' belief in the work of teachers and children, their shared research, and their great potential and human right to learn in diverse, rich, and deeply meaningful ways using many languages. We hope that this book brings these attitudes to life for readers and inspires you, as it has inspired us, to think deeply about the power of the expressive languages when placed in the center of teaching and learning.

REFERENCE

Malaguzzi, L. (1998). History, ideas, and basic philosophy: An interview with Lella Gandini. In C. Edwards, L. Gandini, & G. Forman (Eds.), *The hundred languages of children: The Reggio Emilia Approach—Advanced reflections* (2nd ed.; pp. 49–97). Westport, CT: Ablex.

From the Beginning of the *Atelier* to Materials as Languages

Conversations from Reggio Emilia

Lella Gandini

The idea of the *atelier* was conceived by Loris Malaguzzi with the intention of bringing about a revolution in teaching and learning in schools for young children. The role of the *atelier* and the **atelierista**, within and beyond the school, has continued to evolve through the research and the strategic thinking of the educators of Reggio Emilia. The purpose of this chapter, and of Chapters 6, 8, 10, and 12, is to trace several important aspects of that evolution through the voices of some of its major protagonists, interviewed at different times in its history over the past 15 years. Our intention is to place these interviews within the stream of narrative of experiences of educators in the United States and to offer the sense of dialogue that has taken place during many years. In this way, we present the experience of exchanging ideas and practices as a complex, intertwined tapestry. This chapter will focus in particular on the fundamental ideas and beginnings of the *atelier*, the organization of the *miniatelier*, and reflections on materials as languages.

It is my strong belief that the narrative describing what has been constructed in Reggio Emilia can broaden our conversations with our colleagues in that city and deepen the reflections of teachers in North America who continue to study the Reggio Emilia philosophy. These interview dialogues speak directly to readers with only minimal intrusions on my part.

In this chapter, we will hear the voices of Loris Malaguzzi, founder and philosopher of the schools in Reggio Emilia, and of two *atelieristi*, Mara Davoli at the Pablo Neruda school and Giovanni Piazza at La Villetta School, both of whom were involved in the design of the various versions of the exhibit *The Hundred Languages of Children*.

LORIS MALAGUZZI'S *ATELIER*

What follow are excerpts from a 1988 interview with Loris Malaguzzi about the *atelier* published in the educational magazine *Bambini*, of which he was chief editor. Malaguzzi's language is rich, complex, and dense; it has many layers of meaning. He analyzes the beginning of the *atelier* in the context of the first 25 years of the Reggio schools. At the time of the interview, he had a very strong concept of what the *atelier* could be, but several years were still required for many of its potentials to develop. Much of what he anticipated reappears in the discussions of each of the protagonists in the interviews that follow in this volume, particularly those conducted in June 2003.

The *atelier* was established right away at the outset of our experience, in 1963, and it was included in our general project of schools for young children from the beginning. The *atelier* was built directly into every preschool and later, beginning in the seventies, within every infant/toddler center as well. The role of the *atelier*, integrated and combined within the general framework of learning and teaching strategies, was conceptualized as a retort to the marginal and subsidiary role commonly assigned to expressive education. It also was intended as a reaction against the concept of the education of young children based mainly on words and simple-minded rituals.

First of all, the *atelier* was viewed as instrumental in the recovery of the image of the child, which we now saw as richer in resources and interests than we had understood before, a child now understood as interactionist and constructivist. This new child had the right to a school that was more aware and more focused, a school made up of professional teachers. In this way we also rescued our teachers, who had been humiliated by the narrowness of their preparatory schools, by working with them on their professional development.

Within our framework of many cultural and theoretical influences, we had to reinvent the original meaning of the *atelier*. For us, the *atelier* had to become part of a complex design and, at the same time, an added space for searching or, better, for digging with one's own hands and one's own mind, and for refining one's own eyes, through the practice of the visual arts. It had to be a place for sensitizing one's taste and esthetic sense, a place for the individual exploration of projects connected with experiences planned in the different classrooms of the school. The *atelier* had to be a place for researching motivations and theories of children from scribbles on up, a place for exploring variations in tools, techniques, and materials with which to work. It had to be a place favoring children's logical and creative itineraries, a place for becoming familiar with similarities and differences of verbal and nonverbal languages. The *atelier* had to emerge as both the subject and the intermediary of a multifaceted practice; it had to provoke specific and interconnected events, making it possible to transfer new knowledge acquired about form and content in the daily educational experience.

Our intent was to drive the school in richer, more complex and rigorous directions, and toward new anthropological and cultural paths. As you can see, this was an ambitious and vast process. From the beginning, we concentrated on the observation of the explorations, of processes, and of strategic theories of children as premises and tools for studying, analyzing, and reflecting on hypotheses, as well as for adjusting contents, attitudes, and proposals for the action of adults [teachers]. We were convinced that, in the case of both children and adults, it was valid to use the rule stated by David Hawkins, who said that it was necessary to become familiar first by using directly what you know and what you have learned in order to acquire further learning and knowledge.

The invasion of the school by the *atelier* and by the *atelierista*, a teacher with preparation from an art school, as organizer, interpreter, co-organizer, and collaborator (a role to be reinvented en route), intentionally created a disturbance for the dated model of school for young children. School, in our case, had already been modified by the presence of two co-teachers in each classroom, by the collegiality of work, by the participation of families, and by the cooperation of the school with the community council. Our school had already guaranteed the practice of working with the same children for the continuum of three years, and had been enriched by the opening of the infant/toddler centers.

The genesis of the *atelier* coincided with the genesis of a new overall educational project: systemic, lay [nonreligious], and progressive. By and by, the *atelier* would find its own nature and its own goals. It would develop through crises, results, the reformulation of theory and practice connected with social change and the historic situation. The one stable element was an equal respect for the plurality and the connections within children's expressive languages. Throughout, it has been necessary to keep battling against the old but solid culture of antonyms, which sets up pairs of opposites and ranks in hierarchical order disciplines, behaviors, intelligence, morality, reason, fantasy, imagination, the individual and the social, expressiveness and cognition.

Technology brought the camera, the tape recorder, the video recorder, the photocopy machine, the computer, and so on into the *atelier*. The school continually needs more tools, appropriate architectures, and wider spaces; it cannot risk falling behind. We have to convince ourselves that expressive competences grow and mature their languages near and far from home, and that children discover with us the friendliness of actions, of languages, of thoughts and meanings. We have to convince ourselves that it is essential to preserve in children (and in ourselves) the feeling of wonder and surprise, because creativity, like knowledge, is a daughter of surprise. We have to convince ourselves that expressivity is an art, a combined construction (not immediate, not spontaneous, not isolated, not secondary); that expressivity has motivations, forms, and procedures; contents (formal and informal); and the ability to communicate the predictable and the unpredictable. Expressivity finds sources from play, as well as from practice, from study and from visual learning, as well as from subjective interpretations that come from emotions, from intuition, from chance, and from rational imagination and transgressions.

Figure 2.1. The stone lion in the square of Reggio Emilia.

In fact, drawing, painting (and the use of all languages) are experiences and explorations of life, of the senses, and of meanings. They are an expression of urgency, desires, reassurance, research, hypotheses, readjustments, constructions, and inventions. They follow the logic of exchange, and of sharing. They produce solidarity, communication with oneself, with things, and with others. They offer interpretations and intelligence about the events that take place around us.

Formulas? There are none. There are only possible strategies. Make sure, above all, that children become familiar in their minds with images; that they know how to keep them alive; that they learn the pleasure of reactivating them, regenerating them, and multiplying them with the maximum amount of personal and creative intervention. It is an essential requirement that the images be good and meaningful for children and for adults. For it is only then that those images, combined and recombined (and not always in a linear or cumulative way) in the form of realism, of resemblances, of logic, of imagination, and of symbolism will become signs that carry meanings. This is the only procedure: difficult and uncertain but, perhaps, the decisive one. (Carini, 1988, pp. 8–14)

THE BEGINNINGS OF AN *ATELIERISTA* AND DEVELOPMENT OF THE *MINIATELIER*: INTERVIEW WITH MARA DAVOLI

Vea Vecchi was the first *atelierista* to work closely with Loris Malaguzzi when she began at the Diana School in 1970. It was Vea who introduced Mara Davoli to the role of *atelierista* when Mara worked as a volunteer at the Diana School. Mara began her job as *atelierista* at the Neruda School in 1973. In the excerpts from this interview, which I conducted in January 1997, Mara describes the changes that took place in the way that the *atelier* was used, first as a centralized space where children would go in groups to work with materials, and then as a more complex organization that helped to connect expressive languages throughout the whole space of the school.

Lella: *What are your memories from the beginning of your work as an* atelierista?

Mara: When I first entered the schools, along with several other *atelieristi*, Malaguzzi was concerned with giving us a particular identity through an accelerated professional preparation, because having us was a luxury—it did cost extra money. Malaguzzi was always very aware of the financial burden of the choices he made. If something like the *atelier* or the *atelierista* was necessary because it embodied the idea of a different image of the child and a different kind of school, he felt very strongly that it was the school's duty to offer a return on that investment to the children, the families, the administration, and the city.

Lella: *Therefore, there was a certain evolution of the* atelier, *along with the evolution of the other aspects of the school.*

Mara: We had the privilege of constructing a path that we shared with other *atelieristi*. Each of us assumed the responsibility of trying things out ourselves, of taking risks, but we never felt alone. There was always the possibility of saying, "I've done this, and I interpret it this way. What do you think?" We had the maximum amount of freedom, and we were expected to experiment and to express ourselves, to take on a great deal of responsibility individually but, at the same time, never to be alone. This is one of the things that made me fall in love with the work; it became, for better or for worse, a philosophy of life in which work and life outside of work are intertwined, and together they formed me as a person.

Lella: *In the early years, how did the* atelier *evolve as a space?*

Mara: When I first started, the *atelier* was already part of the school, and it was the only place where the children experimented with certain languages—for example, clay, paint, and other formal art materials. The classrooms had only drawing materials.

Lella: *Did the children come to the* atelier *in groups?*

Mara: Yes, and this created some problems in the organizational choices that some *atelieristi* made, and here I am using the term *organization* in its true meaning—not as a superficial aspect, but as the content that structures our **overall educational project**. We decided to start working with **project-based work**: small projects, short ones, long ones, projects that were often defined differently from how we think about them now. We needed to construct ideas with the different groups in each classroom. We made what we then called, "work plans." Later, to avoid the tendency to see this as a predetermined planning, we changed the name to "declarations of intent," or the "project base for the year." With the teachers, we laid out these plans. This was one way of proceeding that helped me to understand and to learn more about the pedagogical aspects of teaching that were less tied to the *atelier*, but it also helped the teachers to understand more about expressive languages. Working in this way continues to truly help us grow, not to separate languages, and not to separate the learning taking place in the *atelier* from that of the classroom, even as we construct a variety of projects connected to diverse subjects and experiences.

Lella: *Tell me about the emergence of the* miniatelier.

Mara: Our way of working was still not satisfactory, and in one of the ongoing meetings orchestrated by Malaguzzi, he proposed that we organize working groups with a series of topics and issues to discuss and analyze. One group of *atelieristi*, for example, was to discuss techniques and materials, and another group was to reflect on the environment. Malaguzzi said to the first group, "At this point, we need to understand what techniques children can experiment with, beyond markers and clay, that we know work well. Now, we need to widen the scope of what we know." He asked this group of *atelieristi* to prepare a careful inventory of materials and techniques used and an overview of what was happening in the schools. This process alone was extremely useful for us. As a follow-up, that group prepared a series of technical charts on materials and their qualities as well as suggestions on how to choose them among the variety offered in art stores or other sources.

The group of *atelieristi* who worked on the environment included Vea and me. We were focusing on daily problems and on the organization of time and space. For that purpose, we decided to prepare floor plans and maps of the preschools involved. At the Neruda School, this included the classrooms, the *atelier*, the lunch area, the bathroom, the hallway, etc. We designed these maps with the schedule of the day, by hour, along the side. The presence of adults was marked with a sticker of one color, and the presence of the children with a sticker of another color. By making observations, we were able to see how the spaces were used—which spaces in which time slots, how many children and how many adults. We noticed moments of crowding and moments of underuse.

Figure 2.2. The via Emilia in Reggio.

Lella: *Were the parents also included?*

Mara: Yes, the parents were also included, the cooks, everyone. I remember the variety of colored dots. The discussion of the results showed us how often people gravitated toward the *atelier*, and this insight brought about the idea of creating the *miniatelier*s.

Lella: *This idea developed because you realized that the* ateliers *were very important but that not all of the children were using them.*

Mara: The *miniatelier*, used daily with an adult or without an adult, could resolve this. The *miniatelier* was created and organized in each school, but not immediately. After having presented the results of observations and discussions of our group meetings to the teachers, and after discussing all the details with them, spaces were created within the classrooms or next to the classrooms depending on what space was available. Each school had to find a different solution.

MATERIALS, RELATIONSHIPS, AND LANGUAGES: INTERVIEW WITH GIOVANNI PIAZZA

This interview, conducted in May 1997, is the first of two I had with Giovanni Piazza (see also Chapter 10). Giovanni has been working as *atelierista* at La Villetta School for 32 years. Often present at conferences about the Reggio Emilia Approach around the world, Giovanni in recent years has been developing the connection between children's expressive languages and various forms of digital technology.

Lella: *When educators attempt to interpret the approach of the schools of Reggio Emilia, sometimes we hear conversations about materials and languages that are a bit confusing.*

Giovanni: A first encounter for children with materials to explore and act on them is a necessary step in the children's process of knowing. Through such encounters and explorations, children build an awareness of what can happen with materials, and adults build the ability to observe and support the significance of each particular experience.

Lella: *Can we say, even at this early stage, that the child can be aware of an alphabet or a language of material?*

Giovanni: When we consider a material by itself in the way it is presented to a child, or when we just begin to explore it, it is too soon to speak about the language of a material. Material is static. Of course, it can suggest and inspire ideas, but it would be more appropriate for us to speak about the characteristics or properties of a material considered by itself and, as George Forman [1994, pp. 41–43] suggests, to analyze the affordances of different materials.

It is through interactions between a child and a material that an alphabet can develop. As the children use paper, clay, wire, and so on, different alphabets will develop from different materials. As children use their minds and hands to act on a material using gestures and tools and begin to acquire skills, experience, strategies, and rules, structures are developed within the child that can be considered a sort of alphabet or grammar. This alphabet or grammar, of the use of materials, has to be discovered by children in partnership with adults. It is essential for children to acquire knowledge of materials, gain competence with them, and use them in a variety of ways. They often discover or invent different ways of using materials in the process of experimentation and observing through other children.

Lella: *By "alphabet" do you mean the forms and shapes that one can make with that material, or do you mean the way one can intervene to transform it?*

Giovanni: An alphabet is probably best described as the combination of the characteristics of a particular material along with the relationship that arises in the interaction between the child and the material. It is during the construction of that relationship that the possibilities of modification, transformation, and structuring of the material present themselves, so that the transformed material can become a conduit for expression that communicates the child's thoughts and feelings. In a situation that supports communication, as in our preschools, where education is based in relationship, by transforming a material to communicate (paper, paint, clay, etc.) we structure a language. Each language has a communicative system.

Lella: *You are helping us to note the importance of researching possible transformations and modifications of materials.*

Giovanni: Searching for and discovering how a particular material presents itself and is transformed helps the child acquire knowledge about the material itself—about texture, form, shape, color, exterior and interior appearance. The child gradually learns that a material can be used in many different ways. Children acquire a large spectrum of knowledge about materials, and this gives them the chance to use different alphabets in their individual process of representation and give shape to their own ideas.

Lella: *First, it is important for us to be aware of how we can make it possible for a child to enter into a relationship with materials and therefore to construct several alphabets. Second, we should reflect on how a child can refer to the alphabet of one material that he or she has used and gain the ability to transfer it to another material, understanding the similarities and differences and the need for modifications.*

Giovanni: It is clear that in a space that is prepared and supported by adults with intentionality, the children, who already know some alphabets, will construct others. Children's first explorations of and research on the qualities and characteristics of materials take place in the infant/toddler centers. Then, when

di notte Reggio è bellissima
perché si accendono i lampioni
che sembrano tanti soli,
perché i pali
non si vedono

Figure 2.3. At night, Reggio is very beautiful because they turn on the street lights that look like a lot of suns, because you don't see the poles.

the children come to preschools at around 3 years of age, the slow, progressive construction of knowledge of materials continues. This knowledge is based on the possibilities they have to encounter different materials. We also have to keep in mind that for teachers, one very important point is to understand how to recognize (or, we could say, read) the relationship and exchange between child and material and cultivate the growth of awareness among colleagues to support it. Observing carefully and listening to the children helps us understand the ways of learning with materials that the children develop so that we, in turn, can support them.

CLOSING REFLECTIONS

We started this chapter with the powerful, programmatic message of Loris Malaguzzi. We then heard about the initial formation of the identity of the *atelierista* and the evolution of the space of the *miniatelier* in the interview with Mara Davoli. We have concluded with Giovanni Piazza's conversation on how the essential ingredient of children's relationships with materials gives them multiple possibilities to communicate their thoughts and feelings.

These ideas lead us to the next chapter, in which we enter into a school in St. Louis, Missouri, where Chuck Schwall has become deeply aware of the power of an *atelier*; where ideas are continually refined; and where children feel a sense of ownership, a power that "invigorate[s] the lives of children and teachers."

The space and its organization are described in detail, along with an inventory of materials and the documentation of children's transforming them. It is an invitation to a valuable and constructive visit.

REFERENCES

Carini, E. (1988, December 12). Se l'atelier è dentro una lunga storia e ad un progetto educativo: Intervista a Loris Malaguzzi. [If the *atelier* is within a long history and within an overall educational project: Interview with Loris Malaguzzi.] *Bambini, 4,* 8–14. Bergamo, Italy: Edizioni Junior.

Forman, G. (1994). Different media, different languages. In L. G. Katz & B. Cesarone (Eds.), *Reflections on the Reggio Emilia Approach*. Urbana, IL: ERIC/EECE.

Credits: The drawing on the chapter opening page and Figures 2.1, 2.2, and 2.3 are from *Reggio Tutta* (2000), a collection of 25 postcards with drawings by 3- to 6-year-old children of the Municipal Infant/Toddler Centers and Preschools of Reggio Emilia. © Municipality of Reggio Emilia—Infant-Toddler Centers and Preschools.

The *Atelier* Environment and Materials

Charles Schwall

The St. Michael School *atelier* was designed in 1994 to offer children and teachers a space to extend and support projects and experiences in the classroom, and to explore and combine many types of materials, tools, and techniques. I was hired as the *atelierista* at the St. Michael School in St. Louis in the fall of 1993. Our understanding of the role of the *atelier* has continued to grow and evolve since then. Even after years of work, it seems as if the *atelier*'s potential, like a mine in the earth that holds vast resources yet to be discovered, is still largely untapped. Through our efforts to uncover the teaching potential of the environment we have learned that lasting change is sustained through continually refining our ideas and use of this space.

The gestures of everyday life, when viewed as inextricably connected to a space, have the potential to make, renew, and rejuvenate the places in which we live. John Dewey writes about the relationship between daily events and the tangible objects produced by cultures in *Art as Experience* (1934). He uses the metaphor of a mountain peak to highlight the inseparable connections between the products of a culture and daily human experiences. In his metaphor, the peak of the mountain represents the products or artifacts of a culture, while the mountain below portrays the events of everyday life. He writes, "Mountain peaks do not float unsupported; they do not even just rest upon the earth. They *are* the earth in one of its manifest operations" (Dewey, 1934, p. 3).

Each day, our *atelier* supports many experiences and ongoing projects that invigorate the lives of the children and teachers. We have learned to slow down and let events and situations influence how our spaces, including the studio, are used. When children live in a space, they own, feel, and find their place within it. Connections that take place between time and space happen through the rhythms of everyday life, connections to past events, and new experiences that reach toward the future. We aim to inhabit our spaces in ways that focus on variation and difference inside of our routines, rather than automatically repeating them. The children and the adults create the *atelier* anew every day as we find the meaning of this place together.

MATERIALS, COMMUNICATION, AND RESEARCH

The *atelier* is a workshop for children's ideas that manifest through the use of many materials. The style of working we have adopted is one of using materials as languages. In this view, materials are vehicles for expressing and communicating and are part of the fabric of children's experiences and learning processes rather than as separate products. Children are innately receptive to the possibilities that materials offer and interact with them to make meaning and relationships, explore, and communicate.

The ways in which children invent with materials are often unexpected and surprising; therefore, it is important for the adults who work with children to adopt an attitude of freedom and open-ended possibility toward the children's work. The *atelier* environment can facilitate new understandings about children's cognitive and expressive processes. The products that children make can also be very useful in revealing their knowledge. In our school, the teachers and I often discuss and interpret children's work and use it to find new ways to support their learning. Words are often not enough. It is very important for adults to consider objects that the children have made so we can share, talk, and search for new strategies together. The products that children have made can help us make these new choices. In some respects, the *atelier* is most of all about communication, because the artifacts of children's learning can enable us to share with others what we have learned. All of this gives back to the teachers a renewed sense of meaning about their role and strengthens the school.

The educators in Reggio Emilia offer many provocative examples and stress that their work is not a recipe. The sophisticated use of the environment and materials found in the Reggio schools is the result of many years of collaborative observation, documentation, and interpretation. Loris Malaguzzi emphasizes that there is no one right answer or interpretation. Can those of us who live in other cultures adopt similar attitudes? Can processes of research help us to find answers about our own school environments and work with materials? Interpretations from Reggio are invaluable; however, ultimately we need to make our own meaning with the children in our culture.

THE IMPORTANCE OF RELATIONSHIPS

The St. Michael School *atelier* has grown and evolved out of a distinct network of relationships and support systems. When I was hired in the fall of 1993, the school did not have an *atelier*. Ashley Cadwell, the headmaster of our school, had just returned from a year in Reggio Emilia with his family. He had lived there while his wife, Louise, completed internships at the Diana and La Villeta Schools (Cadwell, 1997). When Ashley became the head administrator in 1992, he initiated many changes to support and develop the values and fundamentals of the Reggio Approach in our school (see Chapter 13). The choice to create an *atelier* in the preschool was one of many decisions made at that time.

The backgrounds of the teaching faculty also contributed to our unique context. I hold studio fine art degrees and have a lifelong commitment to work as a painter. I began my career in the early 1990s teaching drawing and painting courses to adults at colleges in St. Louis. The preprimary teachers at the St. Michael School have diverse teaching backgrounds with rich histories in experiential learning and developmentally appropriate practice. My collaboration with them began before the ideas from Reggio directly influenced our school. Prior to becoming the *atelierista*, I taught for two years in a part-time capacity at the school. During this time, I formed important relationships with the teachers that later became the basis for our collaboration around the Reggio Approach.

Our faculty also formed relationships with teachers in other schools in St. Louis who were interested in the Reggio Approach. The St. Louis–Reggio Collaborative is a cooperative organization that includes the St. Michael School, Clayton Schools' Family Center, the College School of Webster Groves, and Webster University. Initiated in the early 1990s with a grant from the Danforth Foundation, the collaborative supports study of the work from Reggio Emilia as well as research in our own schools. We host regular meetings at which teachers share current work from their classrooms and encourage one another's growth. Over the years, as transformations have taken place in each of our schools, the teachers have inspired and encouraged one another.

The collaborative was also privileged to have Amelia Gambetti, a teacher for 25 years in Reggio Emilia and a consultant to schools for Reggio Children, work for short and intense periods with us through the 1990s. The passion, expertise, and energy she brought to the work at our school were invaluable; she pushed us in ways that we never thought possible. She taught us to look at the environment with a critical eye and to include the children as we made changes to the classrooms. From Amelia we adopted rigorous practices. She encouraged us "to pretend to be visitors in our own classrooms" in order to see new possibilities and find creative solutions. It was this attitude that gave us the courage to make many changes in our school environment. When Amelia first began working with us, she said that she had found "fertile ground."

TRANSFORMING OUR ENVIRONMENT

Our preschool environment is located in the basement of a church building. When we began to consider the environment, we realized that our basement classrooms were unlike anything that would be found in Reggio Emilia, and the possibility of creating an *atelier* seemed even further away. Because the appearance of our basement environment is so dissimilar to classrooms in Reggio, it has pushed us to think in deeper ways about how Reggio values might take root. At the beginning of our journey with the school environment we were uncertain how our efforts would play out. Our *atelier* in a sense is the result of the juxtaposition of seemingly unrelated elements: a preschool located in a church basement and a desire to embrace the foundational ideas of the Reggio Approach. Joining these elements transformed our situation into something new.

Making changes to the preschool environment was one of the first ways that the educators in our school chose to begin exploring the values from Reggio Emilia. I think this happened because the school environment is very tangible and can be improved by having meetings, making lists, and carrying out plans. Our first attempts at change were small ones. We started by looking closely at slides of environments in Reggio Emilia and learned to become critical observers of our own classrooms. Some of our teachers had visited Reggio on a study tour and shared firsthand accounts of beautiful classroom environments filled with interesting and engaging materials. In each area of our classrooms, we asked one another questions about what worked well, what the difficulties were, and then we imagined new possibilities. These meetings often led to cleaning, painting, and moving furniture and resulted in classrooms that were more beautiful and functional. These types of small improvements gave us genuine satisfaction and confirmed our beliefs about the value of change.

Our successful first steps gave us confidence to dream of bigger intentions. We wondered if part of our basement preschool could be transformed into an *atelier*. We were inspired by Louise Cadwell's experience at the College School, where she and her colleagues transformed one room of their preschool into a beautiful and dynamic *atelier* (Cadwell, 1997). As we carefully considered our entire preschool environment, it seemed as if an area located between two classrooms held the potential to become a studio. It was a small space, approximately 11 by 25 feet, with no windows and poor lighting, but its close proximity to the preschool classrooms offered the promise of a more connected space. The teachers often referred to this space as the "wet area" because it contained the only two sinks in the preschool. Although it was used regularly by children and teachers, it was disorganized and full of clutter. While many people used the space, nobody was responsible for maintaining it. As we cleared out containers of old materials and equipment that had piled up, the space began to open up, but even though it was in the center of the preschool environment, it still seemed isolated and cut off. It was evident that we needed to make structural changes (see Figure 3.1).

Ashley Cadwell worked with a parent architect to design an *atelier* that embodied Reggio-inspired values. They developed a plan to replace the wall that divided the studio and the adjacent classroom with large windows. Windows in this location would create visual connections between the two rooms and would reflect the values of openness and reciprocity (see Figure 3.2).

Figure 3.1. The space designated to become the *atelier* in 1993.

A father who owned a carpentry business was hired to construct the design. By the end of 1994, the *atelier* was completed, and an open, spacious, and inviting space emerged (see Figure 3.3).

A Tour of Our Atelier

Our *atelier* is made up of many elements that each holds unique identity, purpose, and possibility. It is a symphony of individual parts balanced to create a whole that is diverse and stimulating but also amiable and harmonious; a multisensorial place that invites interactions by engaging the mind, hands, imagination, and senses. It is an environment that offers children high-quality materials, tools, and techniques that translate into numerous possibilities for experiences. We believe that these elements of the environment give dignity and respect to children's experiences and play a crucial role in their education. Many of these items are visible the moment one enters the studio and stand out as valuable parts of the environment. The inventory of materials and languages available in our *atelier* is always changing and evolving, never static. The teachers and I continually update the materials, tools, and organization based on the needs and desires of each class. We regularly make lists of items that we have used in the past, as well as of new materials we want to try. This process helps us to evaluate and consider the many roles materials play in our school, now and in the future.

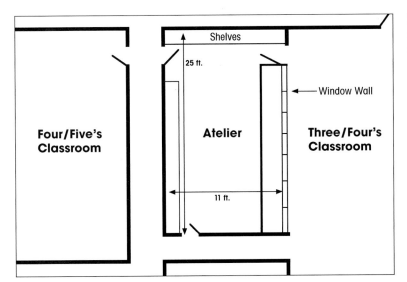

Figure 3.2. A plan of the preschool environment.

Figure 3.3. The St. Michael School *atelier* in 1996.

An Inventory of Materials and Collections

A free-standing wire shelf located in the center of the *atelier* defines the space. It is filled with a variety of interesting materials of many types in open jars, baskets, and trays (see Figure 3.4). These collections, such as flowers, sticks, shells, leaves, folded paper strips, and small wood and metal items, contrast and complement one another and vary greatly at any given time, depending on the focus of our work. On the bottom of the shelf, a basket holds many kinds

Figure 3.4. A shelf for collections of materials defines the *atelier*.

of wire, including soft armature wire, thin copper wire, and telephone or computer wire. It also contains small items such as beads and small nuts and bolts and materials for twisting, such as foil paper and screen-door mesh. Materials presented in this enticing and inviting manner send a message of complexity, connection, and openness. Open or transparent containers communicate to children that these items are for them to use.

The children make many of the items on this shelf. A small basket of paper figures recently made by the kindergarten children occupies a prominent place. Some children were fascinated with drawing people, cutting them out, and folding the paper so that the figures could stand up. They decided to share their "paper people" by placing them on the shelf for other children to use in their play. When these children went on to first grade, they chose to leave their paper people as a gift to new children who would soon use the *atelier*. It is this type of gesture that contributes to the particular culture of the place.

Collections of materials in other areas of the studio invite children to explore. One shelf near the large work table is filled with many tools for graphic representation, such as markers of many kinds, pens, soft and hard lead pencils, various sizes of chalk, oil pastels, color pencils, and several varieties of black fine-line markers. Below the drawing shelf are many types of paper, including white drawing paper in various sizes and weights that is often used for drawing or painting.

Close by, another shelf displays ceramic tools, scrapers, and other items for clay modeling. A stack of small boards, either masonite or plywood covered with canvas, are also stacked on the shelf. These make excellent work surfaces for children because wet clay will not stick to them; they also provide a good base for moving or displaying finished work.

Various looms are offered for weaving, some large and some small, made from sticks, chicken wire, mat board, or cardboard. Large wooden looms allow two or three children to work at one time. Containers of fabric strips, yarn, and paper cut into strips attract children to try them. One year, a parent and I became interested in exploring weaving with children. She had a background in the textile arts and knew many weavers in the local weaver's guild. The fiber arts were new to me, but I learned more about them by attending a weaving workshop at the St. Louis Art Museum. This experience enriched my understanding and gave me many new ideas and techniques for weaving with children.

Easels Inspired in Reggio

An easel occupies the place next to the materials shelf. On my first visit to Reggio, the beautiful easels I saw in many of the *ateliers* and *miniateliers* captivated me. These easels were much larger than the ones usually available in the United States and had work surfaces that accommodate many sizes of paper. When I returned to St. Louis, I worked on an easel design inspired by what I had seen in Reggio. One of the fathers in our school was a professional furniture builder and donated his time, energy, and beautiful pieces of cherry wood for the project. We worked with several other parents to build three easels for the school. The results of our efforts are easels that look and feel more like furniture and are quite different from easels purchased through a catalog. Our easels are 25 inches wide and 48 inches tall, large enough to accommodate a 24-by-36-inch piece of paper. The tray that holds the jars of paint is low, about 14 inches from the floor. This design works well for the height of most young children and provides a larger work surface (see Figure 3.5).

Near the easels, numerous jars of paint are stored on a cart that rolls under a shelf. This rolling paint cart, also made by one of our parents, has casters on the bottom and can easily be rolled to any location in the preschool. It has an open top for jars of paint, while gallons of paint are stored on a shelf below. We keep this cart well stocked with a wide spectrum of hues and tones of color. Brushes of many sizes, types of bristles, and varieties are stored on a shelf near the easel. Some are large, round or flat, easel brushes, thick ones that will make washes, and some are tiny for more detailed work. I often place containers of brushes near the easel when the children are painting so they can choose which brushes they want to use. Children help maintain the colors that are on the paint cart. When the paint jars are empty or the colors become worn out, we invite groups of children to mix new paints into empty, clean jars. This

Figure 3.5. Easels inspired in Reggio.

experience always has a life of its own; children delight in the process of drib-bling one color into another and take ownership by deciding which colors will become available for everyone to use.

Clay Memories

Through the process of revisiting documentation of past experiences, we reach back into our own history in order to use it to rejuvenate the present. On the wall in the studio, two panels serve as memories of pivotal experi-ences with clay. One panel, titled "Making a Figure with Clay," hangs on the wall next to the large worktable in an easily visible location. This panel tells the story of how one boy built an action figure with clay, including his strug-gles, the adjustments he made during his work, and his perseverance (see Fig-ure 3.6). During Amelia's work with us, she encouraged us to "follow" chil-dren's learning processes by documenting them. She asked us to become attentive to, and write down, the sequences of events that occur within chil-dren's learning experiences. The panel in the studio documents one boy's building strategies as he worked with clay. It was inspired by an experience conducted by Vea Vecchi, *atelierista* of the Diana School in Reggio Emilia, and that was included in the exhibit *The Hundred Languages of Children*. On the other side of the studio, shelves display clay work made by the children (see Figure 3.7). These are not only beautiful and provocative to look at, but they also spark detailed conversations among children about how they were made and what they represent.

One year, our culture of working with clay became even richer when a parent observed the children's interest in building animals with clay. Because of his background in operating a local art gallery, he was acquainted with an internationally recognized ceramic artist and made arrangements for this artist to visit our school. During a morning in the *atelier*, the artist demonstrated and conversed with the children about techniques of building with clay. Traces of this experience remain in the studio still, through figures he made and a panel that tells the story. Even years after this memorable day, children often speak of his visit. Artifacts made by children can easily remain isolated and not touch other parts of our lives at school. However, our work to document experiences has taken us further. The process of making learning visible through documentation, and taking time to revisit it, has rewarded us by supporting the continual learning processes of children.

Making a Figure with Clay

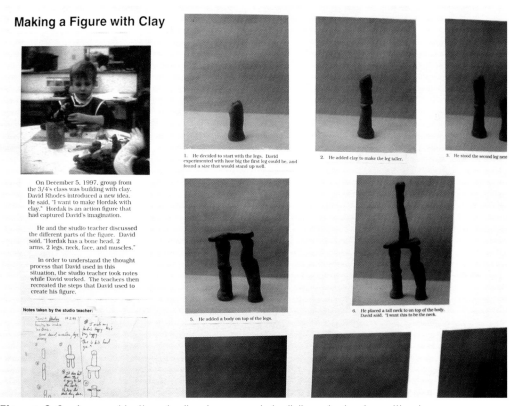

On December 5, 1997, group from the 3/4's class was building with clay. David Rhodes introduced a new idea. He said, "I want to make Hordak with clay." Hordak is an action figure that had captured David's imagination.

He and the studio teacher discussed the different parts of the figure. David said, "Hordak has a bone head, 2 arms, 2 legs, neck, face, and muscles."

In order to understand the thought process that David used in this situation, the studio teacher took notes while David worked. The teachers then recreated the steps that David used to create his figure.

Notes taken by the studio teacher:

1. He decided to start with the legs. David experimented with how big the first leg could be, and found a size that would stand up well.

2. He added clay to make the leg taller.

3. He stood the second leg next

5. He added a body on top of the legs.

6. He placed a tall neck to on top of the body. David said, "I want this to be the neck.

Figure 3.6. A panel in the studio documents building strategies with clay.

Figure 3.7. Clay memories.

The Presence of Technology

Technology has a significant presence in the *atelier*; a computer with graphics and page layout software, a scanner, and a printer have become essential tools for our style of working. Teachers use technology on a daily basis to process numerous documents, such as children's conversations, letters to parents, photos taken with digital cameras, and documentation that will be placed on the classroom wall. The computer in the *atelier* functions as a server and can be accessed from other computers in the classrooms. This has added efficiency to our work, as teachers find time throughout the day to work on documentation and are able to access all of their files from any computer. The *atelier* is a space that can support the production of documentation, as well as push us into new forms such as video, various types of books, and other digital media. The children also use technology in powerful ways in the *atelier*, and we are learning to interweave it with traditional media. We know that we are at the beginning of this journey and are trying to take a few steps each year. During the 2003–2004 school year, our kindergarten children used digital media to enhance and develop self-portraits they had started with fine-line markers on paper. From the teacher's point of view, it was an effective strategy to begin with something familiar, such as self-portraits, and attempt to extend it with digital technology.

THE MAGIC SNOWFLAKE: LANGUAGES THAT OVERLAP

One Morning in the Atelier

The Sunlight and Reflection Project, which occurred during the 2002–2003 school year and is narrated in Chapter 11, influenced the culture of our preschool in many ways. For example, it caused Frances Roland and Christina Adreon, the teachers working with the 4- and 5-year-old class that year, to wonder about ways that light could become a meaningful material for their children. As Frances and Christina formed initial hypotheses, their questions centered on uncovering the potential that artificial sources of light offer to children. They organized new situations focused on children's use of the overhead light projector to explore and discover light. Among these were initial encounters with the light projector, placing it in the block area to encourage children to investigate shadows in relation to constructions and using it to project light on a large shadow screen that could be integrated with dramatic play experiences.

After several weeks of exploring the light projector in the classroom, the projector was moved to the *atelier* in the hope that it would support these intentions as well as provide opportunities for new connections. After talking with the teachers, I set up the studio environment by placing the two easels next to each other on one side of the room. The projector was located on the other side so that light would shine onto the easels.

On this particular morning, four children—Noah, Schroedter, Jack, and Madeleine—came into the *atelier* to explore the light projector in its new context. We sat on the floor together, and I asked them to remind me of some of the ways they had used the light projector in the classroom. The children told me several of their favorite scenarios, and some gave detailed descriptions about how the projector functioned. The children and I talked about how the projector was set up to shine light onto the easels. They were very aware that small objects placed on the projector would be enlarged. They had experienced this in the classroom and were eager to try it again.

After our conversation, I invited the children to go on a treasure hunt around the studio to look for objects to place on the projector. They found many small objects to try, such as beads, shells, plastic geometric shapes, a spoon, and a pair of scissors. The children were thrilled to watch the effects of each object as they placed them on the projector.

The experience was a dynamic one, with lots of movement. The children moved their bodies in and out of the light to create different effects, and projections of the objects would often shine on their clothing. The children also placed their hands on the projector and watched with delight as they were enlarged on the wall. "My things are getting big!" exclaimed Jack.

Madeleine walked around the room, continuing to search for new objects. At a certain point, she discovered a round paper doily on a shelf, and instantly it seemed precious to her. She carefully rubbed her fingers over the soft paper to feel the texture of its intriguing pattern. She then took the doily to the light projector and dropped it onto the glass top. Immediately, a large, intricate pattern of light appeared on the easels. The children were delighted. The effect was of one large circle made up of many tiny shapes of light. Madeleine was fascinated by it; she went to the easel and carefully touched the complex pattern of light with her fingers. After a few minutes, she said that she wanted to trace the beautiful shape.

Madeleine chose a thin marker and carefully began tracing around each spot of light (see Figure 3.8). It was a big job, and she invited the boys to help her trace. When they had finished their effort on all of the small spots inside the circle, they drew the line around the outside to complete the shape.

I was unsure of what would happen next when Madeleine said, "I want to color the shapes in with bright colors." The boys loved the idea and eagerly agreed. I thought for a minute and suggested tempera paints. The children and I pulled out the paint cart. The paints had recently been mixed and offered a wide range of colors to choose from. Because there were four children who were all going to work at once, I suggested that they move the drawing to the large table in the center of the studio. Madeleine suggested that the circle be cut out with scissors before everyone began painting. She chose a pair of scissors from the shelf and carefully cut it out. The children selected the colors of paint and small brushes and began carefully filling each shape (see Figure 3.9). As they worked together, the children began to share their thoughts and ideas. Jack said, "I think this is a snowflake. It's the snowflake that the Snow Queen flies on," referring to a Hans Christian Anderson story that the children had recently seen performed at a local theater.

"It's a magic snowflake!" added Madeleine.

Jack affirmed her comment and said, "I think that, too."

Madeleine continued to develop her idea, "It's a magic snowflake that can turn into anything. If you throw it up into the air, your wishes will come down from the sun!"

"Yeah, it's a snowflake that will give you anything you can imagine. Like bubble gum or candy!" Schroedter added.

"Yeah, it will hit the sun and everything you want will become real!" exclaimed Noah.

Looking at the bright colors of paint, Jack said, "I would want the snowflake to give me candy." He pointed to the various colors and said, "This one is strawberry; this one is lemon, or maybe lime."

Madeleine added, "I think I would want tangerine."

An Environment That Supports Creativity

At the end of the morning, after the group had finished painting, Madeleine sat quietly at the table and looked at the magic snowflake. The boys had moved over to the computer to work on drawings they had previously begun. Madeleine told me that she thought the snowflake needed one more thing;

Figure 3.8. Tracing the beautiful shape.

Figure 3.9. The children chose colors and carefully painted the shapes.

she needed to draw a flower in the middle. She and I asked the boys what they thought. They agreed, and Madeleine took it upon herself to finish it. She chose some markers from the drawing shelf and completed the magic snowflake by drawing a delicate, multipetaled flower in its center (see Figure 3.10). Later, when I asked Madeleine why she added the flower, she said, "I think it looks like a snowflake and a flower. I want to throw it up in the air when it's summertime." Then she pointed to tiny flowers in the pattern on the doily and added, "This has flowers on it."

As the children finished working, it occurred to me that this small episode that began with an exploration of the light projector had evolved into a collaborative event using different areas of the *atelier* and multiple materials to support the ideas. Madeleine's discovery of the doily had invigorated everyone's experience of playing with light and had pushed it into new forms. Once the shadows of the doily were enlarged and traced, it became a catalyst accessible to all of the children's thinking. As they worked, the children continued to develop their ideas in relationship to one another and the familiar materials in the different areas of the *atelier* with a sense of ownership. They combined the precious object with light, drawing, and paint. As they collaborated, the children made connections to storytelling through the comparison of the round image of the doily to the giant snowflake in the Hans Christian Anderson story "The Snow Queen." The experience with the light projector had not been an end itself but a co-created and imaginative experience that transgressed the use of several materials. The rich environment of their *atelier* had supported this experience (see Figure 3.11).

Figure 3.10. Completing the magic snowflake.

Figure 3.11. An environment that supports creativity.

Loris Malaguzzi said that children are the best evaluators and most sensitive judges of the values and usefulness of creativity. He elaborated on this thought by explaining that children easily explore and change their points of view, and that their creative acts are born out of, and are part of everyday life (Malaguzzi, 1998). He also said that "our task is to help children climb their own mountains, as high as possible." Malaguzzi's words bring to mind John Dewey's metaphor that mountain peaks represent a culture's finest work growing out of everyday life and experience. Our school environments and the materials they offer to children on a daily basis are an integral part of learning experiences. When the *atelier* as well as all our school environments are continually developed and used in purposeful ways, they transform our everyday life in school into a living manifestation of the richness of children's potential.

REFERENCES

Cadwell, L. (1997). *Bringing Reggio Emilia home: An innovative approach to early childhood education*. New York: Teachers College Press.

Dewey, J. (1934). *Art as experience*. New York: Penguin Putnam.

Malaguzzi, L. (1998). History, ideas, and basic philosophy: An interview with Lella Gandini. In C. Edwards, L. Gandini, & G. Forman (Eds.), *The hundred languages of children: The Reggio Emilia Approach—Advanced reflections* (2nd ed.; pp. 49–97). Westport, CT: Ablex.

Experiences from a First *Atelier* in the United States

Conversations with Amelia Gambetti and Jennifer Azzariti

Lella Gandini

The 36 inner-city children, ages 3 to 6, who attended the early childhood program at the Model Early Learning Center (MELC) with their families in the early 1990s had a unique experience in the United States at that time, as they lived and learned in an environment that flourished with the innovative ideas of Reggio Emilia. The MELC, part of the National Learning Center (TNLC) in Washington, DC, and connected with the Capital Children's Museum, was indeed a very special place. Ann Lewin, the founder and designer of the school, which opened in 1989, hired Jennifer Azzariti as studio teacher in 1992, and she invited Amelia Gambetti to be a consultant in the spring of 1993 and then a master consulting teacher during part of the school years 1993–1994 and 1994–1995. In the winter of 1995, Ann Lewin resigned as director of the school to get married and moved away. Sadly, the school closed in June 1997. The educators in Reggio Emilia remain convinced that the experience that took place from September 1993 to December 1996 has a value that cannot be diminished by its demise, and that it lives on as an example of the highest quality of work and commitment by educators, children, and parents (Sheldon-Harsch & Gandini, 1994, 1995; Lewin, 1998).

In the series of interviews for the preparation of this book, I felt that the experience of Amelia and Jennifer—with their different and distinctive backgrounds joined in the common goal of inventing and constructing the first *atelier* in this country within a school that had to become respectful of the children, teachers, and families involved—needed to be revisited and to become part of our collective narrative about the *atelier*. Amelia Gambetti is now executive coordinator of **Reggio Children** and liaison for Consultancy to Schools in the United States. Jennifer Azzariti divides her time between her special role of mother of two young boys and her role of consultant to schools inspired by the Reggio Emilia Approach where educators want to develop an *atelier*.

DEVELOPING COLLABORATION:
INTERVIEW WITH AMELIA GAMBETTI

On several different occasions I have had the opportunity and time to observe Amelia Gambetti at work with a group of teachers in the environment of a school, and I have been impressed by her way of "being there." For such work to begin, all participants must establish a serious commitment to examining together the situation and way of working; it is only at that point that reciprocal trust can be built. It is then that Amelia is able to begin to be completely present; observing and listening, silent and alert, she becomes cognizant of what is around her and what is missing. She tries to understand the way the day flows and the way the interactions take place, as she looks for connections among her own experience in Reggio and other experiences in the United States. Amelia "reads" how space, materials, and routines, and how children, teachers, and parents, are part of the life of a particular school. This is the premise upon which she can begin an honest dialogue with the teachers, who are acutely aware that Amelia has been observing them and their environment.

My intent here is to underscore the value of deeply observing one's own environment and one's colleagues to share observations and to help one another see and understand weaknesses and possibilities. The aim is to work together to build a culture of learning and collaboration.

I recall that Mary Beth Radke, while teaching with Amelia at the University of Massachusetts Laboratory School, said:

> This was a point of real learning for me—I understood that the motivation for everything that you do is so critical. Not only do you need to go back to guiding principles, but also you need to go back and ask yourself: "What is the problem here? What is my goal? What motivation is there for doing what we are trying to do?" The asking of questions is so important. It keeps you somehow focused on the essential things that you are trying to accomplish with children. I really learned and grew and changed as a teacher and as a person. We were not trying to translate or reproduce Reggio. Amelia was trying to do something for the people in this school.
>
> We were learning to look at the important things about children that lent something to our understanding and our ability to help them learn. What were their interests? Who did they play with? Things like that provide really important information for teachers.
>
> Start with respect for children. Question what it means to you and how your actions reflect your image of the child. How can you improve consistency about respect for the child through what you do every day? Look at collaboration among all adults in the school in a new and different way—try to learn to question things together, and to exchange ideas and trust each other.

It's not so scary to focus on process and not know where you're going if you have true collaboration, if you are together and are sharing responsibility in a true sense. It's a great joy and pleasure. It's great to be able to say, "I'm stuck. I'm having a problem. I just can't," and to have someone there to back you up, not to judge you. (Gandini, 1994, p. 65)

I believe that these considerations are a fitting introduction to the conversation that Amelia and I had in November 2003:

Lella: *Will you tell us about the first time you went to Washington, DC, to visit the MELC, where Jennifer Azzariti worked as the* atelierista*?*

Amelia: The first time I visited the school, I stayed for four days. Ann Lewin had asked me to observe all that went on in the school. In the afternoon I was to meet with the teachers, who would be presenting their projects. Just before the presentations, I found Jennifer crying in the hallway; she was in crisis over the afternoon meeting. I asked her what the problem was, and she answered that the teachers all had projects to present, but she, the *atelierista*, had nothing. After hearing Jennifer's concern, I tried to set up an afternoon meeting so I could understand more about the organization of the school and its staff. I was told that each project "belonged" to a single teacher and that the *atelier* was considered a space separate from the rest of the school. There did not seem to be collaboration among the teachers, and above all, the school was not in the position to ask itself what the *atelier* could offer to the classrooms and vice versa. The organization of the space reflected this, as well. The school was not considered and lived as a whole; instead, the spaces were separated. There was a space for the Montessori materials on one side, a space for the letters of the alphabet to trace on the other side, the science room, and the library. It was all divided up by sectors, like many islands.

Lella: *When you began this collaboration, what strategies did you use?*

Amelia: I visited the school for the first time in 1993 when I went to Washington with Loris Malaguzzi for a conference in honor of the Reggio schools. Malaguzzi visited all of the spaces at the MELC, but he didn't say anything about the experience. In September, as I prepared to leave Italy to begin my consultation in Washington, DC, I asked for help and advice from Malaguzzi. He answered that he didn't have anything to tell me; he told me that I already knew what I had to do. I insisted he share his thoughts, and Malaguzzi replied that it was a school where one did not see the children, where the children did not exist. I put together all of these impressions: the isolation of the various sections of the school, the invisibility of the work, the separation and the bareness of the *atelier*, and the absence of a connection between materials and the projects of the individual teachers. I observed the work in the school and decided that the first thing to do was to find a way to give visibility and presence to the work that they were already doing. We began to understand what possibilities

Figure 4.1. Collaboration, analysis, and discussion.

already existed in the school, and how much of this could be woven into the activities of the *atelier*, to bring it as close as possible to the expression of the languages of the children. We began to discuss what collaboration meant and the idea of the school as a system of relations and interactions [see Figure 4.1].

We put a lot of work into analyzing and discussing what happened every day and, at the same time, we acted on what we saw. We began to transfer materials from a supply closet, which was full and always closed, to the *atelier*, where the materials became visible and available. We began looking for other useful materials inside the museum. We decided to involve parents in bringing materials to school, creating a "presence" for the parents through the materials they brought. All of this began to transform the *atelier* into a "lived" space. We worked on the organization of the space, to transform the environment, to find the thread that would hold together all of the spaces. For example, the science room remained, but connections were created with the work that was going on in the other spaces. The objective was to use materials to show that the experiences in the school could be expressed in many languages. This took a lot of effort but involved the teachers, and the diversity of their identities emerged. Everyone tried to bring out the particular aspects of their own character, both positive and negative. The goal that we set for ourselves was to create a school that was a community of people that together constructed an experience.

Jennifer's identity was defined by her understanding of materials, her ability to use her hands, and her capacity to weave together her experiences with the experiences of the children. The exploration of materials, which can become languages and can be combined with experiences in the making, became the strength of her participation at work.

Lella: *You spoke about the particular characteristics of the context, which were valued to strengthen the identity of the school. Can you clarify this process for me?*

Amelia: When I began collaborating with this school, I had 25 years of experience as a teacher in Reggio Emilia. To learn how to bring this experience into dialogue with others means knowing the new context and the culture from which it was born. In this exchange, I myself had to grow. Growing did not only mean visiting the schools, participating in conferences, but "being" in each new context [see Figure 4.2].

I think that, through the years in the United States, this exchange has given me a way to see the strength of the schools with which I have collaborated. At the MELC, the significant features of the school remained. What we did was give an identity to these features by observing and listening to what happened there and, above all, through interaction with the children. This process did not radically change the way the community of the school related, but there was greater attention to others, to different points of view and other possibilities.

Figure 4.2. Amelia Gambetti participating with the children in school.

Lella: *This seems like a fundamental way to respect a complex situation.*

Amelia: Certainly. I have supported many collaborations with teachers and schools in my experience in this country. I believe that the collaborations with the most positive outcomes were among educators who carefully read and evaluated their own context and were able to understand the richness of their own identity and how to enter into dialogue with the context of Reggio Emilia. For example, the First Presbyterian Nursery School in Santa Monica has an *atelier* and two part-time studio teachers. Each of the classroom teachers offers her own competencies in the use of the space and its materials. Other schools focus on the *miniatelier*. There is a school in Miami that is based on the idea of a laboratory where things are constructed. In this context, we are trying to weave together the laboratory experience with that of the classrooms. The value of collaboration is that it unites all of the various experiences, but the strategies to put them in motion are different. I have learned to listen, to wait to give my contribution, and to analyze the identity of the context along with the people with whom I am collaborating. This way, more importance is given to time, to process, and to the action of thought. Space is given over to creativity. In this conception of work, creativity is no longer something that belongs only to art; it begins to become a way of thinking that takes the processes for building knowledge into consideration.

Lella: *I would like to go back to the evolution, the changes that Jennifer went through. How did you see her in terms of her role in the school?*

Amelia: Jennifer has many strengths; she is very candid and honest, and this is how she related to the children. She trusted them and, as a consequence, was trusted by them. Jennifer had a very constructive relationship with the children; they worked together. She gave them responsibilities, and the children felt involved in the work that they were doing. This was a beautiful thing. Jennifer really liked following children's processes in working with materials. I remember when she observed the construction of a painting in tempera by a little girl and made 80 small sketches, one for each step the child took during the process.

Jennifer was capable of discussing the children's work with them and capturing their reflections in writing. She had a great ability to respect the thoughts of the children and to involve them in understanding the process. We would use this material when we prepared documentation to render visible the children's processes of learning along with our own. In fact, she learned to use documentation as an instrument, no longer as a product [see Figure 4.3].

In addition, Jennifer had a great passion for the use of materials, and she was able to transfer this passion to the children. From this the dialogue was born among Jennifer, the children, and the materials. Thanks to this way of working, the school became a laboratory. The collaboration between teachers and *atelierista* grew.

In my opinion, the role of the *atelierista* becomes stronger when the teachers have a good understanding of the *atelierista*'s intentions. If the teachers and

Figure 4.3. Preparing documentation together.

the *atelierista* are kept separate, the risk is that there will be little communication.

Lella: *Can you elaborate on this point?*

Amelia: When Malaguzzi began as the director of the first school, which opened in the early '60s, he was seeking to transform the education and teaching of the time. Toward this end, he felt it would be necessary to introduce the *atelier* and a teacher with a visual arts background who could teach using more than words. In Reggio Emilia, we continued to re-elaborate the concept of the *atelier*. Exchanges of initiatives were organized in which the *atelieristi* who had different specializations (in printing, in sculpture, in painting) introduced these techniques to the teachers. As a result, the teachers began to share more and in different ways what took place in their dialogues with the children. We decided at this point to create *miniateliers* in the school or in the classrooms. The *atelierista* began leaving the *atelier* to work within the classrooms. We had many materials in the *miniateliers*, and there were projects that were born in the classrooms and continued in the *atelier*, and vice versa. There were parallel experiences that developed in different classrooms, creating a complexity of meanings, a dialogue that was more open and more articulated. It was then that the school began to present itself as a laboratory.

Lella: *Tell me how the openness to external resources enriches the school.*

Amelia: I will tell you about an experience I had with Chuck Schwall in Saint Louis. When I visited his private studio, I did not see any traces of his work with the children. I asked him why he maintained this separation between his own work and his experiences at the school. After we talked together, he decided to bring one of his own oil paintings to the school. The strong points of our various identities need to be defended; otherwise, we run the risk of homogeneity that does not allow for the richness of diversity. The richness of diversity gives dignity and identity to an experience.

Lella: *Do you have any parting advice after these strong and helpful reflections?*

Amelia: It is easy to fall into repetition when you collaborate in various situations, but the risk can be lessened if we begin to listen. Once we have learned how to give strength to these new contexts, we can avoid that danger.

Regarding the worries of the parents, and the pressure placed on the school to teach reading and writing, I think that when attention to process and to the construction of the thought system of the child becomes evident, the families realize that the work that teachers do with children is much more than reading and writing. It is a preparation for life. But this "much more" has to be visible. Otherwise, we are not capable of communicating this different way of learning and teaching.

GROWING AS AN *ATELIERISTA*: INTERVIEW WITH JENNIFER AZZARITI

Jennifer Azzariti, after working with Amelia Gambetti for several years as the *atelierista* at the Model Early Learning Center, helped to create an *atelier* at the Cyert Center for Early Education at Carnegie Mellon University in Pittsburgh. She also worked as a consultant to develop the *atelier* at the World Bank Children's Center in Washington, DC. Through the years, Jennifer has presented her work and collaborated with other *atelieristi* with great success at various conferences and seminars. She is now writing about her experience. This interview took place in December 2003.

Lella: *How did your interest in art develop? Did you take art classes when you were a student at Smith College? How did your work in Washington, DC, begin?*

Jennifer: As a young child, I was always making things, from mud pies to elaborate costumes, playing in nature and with nature. Even then, I had a passion for collecting and organizing that is with me to this day. My parents nurtured my interest through private and group art lessons—clay, watercolor, oil painting, even macrame. I did take art classes at Smith, but I decided, regretfully, not to major in fine art. I was influenced by a late 1980s mentality that a career in art wasn't important or lucrative enough.

After college, I interviewed for an internship at the Capital Children's Museum, thinking that exhibit design could be a good place for a government major. The interviewer, Susan Albers, noticed my minor in Italian and mentioned that the museum was featuring an exhibit, *The Hundred Languages of Children*, from a small town in Italy. She mentioned your connection with the exhibit, which was quite a coincidence, since I had spent my junior year of college in Florence with you and your husband, Lester Little. She then asked me if I was interested in an internship as an art teacher in the preschool upstairs. I decided to give it a try.

Lella: *How did you learn about the Reggio Emilia Approach?*

Jennifer: In addition to having the *Hundred Languages* exhibit in the museum, our director, Ann Lewin, gave us articles about the Reggio Approach to read. We began going to seminars, but at a certain point Ann felt that she had taken us as far as she could. At that point, she urged Amelia Gambetti to work with us in the school.

Lella: *How do you remember your first impressions of Amelia's presence at the MELC?*

Jennifer: I was curious about her. For a long time she didn't say much; she observed for two weeks. Then, at a staff meeting one afternoon, the dialogue began. Amelia never said, "This is how you do it" or "You're not doing that right." She built relationships with us, shared her experiences, and helped us look at ourselves from a new perspective. She considered our context and framed her comments, questions, suggestions, and insights with her years of experience in Reggio and our particular situation in mind.

Lella: *Was it difficult for you to change your approach to using materials with children from an "art room" to a studio/atelier?*

Jennifer: Actually, I think it was fortunate that I hadn't taught children before. I'd never even set foot in an education class, so change wasn't that difficult for me. I was desperate for guidance about how to work with children. Before Amelia came, I relied on what I knew from my own childhood experiences and from what I saw in other schools . . . traditional early childhood "art," using traditional store-bought materials. I didn't know what else there could be beyond finger painting. I didn't realize the potential and capabilities of young children. Once I saw images from Reggio and began to think about other ways of working, I flourished. It was a revelation to put the same thinking, organization, and care into working with materials and children that I would into my own work. It was liberating to think and make choices as opposed to following recipes for art projects; to work and learn alongside children instead of teaching something to them. I appreciated the back-and-forth nature of the relationships with children [see Figure 4.4].

I don't want to make it sound like change was easy, even with Amelia there beside me. I had to figure out what I was doing and why; it's not as if she handed me solutions. I made many, many attempts and had countless disappointments along the way. It was a challenge to change, and at the same time it was exciting and alive and new. There was an incredible energy throughout the school and in my life. I was being asked to think, and I felt respected, especially as a 22-year-old novice teacher.

Lella: *What were the aspects that captured you and your imagination?*

Jennifer: I especially enjoyed collecting and preparing materials for the studio. In my own work, I had been using a lot of found objects, so bringing this

Figure 4.4. Working alongside children.

to the children was a natural extension. I also loved to think about how to translate an idea or theory into something visual, to determine with children what the best material would be for the expression of a thought [see Figure 4.5].

Lella: *Would you tell me about the construction of relationships with the other teachers?*

Jennifer: This started off slowly. In the beginning, there was a lot of separation, many closed doors. I was alone in the studio, and the work we did was not connected in any way to the life of the classroom. All of us decided what we were going to do that day and did it, without much sharing before, during, or after an experience. A big step for us was finding a forum to talk together and build trust. Documentation helped us to share experiences in a more meaningful way. We began to rely on each other, until it became impossible to work alone; the interconnectedness of experiences and relationships did not allow it. Some other experiences that helped our relationships develop were being observed by a colleague or observing her; working together on a project, a drawing, or a panel; and questioning each other's motives and decisions.

Lella: *I know that the use of documentation was an important development for all of you. Can you reflect on the process of learning about using documentation in a way that could help a young teacher?*

Figure 4.5. The children translated their ideas and theories into visual expression.

Jennifer: I remember boxes of photos waiting to be organized into panels months after they were taken. I remember panels that told the story of what happened, with no evidence as to how or why. I remember sticking tape recorders in the house and block areas and the communication center, hoping to "catch" something useful, and piles of notebooks with unused notes from my observations of children. These memories point to issues of organization and intention, strategy and clarity.

There was no particular moment when I said, "Oh, now I get it," but there were certain experiences that led to advances in my thinking about the process of documentation. One that stands out is my first study tour to Reggio. I watched a presentation by Vea Vecchi about her process of documenting children as they built horses in clay. She showed examples of her notes, a progression of sketches of the process of the child. She drew as they worked and videotaped to use as reference later.

When I returned to our school, I immediately set up a situation where I could practice what I had learned. I videotaped the children and myself and asked the other teachers to look at the video with me. I transcribed my notes as I had seen Vea do. This might not seem like a big deal now, but for me and for us it was an important and difficult step. Inviting other points of view, paying attention to the experience as it unfolds as well as the particular details and mini-stories throughout, and chronicling the thinking of children to make it visible to others. These strategies were all new to us.

The best advice I can give to others, as they begin to attempt this way of working with children, is to consider the importance of thinking about and through an experience before it happens. It is equally important to be intentional about what you are documenting and why, articulating choices and motivations, and organizing and preparing beforehand. Maybe this seems incongruous with the idea of emergent curriculum, but I have found that narrowing the focus, framing questions, and uncovering the many layers of an experience has led me to richer documentation.

Lella: *Can you share some of the occasions when the families became participants, those you remember with anxiety and those you remember with joy?*

Figure 4.6. The first working parent meeting.

Jennifer: The anxiety-filled occasion is an easy one to remember. Amelia encouraged me to organize a working meeting with parents for the first time. We planned to make light boxes for the children as a present for the holidays. I set up the studio very carefully and had all the materials ready to go. I was a nervous wreck. I sort of knew what I was doing with children, but not with a roomful of parents. I had no idea how many parents, if any, would show up; how I would explain myself; or how I would interact in this situation. I think about five parents came, and it was uncomfortable at first, but as we began to work we all relaxed a little [see Figure 4.6]. The parents were so proud of the work that they had accomplished and were waiting to see how the children would use the light boxes. The meeting helped me to know parents on a whole different level, and they in turn became more interested in the work of the studio. Now, working meetings are some of my favorite times.

As for the joyous occasions, I remember standing in the corner at our holiday party with happy tears in my eyes. That year, music had been a big focus in the school, so we centered our celebration on music. Parents made musical instruments for children (another working meeting); children illustrated a songbook; and parents and children sang songs to each other. I was touched by all the preparation and enthusiasm on the parents' part. They tried so hard to make this exchange meaningful and rich for the children. They used the school, its materials, and its teachers as resources and were involved in the creation of the event from start to finish. For the first time, I felt like some pieces were coming together [see Figure 4.7].

Lella: *You have worked with several other schools to begin, transform, or support the life of a studio. What are your reflections about your development as a studio teacher and a learner? What advice can you give to teachers who want to open up their way of working with materials and media?*

Jennifer: In terms of materials and media, one of the most helpful things I do is frequent contemporary art museums and shows. There is such an incredible wealth of examples of different uses of materials. I never fail to leave a museum without one or two new ideas for work with children. My other, very pragmatic advice is to throw out prefabricated materials for children found in catalogues and to start looking for materials in other places: Grandma's attic, flea markets,

Figure 4.7. The parents, children, and teachers at the holiday party.

Figure 4.8. Listening and learning from one another.

beaches, hardware stores. What I did with children depended on what I found in the schools. Every collection was different, so it changed the nature of how I worked and sparked new ideas. Of course, there were similarities in the experiences, but each school developed its own personality in part because of the kinds of materials it held.

Since my days with Amelia, I have had two children of my own. When I sit with my sons and watch them build or draw, or listen to them talk and think out loud, I feel the relationships tug—back and forth. Back and forth; we listen, we learn from each other. I recall most often a similar feeling about working with the children at the MELC [see Figure 4.8]. There was a comfortable ongoing dialogue—an exchange of techniques, ideas, theories and opinions that throws the teacher–student paradigm out the window.

CLOSING REFLECTIONS

Amelia and Jennifer have brought back to life the historic experience at MELC that gave children and their families the joy of learning and a concrete sense of worth that we hope they have carried with them beyond the disappointment of the closing of the school. Some of us have followed the experience close up, and many other educators were touched by it. Now we can reflect in new ways, given the distance in time and our personal journeys, as we revisit

Amelia's and Jennifer's ways of observing and being observed. Amelia and Jennifer give us the chance to witness a group of teachers looking within themselves and, at the same time, to each other for strength. In this way, they discover unusual solutions, a diversity of ideas, and cooperation. Through this work, they were able to sustain hope and support the great potential of children and their families while holding high expectations.

The emotions of reemerging memories and of the first encounter with an *atelier* and an *atelierista* in Reggio Emilia also open the next chapter, by Barbara Burrington. She guides us through the details of the creation of a new place in an unexpected space. We learn about possible ways of transforming what we have, even when it seems that there is no extra space. She also presents her fine views of the *atelier* as a connecting "geography of the imagination" for both adults and children.

REFERENCES

Gandini, L. (1994). What can we learn from Reggio Emilia? An Italian–American collaboration. Interview with Amelia Gambetti and Mary Beth Radke. *Child Care Information Exchange, 3*(94), 62–66.

Lewin, A. W. (1998). Bridge to another culture: The journey of the Model Early Learning Center. In C. Edwards, L. Gandini, & G. Forman (Eds.) *The hundred languages of children: The Reggio Emilia Approach—Advanced reflections* (2nd ed.; pp. 335–357). Westport, CT: Ablex.

Sheldon-Harsch, L., & Gandini, L. (1994). The Model Early Learning Center: An interview with teachers inspired by the Reggio Approach. In *Innovations in early education: The international Reggio exchange,* Part I, 2(4), 1–6. Detroit: Merrill-Palmer Institute.

Sheldon-Harsch, L., & Gandini, L. (1995). The Model Early Learning Center: An interview with teachers inspired by the Reggio Approach. In *Innovations in early education: The international Reggio exchange,* Part II, 3(1), 2–8. Detroit: Merrill-Palmer Institute.

Melting Geography

Reggio Emilia, Memories, and Place

Barbara Burrington

The first stories that I remember were those that my mother and father shared about their personal experiences in World War II. They were stories of challenge, of courage, and of hope. My mother left Framingham State Teachers College on July 3, 1945, to join the U.S. Marines, and forever after my mother was a teacher, bus driver, farmer, cook, and corporal. My father, destined to farm the land of his father and forefathers in the Northeast Kingdom of Vermont, was determined to "help free Europe," and he joined the Navy on May 10, 1943. He became a navigator on an LST (landing ship, tank) boat that delivered supplies and men between England and France. He saw the beaches at Normandy, and he brought those vivid memories and deep emotions to the dinner table. Together, with great passion and compassion, my parents regaled my siblings and me with stories of determination and heroism, desperate tales of homesickness and being afraid, but most of all, stories of enormous confidence.

The first time I visited Reggio Emilia, Italy, I cried. Actually, I cried twice. The first time I cried, I was sitting in the meeting room at the Martiri Di Sesso School, listening to one of the original founders, a brave old woman. "In 1945, the most pressing problem for a population that had just come out of a war was that of rebuilding materially, socially, and morally. . . . Above all, the people felt the need to see that their children would never experience anything as terrible as the war had been for themselves" (p. 6). It was this climate of "'enthusiastic solidarity' and faith in sociopolitical change that . . . gave life to the School (p. 9) (Martiri Di Sesso Centro Verde Preschool, 2002). At that moment, my father's spirit and life were embodied and important in that little school far from East Burke, Vermont, and my mother was part of their story, too. All the stories were one tale of bravery, and all our histories were related. My eyes were too wet to hide, and I fell in love with the place.

I cried later, too. In the same school, I entered the *atelier* and listened to the *atelierista*, Max, quietly describe his work with children. Everything in the room held meaning—clay monsters with oversize features, paintings of faces, weavings from cloth and ribbon, dried grass and flowers, handmade books with sculptured covers, vases of wildflowers, collections of seeds and leaves, things made from wire and woven with fabric, clay people suspended in motion on a table top. All of a sudden, my body started to tremble—at first only a little; then I was wracked with the full force of crying, and I could barely breathe. My friend Lauren asked if I was all right. I can't remember what I said.

Thinking back now, I know that it is rare for a place to carry such deep meaning that it moves a person, through her memory and imagination, to other times. I had been similarly moved when I revisited the house I grew up in and the cemetery where my grandparents, my father, and my oldest brother are buried. This, however, was the first living place—for children and teachers—that moved me so. I recognized how special a particular place can be, exaggerated not in my imagination but by the reality in front of me. In that moment I was faced with a place that exceeded my dreams. I knew then what I know now: that the *atelier* is worth thinking about. In Max's *atelier* I could stop romanticizing about the *atelier*s in Reggio Emilia and begin to cultivate a relationship of my own with the idea of creating a place dedicated to expression.

WHY A STUDIO?

In February 1999, my colleagues and I at the University of Vermont's Campus Children's Center made a wish come true. We raised enough money to participate in a study tour delegation to the preprimary schools in Reggio Emilia. Our experiences and observations in Reggio Emilia created a broad stage for self-discovery and led us, in one week, to what felt like an accelerated process of personal and professional renewal.

Back home, we made a collective decision, based on our observations of our own children, that our center needed an *atelier* or studio space for children. We agreed that such a space would support our interest in scaffolding children's fluency with multiple symbolic languages, create a context for looking deeply at what interests children, and allow us to understand better children's processes for learning. So we began the slow process of transforming our staff room into the "studio." The place where we had previously had discussions and shared meals with one another, or simply rested, was to become a more intentional environment with new purposes.

Our center has eight classroom teachers and 40 children between 6 weeks and 5 years old. Each year we educate approximately 22 undergraduate students in early childhood education in their first fieldwork placement. Discussions among teachers were filled with big hopes for the studio and for all of the various people who would inhabit it.

The teachers felt protective of the space and wanted to be sure that it was developed and utilized with thoughtfulness and purpose. We wrote a vision statement and posted it on the door. We created a journal for our communication in which we would record our questions and shared ideas for environmental changes. Each week, we devoted time during our staff meeting to the development of our practice in the studio. Michelle, a teacher of toddlers, reflected on the collaborative nature of the space:

> I think one of the challenges we have in the room is making it accessible to children of different ages. It is also exciting to have this room where children can cross over and do projects with a child from the Preschool, a child from the Young Toddler and Older Toddler rooms. It is amazing to be transcending the boundaries. I think it is so exciting to work as a whole staff on this one space together. It is working to make us better collaborators, better thinkers together. The process has helped us become more of a community. We are going to be inventing our roles together. We will need to dedicate a lot of time to talking about it, to share our experiences and help each other learn and think together.

In my opinion, the *atelier*, or studio, is not only about the arts. Neither is it about something in addition to the work we do in the classroom. Rather, it is about linking the experience of our lives as teachers with the children's lives and waking up together in the world of a new geography.

This is a geography of the imagination. The territory is defined by sensations felt within children and indelible impressions made by each encounter with materials. The landscape reflects lasting, essential memories the children will carry through life of color, of the way things feel, of how something appears; a place where memories are created deep within the child, shaped through everything made there. The studio is a place for learning all kinds of techniques, and a place for research (see Figure 5.1). "The studio space is not an isolated place where artistic things happen. It is a laboratory for thinking" (Topal & Gandini, 1999, p. 24). Amanda, who teaches toddlers, refers to the studio as "Our Sacred Materials Headquarters." Marley, age 4, said, "It's a fun place. It's not so AHHH! screamy, so we can be a little quieter." Blair, also 4, added, "And there are treasures."

Figure 5.1. Madeline, 2.5 years old, working with clay.

DEVELOPING THOUGHTFULLY

Since we were transforming the space ourselves in our spare time, with help from parents, the project naturally proceeded slowly. This was a positive thing. It created time for us to consider how we could best set up the space and how to work in the space. The process of painting the walls, building shelves, retrofitting tables, and gathering containers for materials took months. We were buoyed by our hopes for the space, and each effort to organize and furnish the space was necessary for developing a relationship and an understanding of the space. As described in *Beautiful Stuff* (Topal & Gandini, 1999), we asked all the members of our community—each teacher, student, and family—to find, scavenge, save, and contribute materials. Our letter to families reflected our values:

> In keeping with our commitment to promoting care and respect for the natural world, we would like to use as many natural and recycled materials as possible. We hope that you and your family will become engaged in an ongoing treasure hunt that will help strengthen the children's connections to both the natural world and the studio space.

We were delighted by the enthusiastic response, and our first encounters with materials lasted months. Sorting, categorizing, and displaying found and donated materials and objects became our introduction to understanding the important elements of the studio space. The studio space is dynamic; it changes over time with the addition of new members in our teaching community and the evolving interests and questions raised by different groups of children. Unlike the *ateliers* we had visited in Reggio Emilia, which often reflected the particular strengths and style of the *atelierista* in that school, our studio became a personal statement about a group of teachers (see Figures 5.2 and 5.3).

We share the studio with our student teachers, as well, and need to be mindful of the fact that many have never touched clay or learned how to spread paint. Many have not had the experience of drawing, sewing, or becoming visually literate with any media or space. All of us struggled, and struggle still, to be unafraid of experimenting with materials and media.

We need to have systems that support scheduled use of the studio as well as spontaneous situations that require us to visit. We have to be accountable for leaving the space the way we want to find it ourselves when we arrive with a group of children. Our emerging shared vision for the space; our values, practices, and attitude of research became common ground for viewing the space as special, even sacred, and provided a shared motivation to create a clean and beautiful place for all who entered. I do not want to imply that it has ever been easy. I am suggesting that perhaps the struggle itself added value, maybe even held out hope to us. In this case, optimism is reciprocal—from the studio to us, and back again.

Figures 5.2 and 5.3. Two views of the studio.

MAKING MEANING

Our early observations of children exploring materials in the studio are thick with anecdotes of children who took long periods of time to become familiar with the characteristics and possibilities of different materials.

Our first piece of documentary work regarding the studio was titled, "Realizing Our Right to a Sanctuary." It tells one of the first stories in our history through the thoughts and images of infants, toddlers, and preschoolers. That documentation reflects our success in creating a peaceful environment for our community of learners. It begins:

> The studio has become an integral part of the shared identity of our little school. We have actively and mindfully supported its continuing evolution and, in turn, the studio serves to inspire the hard work of children and teachers.

Subsequent documentation titled, "Getting to Know Materials, Ourselves, Our World," reflects children's processes as they look closely at materials. Our early observations led to more complex stories of encounters between partic-

Figure 5.4. Oia, 5 years old, sketches a flowering plant. Her friend Lucia comments, "When you draw something that doesn't move, it's a still life, but when you draw people, it's a move life."

Figure 5.5. Intersecting passions. Sean, 2.75 years old, with trucks and paint.

ular materials and the children from the preschool classrooms. We documented the relationships between materials that "sparkled" and "gem stones" and children's personal narratives about their concepts of "love, beauty, and family." The children's questions seem to revolve continually around their very attentive noticing and an internal quest to understand "What is beautiful?" We observe repeatedly that children see the inherent "beauty" in materials first (see Figure 5.4).

Over the years, the plots have thickened along with our individual and collective competencies with different materials. We now have a recorded history of stories, personal narratives, and reflections told in many, many languages through tempera, watercolor, and acrylic paints; collage; puppets; sewn objects; clay structures; masks and totems; wood sculptures; pastel portraits; drawn theories in pencil, ink, marker, and oil pastel; photographs taken by children; and beautiful paper hand made by children and their teachers (see Figure 5.5).

We have discovered a **cycle of inquiry** that constantly re-emerges: an encounter between children and materials coincides with their imagination or interest, is recorded by a teacher or saved in an artifact, and is retold by children and teachers, which becomes a provocation to pursue the encounter into the future. It is a continuous cycle of perching and flying. Like birds landing and taking off, children and teachers survey the terrain and ascend in order to gain a new perspective.

Teachers who visit our school most often ask, "How did you all agree to make a studio?" as if agreeing were the hardest part. Maybe it was, but only for a minute. Each day presents dilemmas. We face them all through dialogue, in arguments, in notes to one another, by reading one another's documentation, by listening, by observing children, and by sharing the questions our children and teachers pursue. We face them with the kind of dignity that is blessed in an *atelier*.

BENDING OUR EYES TOWARD THE FUTURE

Sergio Spaggiari quoted these words by Loris Malaguzzi in his welcoming speech to the United States teachers' delegation: "Education must stand on the side of optimism or else it will melt like ice cream in the sun" (personal communication, November 2000).

After September 11, 2001, we had to listen even more closely to the children and their families. We had to think deeply about our community, and we had to consider how we would respond to the anxiety and sadness around us. Our own doubts and uncertainties compounded this very difficult time of crisis. During the days following September 11, the University of Vermont undergraduate students who live in the suites surrounding our center invited us to collaborate with them on a mural. The students had chosen to create a "Community Peace Mural" with painted images and poetry in response to the September 11 tragedy.

This was very provocative for us. Our young children were not unaware of the crisis and anxiety around them, and their lives, too, were changed because of our proximity to the Burlington Airport, which is just one mile from our center. Our playground is beneath the flight path for planes taking off and landing every day. It is very common for the children and teachers to look up when a low-flying plane casts its shadow over the yard.

The airport also serves as the station for the air unit of the Vermont National Guard. Usually once each morning and once each afternoon, the guard fly mission-combat air patrols over the Northeast corridor from Washington, DC, northward: F16s in formation. After September 11, they flew around the clock for 122 consecutive days, and our little playground shook.

We had to act on our belief that the multiple representational languages of children can be much more profound than simply talking. We know that the arts are a powerful way to communicate. We believe that throughout history, people have used the arts to convey their culture, identity, values, feelings, and ideas, and to define beauty. Art is a mechanism people use to mark time, to understand one another better, and to express and learn about the rich inner lives of individuals. As teachers, we felt that the mural project provided a rich opportunity to respond to incredible sorrow and fear in the context of community and metaphor.

On October 5, 2001, we began our participation in the evolution of the community mural project on the east side of the Living and Learning Complex (see

Figure 5.6). The preschool children were given a special section of the wall between our studio and the pottery cooperative. We had spent the weeks leading up to the actual painting discussing which symbols would best represent the children's ideas of happiness and peace. The children agreed on rainbows "because they are pretty and they make people happy!" Over the years, we have become very familiar with the powerful nature of rainbows to young children. We often observe children making rainbows to express hope, beauty, happiness, and love. We agreed with the children and set up the studio as a warehouse for all the materials we would need to paint outside on the concrete wall.

The children worked tirelessly, taking short breaks from their own painting to watch the older UVM students paint, listen to their music, relax, reflect, talk, cry, and hold one another. The excitement became contagious, and children in the other classrooms wanted to join the process. The toddlers, young

Figure 5.6. Preschoolers composing the September 11 peace mural outside the studio.

preschoolers, and infants contributed strokes of paint, handprints, and energy to the mural. The infant and toddler teachers added words to represent the often unheard voices of young children.

The mural symbolizes the values that moved us to build our studio and announces our presence to everyone on campus. It is a welcome message linking images, places, people, and events. If it could speak, I believe it would quote Cicero: "Be kind, for everyone is fighting their own quiet battle."

Over time, we continue writing our history, evolving our future, and unpacking our memories and impressions from Reggio Emilia. This process is not something we think about continuously because it is part of being absorbed or consumed by the contentment work brings. And our studio nourishes that peace of mind.

OUR LITTLE STUDIO GETS A SOUL

Figure 5.7. Natural materials gathered by children and available to everyone on the studio shelves.

After three years of growing and developing, our little studio's soul became obvious. Early on, the space had a physical essence and it served many people and purposes, but it had lacked enchantment. The studio needed to be invented first, and then it needed to be lived in to absorb some spirit so that it could, in turn, inspire others.

Our studio has become a real place, not an imitation of a place. Its uniqueness seems to be a good starting point for imagination and invites us to reside in it because it has a history. It is a vessel for hope; it holds stories and translates its intentionality and all the values we hold dear.

One value is evident each time we refer to the little room as our "studio," a name that implies work, study, and art all in a breath. Other values are communicated by the space, as well. Our studio is simple. We have discovered a kind of richness in simplicity, displaying that which we really use; things we are connected to; things we consider beautiful, from nature and from one another (see Figure 5.7). The

Figure 5.8. Gemma, 1.5 years old, visits the peace mural.

invitation to work outside the studio on the mural for peace is a constant reminder to us that we can extend our borders (see Figure 5.8). This was the promise of enduring hope first nurtured in me by my mother, inspired in all of us in Reggio Emilia, and integrated into our little studio through the spirit of collaboration, an attitude of optimism, strongly shared values, and an abiding belief in the power of the arts.

REFERENCES

Martiri Di Sesso Centro Verde Preschool. (2002). *Along the Levee Road: Our school turns 50—From nursery school to municipal Centro Verde Preschool, 1945–1997* (English ed., pp. 6, 9). Reggio Emilia, Italy: Reggio Children S.r.l.

Topal, C. W., & Gandini, L. (1999). *Beautiful stuff: Learning with found materials*. Worcester, MA: Davis Publications.

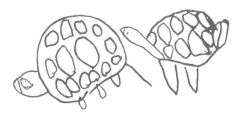

The Essential Voice of the Teachers

Conversations from Reggio Emilia

Lella Gandini

At times, through the questions posed by educators from the United States and the conversations that take place about the *atelier* when they visit the schools of Reggio Emilia, it appears that the connection of the *atelier* with the work of the teachers and the cooperative aspect of their construction of the learning experience is undervalued. In this chapter, first two preschool teachers, Laura Rubizzi and Paola Barchi, will speak about their long experience and understanding of the importance of this connection; then Lucia Colla will give her perspective as a young teacher from the Infant/Toddler Center Bellelli; and to conclude, Tiziana Filippini, pedagogical coordinator, will offer her reflections.

THE *ATELIER* AND DOCUMENTATION: INTERVIEW WITH LAURA RUBIZZI AND PAOLA BARCHI

In June 2003, I interviewed Laura Rubizzi of the Diana School and Paola Barchi of La Villetta School, two teachers who have documented their work with great care and presented their documentation internationally.

Lella: *Would you try to reconstruct the evolution of the* atelier *from its birth to the experience of today?*

Laura: I have 28 years of experience, 25 with the same *atelierista*, Vea Vecchi. In the last three years I have worked with a very young *atelierista*, Isabella Mennino. In the beginning years of my work, the *atelier* helped me to find a concrete relationship between pedagogical theory and didactics [teaching practice]. I also grew to understand this concrete relationship through the orchestration of and reflection on projects. Then there was the very important transition in our ways of documenting when we searched for a way to make the actions and processes of children more visible. I learned communication techniques from the *atelier* that I had not learned in my preparation as a teacher.

In the very first years, teachers and *atelieristi* worked consistently on exchanging abilities and techniques, and this modified my way of working, as well. I learned a great deal from Vea. She is a professional with preparation, interests, curiosity, and a culture different from mine. Over time as a teacher, I have acquired more autonomy in planning and in carrying forth my work, but the relationship with the *atelierista* has always been intense during the planning, documentation, and verification of the project work.

The arrival of a new *atelierista*, Isabella, has determined the beginning of a new relationship. She has experience in fashion, in advertising, in digital media. She has a very up-to-date understanding of a variety of different languages that we teachers do not possess. Isabella needs to construct her experience working with the children, but she knows that she can count on my experience. What I find most fascinating is the idea that the *atelier* and each *atelierista* offer us the opportunity to continue to learn over time.

Furthermore, rather than only a physical space, I think that the true *atelier* is a mind-set, one that slowly enters into your understanding as a teacher, into your way of organizing spaces, of observing children, of carefully taking notes on the learning processes, of working on documentation, and of communicating what the children and teachers are doing [see Figure 6.1]. The research of the children and of the teachers is very important, and the *atelier* is a great support in this respect; it makes the relationship between art, emotion, knowledge, and creativity more clear. By bringing in art and poetry, the *atelier* gives a great deal of hope, especially when society finds itself in a difficult moment.

Figure 6.1. Teachers meeting at the Diana School: Laura Rubizzi, Marina Castagnetti, and Paola Strozzi.

The *atelier* is a sort of multiplier of possibilities, of explorations, and of knowledge. For the children, this is evident because they can continually exercise their creativity, communicating it through the objects that they produce, and through their thought processes. They also can refine many languages as well as exchange different points of view. The *atelier* also gives parents the chance to see the creativity of children in a different way. With regard to teachers, the *atelier* gives us fresh ideas for offering learning experiences, thanks to the value given to the playfulness that the *atelier* brings into our daily work.

Then there is the subject of constant updating and researching new forms of communication. If we do not communicate, if we do not document, it is as if the things we do as teachers and the things that the children make do not exist, or they would exist for a brief time and only within the cultural context of their school.

Lella: *What has been your experience, Paola?*

Paola: I have worked for 17 years with Giovanni Piazza, the *atelierista* who has worked in my school for the past 32 years. Over the course of the years, we have always searched, *atelierista* and teachers together, for new tools and new forms to construct documentation. Notes presented in different types of observational charts, as well as with digital cameras, computers, and scanners, have modified our approach to documentation and research. The tools and the strategies for documenting are in constant evolution, changing in relation to different contexts in which we work with the children.

Personally, I began by working in private preschools in which the *atelier* did not exist. The *atelier* was a huge discovery for me. But most important for me was discovering that the expressive languages can contribute to our own learning as teachers and to children's learning in multiple ways. Throughout my time of discovery, I have felt the desire and the need to know and understand different materials and their narrative possibilities. Therefore, my formation was shared with the *atelierista* and with my colleagues, but was also made up of individual moments, in solitude, in trying, understanding, and experimenting. This helped me, I think, to learn how to put my knowledge into play and to listen more carefully to the processes of the children as they construct their understanding through materials [see Figure 6.2].

Lella: *Laura, you said that, at a certain point, documentation became a very important tool. How did you become aware of this?*

Laura: Loris Malaguzzi was very aware of the need to document from the beginning. His idea was to create a *transparent school*, visible and in dialogue with contemporary culture. In my personal history I think that the change took place when we began to focus on the evolution of the learning process of the children, by documenting it. Before that, the projects, though articulate and carefully considered, kept this part hidden. From the moment that we accepted

Figure 6.2. The teacher, Paola Barchi, takes note of a 5-year-old girl's thoughts and choices as she selects images for placement in her digital portfolio.

this challenge, showing the product accompanied by what we had observed, the change took place.

The strategies to communicate learning processes are still a very open area of research. The farther we go on, the more we understand that many levels of documentation are possible: basic documentation, with keywords, gives a certain type of information. But to articulate the communication, one must enter inside the processes of learning, getting to know the tools that the teacher uses, reading the discussions of the children, seeing the growth paths that the children follow.

Every time teachers evaluate themselves through revisiting the documentation, they learn something more than what they had learned with the children. Moreover, revisiting with other colleagues the analyses of the experience and the exchange of ideas can lead to a valuable assessment.

Working together on documentation is a fundamental experience because it represents the synthesis between the competencies of the teacher and those of the *atelierista*. It provides a way to get to know each other and appreciate each other. The *atelier* guarantees that languages and techniques make their way to the teachers who do not possess them. In general, young teachers do not have very good preparation, but they know how to offer new points of view that can enrich our collective experience. I think that it is fundamental to considering the aspect of intellectual curiosity that the *atelier* nourishes.

Figure 6.3. Two teachers discuss with the *atelierista* Giovanni Piazza a documentation in progress at La Villetta School.

Lella: *Do you agree, Paola?*

Paola: I think that exchanges with our colleagues regarding documentation carried out during a project sometimes bring up problems and questions. Naturally, this can be a source of conflict that requires being open to negotiation and valuing other people's points of view. But it is also true that the different roles within the work group can lead to productive and rich exchange [see Figure 6.3].

Laura: Another very interesting aspect of the past two years is the experiences we have had with the elementary schools. They are very different in their didactic structure from the preschools, because the *atelier* and documentation are not present. Working with schools different from the one in which you work is very stimulating.

Lella: *Does the exchange with other schools happen on a regular basis?*

Paola: This year we had various meetings about *miniateliers*. The plan designed by the Documentation Center [a center created to support professional development for all the educational programs of the municipality] was titled, "Thinking with the hands." It promoted a course for the state, private, and municipal preschools. The theme of the seminar, which I helped lead, dealt with the identity of the *miniateliers* on both a technical level and a practical–organizational level.

This was an occasion for exchange and development. We asked ourselves what aspects of the *miniateliers* could be interesting to the other teachers. Teachers almost always talk about the big problems of organization that the *miniatelier* creates and the administrative difficulties that they come across in setting them up, but the thing that had the greatest impact on me was seeing the enthusiasm of the young teachers who were ready for this change. The *atelier* opens teachers to a different way of working. The *atelier* offers us the chance to continually imagine a healthy utopia that is fundamental for those who work with children.

Laura: Another aspect that is very important for the teachers that Paola and I have come across is a need to test themselves as leaders in professional development. A seminar with teachers from the elementary schools that I led was called "Documentation on the Walls." The elementary school teachers were perplexed and irritated when they considered this idea: the materials seemed excessive to them and difficult to create.

Then someone started to make comments about the experience of the children within the elementary school: "Maybe the school does not have very much faith in the children." After this first observation, others followed: "The elementary school does many things, but without documentation; nothing remains, only the written evaluations, but these say nothing about the learning paths the children followed, and nothing about the teaching, either." Then a discussion started about the desire to better understand what kind of documentation might work in an elementary school. Right now, a group of elementary school teachers are enthusiastically documenting the processes of their work with their students that they will show in an exhibit on the expressive languages of children and art.

Lella: *Will these experiences with other schools continue?*

Paola: These are the first attempts, but they are experiences that are very enriching for us, and we hope that they can become so for all of the people involved.

THE RELATIONSHIP OF THE *ATELIERISTI* WITH THE INFANT/TODDLER CENTERS: INTERVIEW WITH LUCIA COLLA

Vea Vecchi has suggested paying particular attention to the work done recently in the infant/toddler centers with regard to documentation of the encounter of very young children with materials. She said in a conversation in May 2003:

I believe that observation of the youngest children requires even a more refined way of listening. By understanding the power of documentation, it has been possible for teachers to thoroughly observe and truly understand infants' and toddlers' processes at a profound level. As a result, they are able to reflect deeply on the identity of these very young children and accredit them further than before for their potential; then they are ready to make this understanding more visible through images.

Therefore, in June 2003 when I interviewed Lucia Colla, a teacher at an infant/toddler center who is very active in documenting projects presented at international conferences, I was ready to ask her many questions.

Lella: *How long have you been working as a teacher in an infant/toddler center?*

Lucia: I have worked in Reggio for 13 years. I have always liked my work, but before coming to this city I was not very satisfied. Once I got here, I understood why.

Lella: *You found an environment where children, teachers, and parents learn together in harmony. How do you experience, as you work, your identity as a teacher in the infant/toddler center in relation to the* atelieristi?

Lucia: As you know, the position of *atelierista* was not included in the infant/toddler centers, although the *atelier,* as a space, was part of our buildings. However, over time, meeting periodically with an *atelierista* became an essential support for the teachers. This encounter between two types of professionals who have different knowledge enriches and helps form the identity of teachers at the infant/toddler center. The identity of the teacher at infant/toddler centers is more fragile than that of a preschool teacher. A stereotyped culture prevails about the natural tendency of women to care for very young children, and education is not considered relevant at this stage of children's life. This view has repercussions at times on the image that we have of our work and ourselves. Therefore, our professional development, particularly with the *atelieristi,* gives us the strength to continue with our overall educational project. Through these exchanges with the *atelieristi,* the teachers from the infant/toddler center gain experience and autonomy in learning to read and interpret the expressive languages of children.

Lella: *How did the particular sensitivity of the infant/toddler teachers mature, allowing you to be more attentive but, as you say, also autonomous in the interpretation of the languages of very young children?*

Lucia: I think that the infant/toddler teachers grew tremendously thanks to this network of ideas and professional encounters with teachers from the schools of children age 3 to 6, with the *atelieristi* and with pedagogical coordinators, and also thanks to the interdisciplinary approach of the project-based work. All of this prepared us, made us grow, and made us sensitive to research beyond pedagogy. In our way of working, and in our professional development, there is this extraordinary capacity to intertwine our shared knowledge with attention to the contemporary culture that surrounds us, to widen our horizon. Each individual is also engaged in his or her daily actions, since it is our role to take care of the daily routines of children so young. Each situation, from lunch to getting ready for nap time, can be a moment of research, because all of that constitutes an increased attention to the environment, to the preparation of materials, and to the contexts for research.

Lella: *How do parents consider the experience of their very young children with materials?*

Lucia: With regard to the parents, I would say that their participation is fundamental. Last year, we maintained a connection with the parents through meetings in which they would tell about their concerns and we would tell them the things that perplexed us. In a meeting with them about expressive languages—when several teachers from different levels of schools were working on a large project called Children, Art, Artists [Vecchi & Giudici, 2004], centered on the work of the famous Italian artist Alberto Burri—a father said to us, "But what is my 8 month old son going to do with exposure to the art of Alberto Burri?" He was asking himself what we had asked ourselves at the beginning. Trying to explain the sense of our work was not easy. Later, the mother told me that the father came to understand our work during the summer when, at the beach, he saw his son making not only forms but also actual compositions out of the sand. Our discussion had changed his way of looking at his son. Thanks to the meetings that we had with the parents, in which we kept a positive attitude and openness to questioning, an atmosphere of solidarity was created at work in the infant/toddler center and at home with the families.

Lella: *What is your relationship with the* atelieristi, *and how do they support you in your work?*

Lucia: It is a relationship of mutual respect and alliance. Vea has supported us in dialogue, in various projects, and even with small documentations. Tiziana Filippini, always a very precious presence as our pedagogical coordinator, has supported us all along and given us the vital suggestion that we contact other pedagogical coordinators and teachers to ask for additional points of view. That way she has helped us create other relationships. We are never alone.

We learned from the *atelieristi* to be more rigorous in the way that we set up experiences with the children and in the way we observe and do research. We have become more refined in the search for and selection of materials. We create situations that are richer and more interesting for the children and for us than before, and these experiences and projects tend to generate new learning and growth [see Figure 6.4].

Lella: *Do the* atelieristi *usually support you in the analysis of your work?*

Lucia: Yes. I remember my first documentary: I had prepared 150 slides. During the presentation things were not going well. I realized that I needed to

Figure 6.4. The *atelier* of the Infant/Toddler Center Belelli with toddlers and teacher Lucia Colla.

be able to use one significant image instead of saying one thing with 10 images. I understood from the *atelieristi* that documentation during the process of an experience is one of the most important elements constructed in Reggio. A prescribed tool for documenting does not exist; it is built step by step. The children are not all the same, and neither are the teachers. Therefore, a single method of observation for all would not be adequate. Each time, in relation to what it is that we want to document, we build observation charts and tools. The tools must be tested, experimented with, and then continually redefined. Observation is essential; we find that it offers possibilities to reflect on our own processes of learning while we reflect on the learning of the children. The more attentive our choices are about materials and space, the more evident are the seriousness and the beauty of the inquiries children make.

Lella: *I recently saw some of the documentation of your Unexpected City project, and it indicates a strong aesthetic sensitivity to the experience of the children with exploration of materials. Would you talk about the experience of the Unexpected City project?*

Lucia: There is now competence in the infant/toddler center to read and interpret the work of the children and the processes of understanding that have evolved recently. Regarding our participation in the Unexpected City project, let me show you a booklet with a title taken from the words of Michele (age 2.5): *I Giardini sono . . . il posto delle ombre, degli alberi paurosi, degli alberi verdi e dei sassi belli* [Gardens are . . . a place of shadows, scary trees, green trees, and beautiful rocks]. Here is the introduction:

> [On May 12, 2003], three spaces in the historic center of the city of Reggio Emilia—Via Farini, Vicolo Trivelli, and the Public Gardens—present[ed] themselves to the eyes of the residents, transformed by unexpected and unusual inhabitants. For one day a multitude of presences, small and large, visible and partially hidden, transformed the city, the ways of walking through and living in these three spaces. What had happened?
>
> In the past months the children of the infant/toddler centers and of the municipal preschools had explored these three predetermined spaces with strategies that have always belonged to children: attention, vibrant curiosity, extremely reactive gestures and senses, capable of strong empathy and reinterpretation of that which they encounter. These are explorations where the physical space, objects, acquires a dimension and significance that is different from that which the adult world usually attributes to them. A perspective that transforms, the children's perspective, is capable of generating a new identity in spaces known by everyone. The project, the intent of the unexpected city, was to have certain visible references to the strategies, to the creativity, and to the imagination of the children, allowing their amused, playful, imaginative perspective to orient and shock our way of looking for at least one day. In the process of the discovery of the public gardens, which lasted for several months, the children of the infant/toddler center investigated with their eyes and with their hands, building relationships with trees, with benches, with sounds, with the weight of stones, intertwining play, humor, and beauty. (Filippini, Ruozzi, & Vecchi, 2002)

Lella: *The booklet documents a beautiful experience. The public gardens gain a new dimension when they can be experienced with the intensity and wonder of the vantage point of children and those who know how to see and listen with them.*

Lucia: In the documentation and in the selection of materials, one has to succeed in giving possibilities for beauty and creativity. As a consequence, it is evident that one also tries very hard to capture images that are at the same level, so much so that the images become more beautiful, more evocative. But they can only be at this level of beauty if there is a very serious study of the process of understanding underlying it. It is the only way of becoming more capable. We grew through this process, which was very difficult and required patience. "We refined ourselves," as you have said. There is the desire to communicate what we have seen, to support the culture of infancy, and to communicate with others, to fascinate them, to involve them, and to enchant them a little.

THE *ATELIER* AND THE ROLE OF PEDAGOGICAL COORDINATOR: INTERVIEW WITH TIZIANA FILIPPINI

Tiziana Filippini, pedagogical coordinator (*pedagogista*) of the Diana School and other centers, is the director of the Documentation and Education Research Center and the coordinator of professional development planning. She has spoken about the schools of Reggio Emilia to educators in various countries. She lived in the United States as a young student, an experience that contributed to her interest in many different aspects of communication in her work. I interviewed her in June 2003.

Lella: *As pedagogical coordinator, how do you work with the* atelier *and the* atelieristi? *How do you contribute to professional development, work with* atelieristi, *teachers, and parents, and coordinate the work among schools?*

Tiziana: Considering my own experience, I find essential, still today, the happy choice that introduced in our schools different professionals who discuss and compare their work within a climate of participation and shared responsibility in making educational and didactic choices. The best results stem from this dialogue taking place on a daily basis and in the more centralized professional development. That is, it takes place in reading, interpretations, assessment of project work, and of particular projects analyzed together.

As our choice since the beginning has been to work without referring to a preset curriculum, we meet to review and discuss the experiences we have lived with the children. On the basis of this review, we hypothesize in which direction to proceed in our work with them. Therefore, when the teachers are working on projects, our meetings are based on *ricognizioni* (surveys, bird's-eye views); this is an attitude connected with *progettazione*. This has become for us a mental attitude, a conceptual structure, and it is done with a view that considers at once and keeps together how ideas translate into practice and how, in reviewing practice, we develop new ideas. To examine the work that we are doing in a way that we consider both theoretical and practical reflection is essential for the emergence of ideas. This process is included in all our professional development.

The *atelierista* helps, for example, to interpret graphic language, to detect other languages that the children have used, to note other languages in the work they have done, to reflect on the connections among various languages, or to highlight which languages should be reinforced. The pedagogical coordinator has the job of pointing out the underlying concepts and of analyzing

Figure 6.5. The transformation of a leaf.

the meaning that the teachers and children have constructed in the course of their work.

The *atelierista* considers the work that takes place in the *atelier* and raises questions for the pedagogical coordinator that point to more complex itineraries. I can give you an example that may seem banal. More or less everyone explores leaves in autumn. Pedagogy suggests working with the children on how to represent the leaf and on the leaf's relationship to the tree through observing the leaf in the natural world. In fact, pedagogy supports an idea of knowledge as a reproduction of an event or an object. Instead, in the *atelier* we encourage the child to enter into a relationship with the leaf and activate processes of reelaboration and reinvention, metaphoric expression, using analogies and poetic languages to build a personal image of the leaf [see Figure 6.5]. We give opportunity to the child to appropriate it on some level through an aesthetic and expressive experience that is not separate from the cognitive one. It is important to stress that this process of elaboration and reinvention is the same one that the individual uses in the construction of knowledge and understanding, a process that clearly belongs to children.

The pedagogical coordinator can help the *atelierista* understand how these processes are not only part of the artistic creation but also of constructing meaning and understanding. In addition, the pedagogical coordinator can help the teachers put different strategies into motion.

Lella: *These complex layers of the processes are probably not obvious to the new* atelierista *or beginning teacher. A very important element in their integration must be guidance by more seasoned teachers or people who have your role.*

Tiziana: First of all, it is necessary to keep our relationships with others open. When we try to explain to others—and, in return, when the others ask us questions—their thought contributes to widening our own point of view. For example, if there is a young *atelierista* who knows very little about the children's process of learning, there is the risk that he or she will make interpretations that are limited or tied to his or her particular area of competence.

Then the pedagogical coordinator *reads* the documentary material along with the teachers and the *atelierista*, with the goal of reviewing together what is happening or what has happened already, to go beyond the more obvious and superficial interpretation. This cooperation helps to gain awareness of the learning that comes from one's own observations (it is part of learning how to learn). It is like offering useful filters to evaluate what we are doing or have done.

Lella: *This way of working also helps in the preparation of the documentary material to be selected—for example, using just a few significant images rather than many.*

Tiziana: There is a great deal to learn connected to visual communication that helps to modify the structure of thought. We like to say that the dance should not be differentiated from the dancer, meaning that the structure of the language influences the content of what we want to communicate in some way. For example, while preparing documentation we make selections of slides considering how to structure visual communication. This requires us to keep in mind not only the technical aspects, but also the expressive ones. This means, at least potentially, that what we have as our final product will give us input that will reflect that which we have put together. In the construction of a documentary we gain a new possibility to read the work done; in fact, as soon as we put together the documentation, we see it in a different way.

Lella: *You can then understand that at times the messages received are not those that you intended to send out.*

Tiziana: Not only! Once something to which we had given a particular interpretation is placed into a certain sequence or new structure, it comes back to us in another light, because the structure of that language has determined the emergence of new details and issues. Furthermore, each transformation gives us more feedback, not simply by adding new elements to a set of known elements, but by restructuring the cognitive, psychological, and cultural fields that belong to the people involved.

When Lucia and I reviewed her most recent work, part of the project titled, "Unexpected City," which was a slide documentary in its first version, we talked about it and interpreted it in one way. But when we prepared a paper version of the documentary for publication, we sort of rewrote the work, because we used a series of excerpts that we had to extract and divide by chapters based on concepts and meanings that had emerged from the written narrative. The whole thing was different from the slide presentation, which had followed a sequence and was accompanied by the voice of a narrator. We had given a new significance to the experience. Extracting other passages, we highlighted other values that we had not been able to distinguish before. Each language has potential and possibilities that can be extracted and focused on when we work with others or when we prepare to communicate with others. Each language gives different images, and when one uses this variety, one has more possibilities to learn. With each passage, one acquires a richer and more complete image.

Passing from the slide presentation to the documentation in a small book, we came across and gained certain aspects that permitted this experience to travel autonomously. Once again, it is a demonstration of what can be learned from keeping the technical and expressive aspects of an experience united. The things that can be learned are much richer and they correspond to and respect more closely the children, who are the protagonists of the experience. In fact, if we examine the artistic processes that are particular to the *atelier,* we see how in tune they are with what the children are asking for, rather than pedagogy that tends to separate different types of knowledge.

Lella: *Do you want to conclude with a particular reflection?*

Tiziana: *Language is a communicable form of thought.* This statement we share and try to understand during teachers' professional development, and it is very much part of our reflections when we try to understand and when we try to support the learning processes of children and adults. This effort to reconnect and to see better, making us give more attention to how we read the experiences in different ways, is, I think, one of the major contributions of the *atelier* to the peculiarity of our educational experience.

The importance of the *atelier* must be connected to the idea of the hundred languages. In a society like that of today, which tends toward the standardization of communication, the hundred languages should be considered an antidote to conformity. We think of the hundred languages as the endowment of the individual, as a metaphor for the construction of knowledge, as democratic participation that goes beyond the single voice by giving a positive force to diversity and to the different languages.

The *atelier* was not introduced as an experience to be added to the other experiences. Instead, it was introduced to modify the pedagogy through a new way of seeing and working; to modify the way of learning within the life stories of the children of the school. This is still the intent and the strength of the *atelier.*

CLOSING REFLECTIONS

This chapter opened with the voices of two expert teachers, Laura Rubizzi and Paola Barchi, who expressed their strong appreciation of the *atelier* as a multiplier of possibilities and as a mind-set. If we consider the interview with Lucia Colla, the teacher of the youngest children, we see how each of these teachers describes in a personal way how the *atelier* has broadened her awareness about children's ways of learning. The *atelier,* they say, offers a true synthesis between the competencies of teachers and those of the *atelieristi* for the benefit of all of the children and adults involved. This process is sustained through documentation, which renders transparent the work of the school and creates evidence of the children's learning and constructions, because without documentation, nothing remains.

Tiziana Filippini concludes this chapter with her keen descriptions of professional development, which she presents as a connecting web for creating collaboration and thinking together among the different professionals working in the schools in order to be open to change. She offers an energetic presentation of the role of pedagogical coordinator as a guardian of communication and connections. She describes connections among different professional roles, among different schools, between theory and practice, and between pedagogy and the *atelier*.

This prepares the way for the next chapter, in which we will follow Lynn Hill's narrative about the frames of mind of courageous teachers who, through cooperation, make formidable changes in their school space. She is eloquent in describing difficulties and reflections accompanying the solution to problems, as she and the teachers take the healthy approach of seeing "the problem as a project." Our colleagues in Reggio do not speak very often about the difficulties, but we know from some of their documentaries (Reggio Children, 2001) how complex it has been to overcome the barriers during their 40 years of developing schools.

In her story Lynn describes the *atelier* as it develops over time to create a sense of community in the school and among generations. She helps us to reflect on the delicate issue of respect for the interests, abilities, and rights of the older generation and shows us the positive relationships and sense of well-being that develops when young and old are offered the opportunity to share in meaningful experiences.

REFERENCES

Filippini, T., Ruozzi, M., & Vecchi, V. (Eds.) (2002). *I Giardini sono . . . il posto delle ombre, degli alberi paurosi, degli alberi verdi e dei sassi belli* [Gardens are . . . a place of shadows, scary trees, green trees and beautiful rocks] (unpublished documentation). Infant/Toddler Center Belelli, Reggio Emilia, Italy.

Reggio Children S.r.l. (2001). *Not just anyplace* (video documentary). Reggio Emilia, Italy

Vecchi, V., & Giudici, C. (Eds.) (2004). *Children, art, artists: The expressive languages of children, the artistic language of Alberto Burri*. Reggio Emilia, Italy: Reggio Children S.r.l.

Border Crossings and Lessons Learned

The Evolution of an *Atelier*

Lynn Hill

In Blacksburg, Virginia, the Virginia Tech Child Development Lab School (CDLS) serves as a site for teacher education and research and provides quality care for children of approximately 90 families who are enrolled in the seven part-time programs. The center offers care and education to the children from the college and local community. The teachers are graduate and undergraduate students who are studying child development or early childhood education. The head teachers (graduate students) typically spend one to two years in the school, and the undergraduates complete an internship in one year as they work six hours per week in the school. So, the teaching members of the community are constantly in flux, which unfortunately often contributes to a lack of continuity, and sometimes even a lack of deep commitment to the school. As the school's director of curriculum, I was one of only three full-time staff members, so each year it fell to me to share the history, rituals, philosophy, and traditions of the school with the newest members of our community. In spite of our challenging context, my most important goal during this orientation process was to emphasize a sense of belonging and a feeling that the Lab School would be a place where they would be nurtured, encouraged, and challenged to be strong, inquiring, and courageous teachers.

To add to the already complex nature of our program, located in our building alongside the CDLS is another program known as Adult Day Services (ADS). This program is available to elderly members of the community who need a place to spend the day—usually while their family members are at work. The ADS enrolls 10 to 20 "residents" who vary in their ability to care for themselves. Many have high levels of dementia; others are more lucid but physically impaired; and most have retained much of their long-term memory but have difficulty with short-term remembrances. Although the programs were side by side (with a large unused space between them), for many reasons the CDLS and the ADS had never been successful in their attempts to relate as neighbors.

The CDLS has been enormously inspired by the schools in Reggio Emilia. Several of us have visited the schools many times and led groups of colleagues and student teachers to Reggio Emilia to engage in thoughtfully constructed and personal **action research** projects. On arriving home, we found that if we were to embrace the ideas from Reggio Emilia, many changes would have to be made within our school. We knew that we would need to think more deeply about our philosophy, structure and organization, space, and way of collaborating with our ever changing community.

Yet change has proved to be a very elusive and difficult concept. Strong feelings of territory and of nostalgia were tightly embedded in our school's culture, and the suggestion of change felt frightening and even sad for some members of the community.

The leadership group (three full-time staff) worked together to consider how change could be enacted without causing even more uncertainty for our community. We believed that, in the case of dissonance or conflict, we should simply consider "the problem as the project" (Hill, 2005). We held tightly to this school motto, like a life raft. This movement to initiate an intentional change in our learning community became our "project." However, while some members of our group seemed safe and content on the raft, others were desperately treading water, and then there were those who were sinking fast. We needed to unite our school so that we could construct a sense of community where everyone would have a comfortable seat on that raft.

MAKING THE PROBLEM THE PROJECT

At the beginning of each school year, every member of our school community is asked to undertake an action research project related to his or her work in the school. In previous years, these individual and group action research projects had led to significant professional development for each of us as well as to a new level of maturity for our school.

As I considered choices for my own topic of inquiry, I remembered the strong, almost magnetic, pull that I had experienced when I discovered the work coming from the *ateliers* in the schools of Reggio Emilia. These special places within each school seemed to contribute to a sense of community and **amiability** (as it is often referred to in Reggio Emilia) that spread throughout the school. There appeared to be a rich transparency and reciprocity between the *atelier* and the classrooms, so that the work in the *atelier* permeated all areas of the school while the classroom experiences fueled the efforts in the *atelier*. This relationship was extremely provocative for me.

Because my formal training in the visual arts includes an undergraduate minor in fine arts and a deep love and continued dedication to creating my own art, I felt that realizing an *atelier* in our school did not require the participation of an individual with more formal art experience. Rather, the project could be initiated by an interested teacher (or group of teachers) who were committed to the power of materials in learning and to the idea of sharing and collaborating with the entire community of a school.

When I announced my intention to study the ideas coming from the studio, my suggestion was met with enthusiasm by my colleagues. The enthusiasm was infectious, and from it a small but determined research team was born. The major challenge with our research topic (which was quickly pointed out by my co-workers) was that our school did not have a studio—or even a space for a studio. I was confused and conflicted about where we might begin our study. My fellow researchers and I began by reading everything that we could get our hands on regarding the *atelier*s of Reggio Emilia. We returned to Reggio Emilia together for more intense observation and consideration, and we brainstormed possibilities. The new school year began with declared intentions to begin the work of developing a studio and to working together in the spirit of community.

GETTING STARTED: CONSIDERING AN ELUSIVE CONCEPT—COMMUNITY

As the research team talked together, we noted that the concepts that were most intriguing to us within our particular research topic included our observation that a strong sense of connectedness, deepened interpersonal relationships, and more beautiful space are evident when an active *atelier* is located within a school. As a way to begin our efforts to realize an *atelier* within our school, we opted to carefully consider the foundation of community, since this essence seemed to be the underlying emphasis in Reggio Emilia and one that was desperately needed in our school.

Thomas Sergiovanni (1992) writes extensively on the topic of school community. He defines community as "people who work in the same place (a community of place), feel a sense of belonging and obligation to one another (a community of friendship), and are committed to a common faith or values (a community of mind)" (p. 63). We immediately recognized that establishing this complex, three-part collaborative network of relationships would take a great deal of dedication and perseverance but would be key to moving from an organization to becoming a community.

Together, as a team, our mutual and early goal was to take a careful and focused look at our environment. We felt that this intense examination of our space would help us develop a richer aesthetic within our school. We believed that the intentional consideration of our space would lead us to expand the ways we think about our entire community and about our philosophy of teaching and learning.

We began to look at our space with new eyes, and many aspects of the school's environment were altered because of this effort. Over the course of several months, our environment changed dramatically. Old and unused materials were replaced with more provocative and natural items. Spaces that had previously been used in less meaningful ways were recaptured and transformed. This was a powerful beginning for our research team and reflected our first steps toward our shared goals of creating a community based on a shared sense of place, mind, and friendship.

GUIDING QUESTIONS

Our initial effort to think and act around the use of our environment naturally led us to the heart of our intended research. We began to make a list of guiding questions that would help us to articulate, imagine, and build the currently intangible concepts of amiability and community, and an *atelier*. Our first questions led to even more questions. We realized that we would have to narrow the list and focus on what was most important for our entire community of learners, and what we might possibly attain. Slow and thoughtful processes were not always common in our school due to a constant feeling that we needed to accomplish goals before our teaching staff left us once again. The sense of floating aimlessly on that raft was palpable.

Although it was a difficult decision for our group, we acknowledged that we would need to start at the very beginning and consider what we knew and did not know about the benefits and values of an *atelier*. Our questions took shape as we carefully reflected together. We realized that we would need to define an *atelier* within the space and systems of our little school, and we challenged ourselves to consider this most basic question. We also wondered how an *atelier* could be created when we did not have an *atelierista* in our school. We struggled with how we would even find the space to create an *atelier* in our already crowded building. How would we know when the space was successfully contributing to the good of the school? We recognized that there would be many borders to cross as we worked toward our goal, and we were committed to finding a way to communicate with others about this new way of thinking, learning, and working together. Despite the many barriers in the way of our goal, we were committed to providing a space for children and adults to think together and to represent thought—an *atelier*.

EARLY EFFORTS: DEVELOPING A STUDIO SPACE

We turned our attention to a room with large windows that had been used to archive old testing materials and quantitative research results. This unlikely room for an *atelier* was filled with natural light but also with filing cabinets that were bulging with ancient, meaningless files. Our new, visionary eyes could see that the room had great transformative possibilities, and although it was rather small, we could visualize it as our first studio. Before we could claim the space for our own intentions, we first had to justify our new philosophical stance, and our certainty that a studio would be a strong and meaningful contribution to our program, to the senior faculty in the Department of Human Development, which sponsored the CDLS. We were surprised and perplexed when our ideas met opposition. These new ideas were not understood and seemed whimsical and inappropriate to the faculty. We had several difficult exchanges before the cabinets were grudgingly moved, leaving the room vacant. In hindsight, we can see that, although we had achieved our goal of procuring the space, our overly enthusiastic way of pushing to move forward quickly led us to miss an opportunity to add new members to our cause. This mistake was vital and would continue to haunt us during the rest of our work to achieve and maintain a studio space. We recognized that we had lost sight of our overarching intent: to promote amiability.

Meanwhile, with mixed emotions we rolled up our collective sleeves and went to work. After extensive effort on this space, we finally had the beginnings of a small studio where we could envision children and teachers researching together.

To get us started, and to add even more members to our collaborative team, we followed in the footsteps of Cathy Topal and Lella Gandini (1999) and began with letters to families explaining the addition of the new studio and requesting that they fill the accompanying bags with interesting natural and recyclable materials from their homes that could be used to stock our studio shelves. Some families were so excited by the treasure hunt that they filled seven or eight bags. It took weeks for us to sort the materials as we marveled over each special item that had been donated and then had to decide how to order, classify, and sort the incredible collection (see Figure 7.1).

Figure 7.1. The first studio space in our small school allowed children and teachers the opportunity to work in intimate concentration and joy.

We noted that our youngest children tended to sort by color, and from this exercise sprouted an investigation of color that extended throughout the year (see Figure 7.2). By the end of the year, even the adults within our community were captured by the stunning idea of color and worked together to create a permanent tribute to the concept as a gift to the school. This affectionate and meaningful offering is now proudly displayed at the entrance to our school (see Figure 7.3).

The older children (ages 3, 4, and 5) were more eager to sort their items by substance and texture, such as paper, plastic, metal, string, wire, and so on. They explained that this style of organizing their materials would help them create the "tall" (three-dimensional) structures that they longed to produce.

This first studio was well loved and well used for almost two years (see Hill, 2005, for details of these first years). It was the source of many exciting projects and of many new relationships. The one problem with this early studio that continued to persist was its very small size.

We reflected on the earlier research questions and were especially drawn to the question: How would we know when the space was successfully contributing to the good of the school? We knew that the children enjoyed the opportunity to visit the studio and to select materials for their plans, and we also felt that the children had become more intentional and thoughtful about their work. We had turned our main hallway into a museum that documented

Figure 7.2. An investigation of color by infants and toddlers grew from the collection of "beautiful stuff" in the CDLS.

Figure 7.3. Adults from our school were inspired by the emphasis on "color" and created this gift to our school: a mural in tribute to tone, hue, shade, and the joy of childhood.

the children's work and respectfully considered each experience. It honored our intent of offering an amiable welcome to all who entered. Anyone who walked down our hallway could have the opportunity to encounter our philosophy of teaching and learning. Our families were pleased with these new ways of representing children's experiences. There was a strong belief among us that the studio had played an important part in helping to create a positive impact on the culture of our school. We were now beginning to think of our school as a collaborative laboratory where we practiced the skills of thoughtful inquiry and documentation.

As we observed the ideas being considered by the children, we noted that the children were helping us to become more thoughtful and analytical teachers. We had developed a more mature means by which to analyze experiences so we could not help but notice, with some concern, that the children were telling us (in their own way) that the size of the studio might be inhibiting them. Sorting and displaying all of the new materials that were being donated to our

Figure 7.4. Ministudios sprang up in each classroom, giving everyone the opportunity to learn through the manipulation of more available and natural materials.

special studio had become an exciting but full-time job. The children seemed to be overwhelmed by the sheer number of options in the studio, and the space was beginning to feel less beautiful and more cluttered. Keeping these new thoughts in mind, we decided once again to rework our ideas for a studio setting in our school. Together, we decided to create ministudios in each classroom. The ministudios were meant to give the children more immediate access to the materials that were contained in the more formal studio (see Figure 7.4).

The evolution of ministudios generated interest and inspired the children. It definitely was a meaningful contribution to each classroom. A reciprocal relationship was becoming more evident between the studio and the classroom (see Figure 7.5).

IMAGINING AN INTERGENERATIONAL SPACE

We continued to long for a more amiable space for our work and turned our hungry and inspired eyes to the only space in our school that was unused, wondering whether it might be accessible to us. This was the space between the CDLS and the ADS. Over the years, the space had been reconceptualized several times to encourage intergenerational activities that were meant to be mutu-

Figure 7.5. Once the ministudios were made available, the children thrilled us with their creativity, expression, and love of multiple materials.

ally beneficial to children and adults. Unfortunately, the many unsuccessful attempts to collaborate had left pessimistic feelings and an even greater schism between the two centers. As a result the space was being used as a storage room for both programs. Our research team saw this as a problem that might be considered a great project for our group. We felt provoked and intrigued when two graduate-level student teachers announced to us that they had decided to explore the possibility of an intergenerational exchange between the CDLS and the ADS. This topic had not previously been considered or studied in depth, so we wholeheartedly embraced the idea and decided to widen our research group to include these new colleagues. We collaborated with the intergenerational research team and from this association we came up with a novel idea: What if we were to choose to use this space as a larger, more beautiful and shared studio where participants from both centers might take advantage of the possibilities that were hiding there? We recalled having seen beautiful studio spaces in some of the schools in Pistoia, Italy that had been opened to the public for after-school use. In that context, this interesting and progressive idea had contributed to a deeper appreciation, respect, and connection between the school and the local community. Could we find a way to replicate the collegiality, amiability, and community between the two groups that we had observed in Pistoia?

We knew that we would have to inspire the other members of the two centers to consider the experiment that we had in mind. Finally learning from our previous attempts to rush in and to claim space, we intended to be more thoughtful and considerate as we entered into dialogue with our neighboring program. Carefully we prepared a presentation for members of both centers proposing that we consider the possibility of an intergenerational studio for the space.

Researching the Values of an Intergenerational Studio

While we admitted that our ideas were experimental, we believed that an intergenerational studio might be designed to allow participants from both centers to share time, materials, and experiences with one another. It might also provide a space that would more effectively serve the best interests and developmental and functional needs of both adults and children. From our research we had learned that:

> it is especially important for preschoolers to experience the benefits of intergenerational programs because many negative and stereotypical attitudes about older people and about growing older are formed during the very early years of life. (Fruit, Lambert, Dellmann-Jenkins, & Griff, 1990)

In addition, we knew that "contact with members of the younger generation is most likely to be positive for older people when they perceive themselves to be meaningful and valued role models" (Dellmann-Jenkins, Lambert, & Fruit, 1991, p. 22). We also remembered having seen an emphasis on the role of the grandparent in the schools of Reggio Emilia. In these schools for young children, a grandparent is often the family member who drops the child off at the school in the morning and picks him or her up at the end of the day. If one is lucky enough to have the opportunity to visit the schools at length, one might also have the chance to listen as grandparents speak articulately about their experiences in the school. These older members of the family are extraordinarily involved in the educational system.

This kind of experience, where children have the advantage of growing up within an intergenerational context, is not as familiar in the United States. Because the United States tends to be a very transient society, children do not often have the daily opportunities to come to know and understand the older generation of their families. We hoped that this reinvented space might allow reciprocal participation in meaningful experiences that could lead to shared life experiences, the opportunity to engage in self-discovery through experimentation with materials, and a chance to build a bridge of relationships across the age span. Thus, we hoped this new and unique studio might emulate a version of what we had observed in the Italian schools and provide a larger and stronger life raft, where both adults and children could climb aboard and consider a route of possibilities and capabilities together.

Preparing a Unique and Complex Studio

After receiving the go-ahead from both programs, we began another reinvention process. With this new evolution of space and place, and keeping in mind how it might affect relationships, enthusiastic teachers, students, and faculty from the CDLS worked late into several nights to prepare the new studio. This period was one of great chaos, confusion, and disorder (see Figure 7.6). It was also a time of deep and thoughtful consideration as we pondered the placement of shelving, tables, and materials, always carefully considering the wide span of ages that would be using the space. Our committed groups of workers

Figure 7.6. Preparing a larger studio—a complex and confusing time as we considered the challenge of creating a place for an intergenerational group.

was extremely dedicated to the possibilities that might lie ahead, and so together we inspired one another to continue the physical, mental, and emotional effort that it took to proceed.

Unfortunately, the staff from the ADS was not initially pleased with the new space. They felt that it was inattentive to their residents and could cause many problems. Now we were learning another lesson. Although we felt that we had carefully attended to the ideas that had been put forward by the ADS in our early conversations, we were finding that many thoughts and concerns had not been voiced in those initial meetings. What had we done to diminish the voices of our neighbors? We were finding that the effort to create such an unusual setting was ripe for skepticism, disillusionment, and challenge. So we did then what we should have done much earlier, as frustrating as it felt to us: Once again, we slowed down and listened carefully, and over the next several weeks we experimented with many changes to the space. We continually rethought the environment and reduced the number of materials that were visible. We reorganized the materials into baskets and tubs that gave the studio a very lovely and home-like appeal. Indirect lighting was added to provide the space with gentle warmth. Surprisingly, even with these efforts some of the members of the ADS remained skeptical of our unique way of envisioning space. In addition, the senior faculty who had disagreed with our original studio aligned themselves with the ADS staff and began to threaten to reclaim both spaces.

It was during this phase of discomfort and fear on our part that we came to realize that one of the problems between our two centers might be that, on every occasion, we had physically taken complete ownership of the revamping of the environment. While we had certainly consulted the ADS staff, we had never included them in our physical efforts to reinvent the space. We realized that we were acting as the esteemed "navigators" of the raft while assigning our neighbors to the lowly occupation of "rowers." Certainly, this style of interaction must have contributed to feelings of invasion of their territory and a lack of respect for their expertise. This was a painful lesson and difficult for us to learn as eager teachers, but in the interest of learning to be amiable, we had to admit that we had been prejudiced and even rude as we envisioned our dream studio. So we went back to work—this time in a more collaborative manner—and this time we included teachers, children, the older adults, and all the residents who would inhabit the space as we worked to find the solution to our environmental problem.

Welcoming Children and Adults into the Space

Slowly and carefully, we began to invite the older adults and the children into the studio to work together around the new table that had been procured for this use. Now both age groups could comfortably reach the table as the children were perched on tall stools while the adults could roll their wheelchairs right up to the table. We had decided (both ADS and CDLS this time) that we would spend the rest of the year exploring materials, but more important, we would focus on attempting to build relationships and a sense of community between the older adults and the children. Now we understood that cultivating community *was* the curriculum, and we hoped that shared experiences with materials in the studio would engender deep understanding, respect, and appreciation for one another.

The earliest experiences around the studio table were quiet. Our detailed observational notes from this time expressed that the children seemed inhibited and even a bit nervous about these new "friends." Some of the adults sat silently as they begrudgingly and haphazardly manipulated the new materials that had been provide for them from our new studio shelves. To say the least, there seemed to be a lack of understanding and appreciation between the generations. There was also an inevitable tendency for the staff of each center to be protective of their own residents. Unfortunately, the division between the centers continued to grow.

Cultivating Relationships

After the early disagreements on space and display, as well as the visible lack of interest between the older adults and the children, the research team planned several events that were meant to offer more moments of intimacy between the adults and the children. We were hopeful that these shared experiences would lessen the nervousness that the children seemed to be experiencing when they were in the company of the older adults.

During their time in the studio, as they "messed around" with an eclectic array of materials, the children and adults were observed quietly comparing hands, arms, faces, and even teeth. So the next several experiences were planned to build on these interests and (we hoped) to bring the adults and children even closer together. One opportunity included reciprocal face painting, where individual identifying traits could be acknowledged from a closer, more intimate stance. Wrinkles, hair color and texture, eye color and shape, teeth, and a variation of noses, ears, and smiles were carefully and affectionately noticed (see Figure 7.7).

At our next research meeting, we shared our most recent observations of the work coming from the intergenerational studio. There was certainly an emphasis on materials each day, but another story that we were witnessing was a growing enthusiasm for being together and for forging friendships. Another observation that was carefully noted in our journal was the parallel development of personal and professional relationships between the CDLS and ADS staffs. We were finally sharing meaningful and authentic information with one another and were taking a shared responsibility for contributing to the planning of the intergenerational experiences. We noticed that our new goals had become building relationships, observing what might inform our next steps, and continuing to support one another.

Figure 7.7. An opportunity to get up close and personal with one another led to a more comfortable pleasure between the groups.

One beautiful day, we worked together to set up many easels on the ADS patio and to offer a wide range of soft pastels to provide a new context for these growing relationships. When the children and adults arrived on the scene, they were immediately drawn to the experience that had been prepared for them. They quickly paired themselves up (an older adult with a child) and began to experiment with the materials (see Figure 7.8).

The next day, we offered visual documentation to the intergenerational group from the experience of working with pastels and easels on the patio. The power of documentation was immediately evident in the room. We found that both the children and the adults were thrilled to see themselves pictured in the documents, but something else was also happening: The couples who had worked together were now sitting together and pointing out remembrances to one another (see Figure 7.9). They also seemed excited and inspired to see their work once again. The enthusiasm expressed by our participants as they revisited their earlier work, reflected on those experiences, and then decided to move to the next level together was contagious.

We also noted that the two groups of teachers were getting along well and that we seemed to share many similar thoughts, concerns, and ideas for our time together. This is not to assume that all was completely agreeable on all occasions, but any dissent between our groups was beginning to challenge (rather than irritate) the members of each group. We were learning that embracing our disagreements and arguments, and the dissonance that came with them, brought our multiple perspectives into light where we could best address them.

Figure 7.8. A chance to work in couples gave us a look at different styles of collaboration.

Figure 7.9. The power of documentation was very evident among this unique group of friends and promoted further investigation of materials.

Figure 7.10. When the older adults suggested a flower-drying experience, the children were enthusiastic partners as they were given the opportunity to cut flowers from the community garden.

Figure 7.11. Within these special and transitional moments, we recognized that the children and adults no longer needed the teachers to guide and encourage their interactions.

RECIPROCAL LEARNING: ADULTS AND CHILDREN

As the year progressed, we saw a shift in the interactions between and among the groups. Now, instead of relying on CDLS or ADS staff to guide the interactions, the children and older adults began to initiate their own experiences. For example, we watched as they shared the delight of picking flowers from their collaborative garden, after which the older adults guided the children as they taught them how to press the flowers, dry them, and make plans for their future use (see Figures 7.10 and 7.11). And finally, as the literature on intergenerational experiences had predicted, the thrill of working as a role model for the children was very obvious during these moments and seemed to inspire a general sense of self-esteem for the older adults (see Figure 7.12).

The children reciprocated by independently suggesting and insisting that the Grandmas and Grandpas (as they now called their older friends) work with them on other projects. Having noticed a distinct interest in nature, color, and treasure hunting among both groups, our teacher team decided to offer a provocative moment to our intergenerational group. One morning, the adults and children arrived at their centers to discover that an enormous tree had sprouted overnight and was now filling a very large space in the middle of the studio. The evening before, the research team had cut down a multilimbed

Figure 7.12. The adults had become role models, and the children were happy and comfortable collaborators.

tree from a nearby farm and had secured it by planting it in a large tub of plaster of paris. Because the tree had seemed to appear magically, there was a great sense of delight and possibility coming from both the children and the adults. The children conferred together and then initiated a treasure hunt to find "beautiful stuff" to hang on the tree, eagerly inviting their older friends to assist them with this new creative process. At the insistence of the children, the two generations divided themselves into committees of "gatherers," "sorters," and "hangers" as the tree grew into a rainbow of eclectic and carefully chosen materials. This experience took several weeks to accomplish, and the enthusiasm for it never diminished. As teachers, we just stood back, observed, and took notes as the older adults and the children claimed ownership and collaborated to create a shared and very colorful sculpture that seemed to be a tribute to their new, diverse relationships (see Figure 7.13).

Figure 7.13. Spontaneous and affectionate experiences were the result of this special and experimental studio.

LOOKING BACK, THINKING FORWARD: THE CREATION OF COMMUNITY

At the end of the school year, the research team sat down together to try to put our closing thoughts on paper. Using our detailed daily journal, which included observations, reflections, photographs, and artifacts of each day we had spent together; we carefully reviewed the story of the multiple studio experiences that had influenced our thinking, and we began to consider specific thoughts for the future. In addition, we reflected on our original guiding questions to determine whether we now had answers to some of the provocative queries that had initiated our project several years earlier. First, we chose to consider Sergiovanni's definition of community.

A Shared Sense of Place

Together, the groups had found a particular way to create an environment filled with eclectic materials that allowed most members to make meaning and to discover the joy of representing their ideas in new ways. Our *atelier* had become a "place" that was not privileged or separate but that had infused each program.

A Shared Sense of Friendship

Although the adults and children were not related, there was now a beautiful sense of togetherness, tenderness, and affection among the members of this new kind of family. While the older adults and children had definitely formed strong relationships, one of the more surprising results of this effort was the formation of parallel relationships between the staff from each center. The earlier feelings of distrust and lack of respect between the staff members had been transformed into a shared loyalty and vision for what could happen when a studio was introduced to a program.

A Shared Sense of Mind

Although we had begun our experiment on shaky ground, it was evident from our notes that most members felt a sense of belonging as the group created together, laughed together, listened and learned together, and finally came to a point of "intersubjectivity," where people have an intimate understanding of one another's minds. In keeping with the research on intergenerational experiences, the children had come to a place where negative and stereotypical attitudes about older people had diminished. Further, the adults now perceived themselves as both collaborators with the children and meaningful and valuable role models.

CLOSING REFLECTIONS

As this project drew to a close that year, we were excited by one more important revelation: The major tenets and principles coming from the schools of Reggio Emilia certainly could be applied to the work with older adults as well as that with young children. As we at the Child Development Lab School worked to define and develop such Reggio principles as our understanding of "amiability," "an education based on relationships," "the image of the child," "the environment as a third teacher," and so forth (Gandini, 1993), we recognized with enthusiasm and the help of the intergenerational studio experiences that these important concepts could also be applied to a very different population.

Our group's research, analysis, and application of the idea of the *atelier* had led us on a creative journey. The experimental intergenerational studio had offered us a great opportunity to learn and grow as individuals and as a group. It had been, at once, an inspiring, frustrating, exciting, painful, and passionate attempt to find new ways to offer the benefits of the *atelier* to a unique group of participants.

While the story of this novel studio will probably differ dramatically from the experiences of those who are reading this chapter, we believe that you can find many similarities in the epic of challenge and change that were addressed along the way. In the end, as our life raft continued to make headway, despite every storm and adversity thrown at it, we recognized that, above all, the studio is about listening, communicating, and community. Developing a community of learners helped us to become more courageous risk takers, and from that stance we all learned and grew together. We are still in the very early stages of imagining and creating a studio space that celebrates the multiple use of materials; however, we know that we have achieved one important piece of that way of thinking: We have come closer to understanding what it means to consider an "education based on relationships." We believe that this is the first and most vital step toward achieving an *atelier* that will cross borders and affect everyone who comes in contact with it. We learned that, by slowly and respectfully encouraging relationships and cultivating community, we had discovered the foundation of the idea of our *atelier*—amiability.

REFERENCES

Dellmann-Jenkins, M., Lambert, D., & Fruit, D. (1991). Fostering preschoolers' prosocial behavior toward the elderly: The effect of an intergenerational program. *Educational Gerontology, 17,* 21–32.

Fruit, D., Lambert, D., Dellmann-Jenkins, M., & Griff, M. (1990). *Intergenerational day care.* Paper presented at the 43rd Annual Meeting of the Gerontological Society of America, Boston.

Gandini, L. (1993). Fundamentals of the Reggio Emilia Approach to early childhood education. *Young Children, 49,* 4–8.

Hill, L. (2005). The amiable school: Incorporating everyone into the equation. In L. Hill, A. Stremmel, & V. Fu. *Teaching as inquiry: Re-thinking curriculum in early childhood education* (pp. 127–142). Champaign, IL: Allyn & Bacon.

Sergiovanni, T. (1992). *Moral leadership: Getting to the heart of school improvement.* San Francisco, CA: Jossey-Bass.

Topal, C. W., & Gandini, L. (1999). *Beautiful stuff: Learning with found materials.* Worchester, MA: Davis Publications.

The Role of the *Atelierista*

Conversations from Reggio Emilia

Lella Gandini

In the Reggio schools, the process of observing children's interactions with materials and listening to them has continued to grow through time in creative methodology and complexity. New developments, the attention to other levels of schooling, and the entrance of new, young professionals are brought into the system of education that, all along by choice, has been a dynamic mirror of social and cultural change. Through documenting the interconnections among children's many experiences and relationships, teachers and *atelieristi* inform us, in depth, about the processes of understanding, learning, and teaching.

The following interviews are linked with those of the previous chapters; they take us further along the narrative about the research done in the schools. We will start with a new conversation with Mara Davoli, *atelierista* of the Pablo Neruda School, and continue with an interview with two young *atelieriste*, Isabella Mennino and Barbara Quinti.

EVOLUTION AND CHANGES IN THE ROLE OF THE *ATELIERISTA*: INTERVIEW WITH MARA DAVOLI

Mara describes the strategies designed to help the transition of new teachers, the opening of professional development to other schools, and the emerging new roles of the *atelierista*.

Lella: *What aspects of the experience and the evolution of the* atelier *are important for you today?*

Mara: To be able to sift through 30 years of personal and professional experience is not easy for me. On one hand, I have the feeling of being rooted in the experience; on the other, the way I live the profession and the *atelier* in my school, and in our educational system, have undergone some notable transformations. The reasons for transformation vary; certainly, the social, cultural, and political mutations are deep. Our city has changed; so have the children and the families. I also have changed. In addition, in these last few years, there has been a great turnover of staff; it is a change that affects all of our institutions, both infant/toddler centers and schools for children age 3–6, but it affected our school in a particular way.

Lella: *The new generations tend to change their profession. The teachers in the United States would understand this. Is it a recent phenomenon in Italy?*

Mara: Yes. Regarding the youngest generations, my impression is that they have a different view of the future when they consider their professional life. I think that this forces us to consider professional development and self-development in a different way. I think that now there is a different perception of time and a faster pace that leads us to find new strategies and new tools for our work.

Another important change in our profession is certainly due to the fact that, during our experience, the number of educational institutions—communal, state-run, and private—has multiplied. The city is more and more frequently taking an approach to inclusive professional development that is carried out in dialogue with different institutions.

Our strategy to cope with the staff turnover was as follows. Knowing, through experience, that all of the parts in a school are vital to the life of the system—the kitchen and the *atelier*, the teachers and the auxiliary staff—we invited the new teachers to participate with us during the professional development and evaluation at the end of the school year in July. We few "survivors" who knew we would be teaching again the next year considered our energy and our strengths, and we tried to divide the responsibilities for the coming year. Regarding the most particular aspect of the *atelier* and my role as *atelierista*, we decided together to dedicate a consistent part of my time at school to working side by side with the two new young teachers who would be coming in August and taking on a new classroom of 3-year-olds.

We pulled out the archived papers and other documents that could be useful for these two new teachers. For example, to get to the course the projects had taken from the 3-year-olds' classroom of the year before, we extracted the elements from the first classroom meetings with the families and two short booklets on the projects that were undertaken with those children. We gave the documentation to the teachers at the beginning of July so they could build expectations and prepare themselves for entry into the school.

Lella: *This strategy must have helped them to start to see what it means to work in a school like yours.*

Mara: Yes. Then in September, I moved for part of the morning to the *mini-atelier* of the classroom so that the young teachers would experience expressive languages as a rich opportunity and, at the same time, as something normal and part of everyday experience. We chose the theme "Variations of Light and Color in the Natural Environment" to be contained within mini-stories connected to one another, as a sort of thread that would lead us throughout the course of the year. This thread would weave a web, a story of what we were exploring, nourished by a number of languages: verbal, visual, plastic, and so on. Naturally, the story of this evolution is very complex, and I cannot do justice to it in a few words.

Lella: *I am convinced of this. But all of this was new for them?*

Mara: Yes. We worked in this way in the *miniatelier*, but then we moved into the big *atelier* in pairs—the two teachers, alternating depending on the part of the project taking place, and I [see Figure 8.1].

The teacher worked with the children, and I observed, documented, and took notes. At the end of the morning, we did a first evaluation of what had happened. Even if the time was limited, these discussions, which took place on the spot immediately following the observation, were very fruitful. We went over them again together in the afternoon, using other documents collected

Figure 8.1. The *atelier* at Pablo Neruda School.

during the experience: ongoing notes, images taken with the digital camera, slides, and tape recording of children's and adults' conversations.

Then in a simple way, to communicate with the families, we constructed documentaries for the classroom meetings, using this long-term project as a base. And even if the documentaries were at a beginning level and needed further collegial elaboration, the experience of working together—from beginning to a first conclusion—to weave together theory and practice, and to give an initial form to a document, was an important step in professional development. But what I remember with most pleasure is the teachers' surprise in considering the richness and potential of children. They discovered an unexpected child.

Lella: *This is a way of constructing a sense of the hundred languages for everyone.*

Mara: Yes, because at the end of the school year, the documents that we used with the families were the subject of discussion and observation in our collective professional development. Therefore, we received the contribution and external perspectives of the pedagogical coordinator and other teachers who came. All of them posed questions or made comments that we had not always been able to bring up within the group of the school.

Lella: *Would you comment on the complexity of your role?*

Mara: Until now I have only talked about the part of my work within the school that has included bringing in different perspectives, including contemporary artistic and visual culture. As *atelieristi* we also work with research groups and professional development groups that bring people from different schools and institutions together. This takes place even in educational institutions with different identities and goals, such as the state schools or the FISM [Italian Federation of Nursery Schools].

Lella: *Can you give an example of the kind of research?*

Mara: This year, during one of these group development sessions, I was asked to lead a laboratory session on daily documentation. (It had been launched by our Center of Documentation and Educational Research.) In this case, we chose a document that is used in different ways in different places: the daily diary or journal, it has different names. Teachers, either during the school day or toward the end of the day, write notes about the daily happening in each classroom; often they add sketches or copies of children's drawings and highlights of conversations. These are placed at the entryway of each classroom to invite parents to find out what happened that day.

We reflected on this journal—on its goals, its conceptual structure, how it is made, who compiles it, and so forth. We gave ourselves a period of time for experimentation. For a month, different people from different institutions produced these daily diaries—some of whom had already done this, but others who were completely new to it. Afterward, we got back together to compare and exchange reflections on what each group had done. This method is very helpful to those who are new to the profession, but it is also extremely helpful to those who have worked for many years, like me; it is a way to help avoid the fossilization of one's thinking. I am 54, an age that is both personally and professionally respectable because next August I will have worked in the schools of Reggio Emilia for 30 years. I started on August 23, 1973. And these young teachers and *atelieristi* who have arrived bring a contemporary view of the world with them that is different from what I can bring myself.

Lella: *Do you find that there are different points of view?*

Mara: Yes, it is normal. I, for example, am cautious in my relationship with new technologies that are fundamental today for adults because of the way that they have encouraged us to think about documentation and the construction of archives in a different way. I began to learn how to use digital technology a few years ago, alongside the children. Luckily, there was a teacher in my school who was competent in this new language, and he helped us all out. He helped me not only to learn how to "do" things but also to try to conceptualize them. I also get a great deal of inspiration and help from Giovanni Piazza, who has been making great strides with the digital language. First, I tried to imagine working with this new language with the children, and then to see if it could be connected with traditional visual languages, which I think should never be lost. I need to understand better how the digital experience becomes part of the process in children's construction of knowledge and, as a consequence, find appropriate strategies to use with them. However, what helps me is the tranquillity and normality of how the children get to know these tools, which are now part of daily living.

Lella: *You are describing both continuity and evolution in thinking about the role of* atelierista.

Mara: The other thing that is happening to a certain degree is a thinking of the idea of the *atelier* in a way that is much more flexible and much more open even to different new languages. Of course, the visual languages remain important, even though the boundaries among different languages are becoming more nebulous, and the **contaminations** between the languages and within the artistic culture are more and more evident.

I hope that *atelieristi* who are dancers or musicians, as well as traditional *atelieristi* like me, work in our schools in the future. I also think that we should stop thinking of ourselves as the *atelierista* of a single institution; we should think of ourselves as a group that is more and more heterogeneous, playing roles that exchange with one another.

Lella: *Malaguzzi wanted a school made up of lots of laboratories.*

Mara: The *miniatelier* has been—at least, in part—an answer for him. But what is happening with *atelieristi*, with different specializations, would be another way to answer to his idea.

Lella: *Our conversation remains open.*

Mara: My wish after 30 years of work is not to lose the important patrimony of relationship, of friendship, and of professional passion built with fatigue and pleasure at the same time. Our conversation remains open, and I like this, because it opens a door for our next encounter and exchange.

HOW TWO NEW *ATELIERISTE* VIEW THEIR ROLE: INTERVIEW WITH ISABELLA MENNINO AND BARBARA QUINTI

Loris Malaguzzi used to say that the tool box of the *atelier* was becoming wider and wider and was producing a larger variety of languages. Mara Davoli has spoken to us about the connection among languages that are part of the cultural world of today with regard to the arts, music, architecture, design, dance, and theater—connections and contaminations—that determine possibilities of fruition of a very rich cultural landscape for the *atelier* and the work in the schools. These observations also connect with the tendency toward interdisciplinary approaches in research and study that have a great following in many disciplines and in teaching. In Reggio Emilia, this awareness has guided the choice of new *atelieristi* in the schools. In June 2003, I interviewed Isabella Mennino, a young *atelierista* at the Diana School, and Barbara Quinti, recently hired at La Villetta School. While they are learning to be with children with the depth of observation essential in the schools of Reggio Emilia, their backgrounds and their interests bring new perspectives and points of view to the daily work and the group meetings for professional development.

Lella: *What are the notable aspects of your experience as an* atelierista?

Isabella: After studying at an art school, I received my preparation in Milan in a highly innovative environment of design. My mentor, A. G. Fronzoni, was a great master of Italian graphics and a great innovator in this field. He had a great love for teaching. We young students had many ideas but little planning methodology. It was with Fronzoni in Milan that I began to understand my own capabilities and acquired the ability to plan and exchange design methodologies with others.

Lella: *What happened after your encounter with Fronzoni?*

Isabella: I continued to develop as a graphic designer. I worked with architects, engineers, and designers. I was in fashion for a while, designing accessories and costumes for theater and dance. Then I met Vea Vecchi. When I arrived at the Diana School, I was deeply moved by entering into such a rich, cultured environment. (Some of the sites of design and architecture seemed mediocre to me compared to this school.) Among the environments I had known so far, this one most reflected the importance of aesthetics. Therefore, I participated in the competition to become an *atelierista*.

Lella: *How did you use the ideas that Vea communicated to you when you began working with her at the Diana School?*

Isabella: The people who teach you, who work with you, who care about you see what you are capable of before you see it. There is another part that belongs to you that is like the seed that still needs to sprout. To put together what the other sees in you and what you see in yourself is a slow process through which you begin to know yourself. The work with children was fundamental. Working while documenting the process, constantly reviewing my own interven-

Figure 8.2. In the *atelier* at Diana School, 4-year-old children prepare to paint a carpet on a plastic sheet for their beloved mountain in the playground.

Figure 8.3. The children place their carpet outside to cover the mountain.

tions, was extremely important for my growth. My first approach with the children was an emotional one. I was very worried about my relationship with them and about how to entertain them. When I began to document, I began to take other aspects into consideration: the thoughts of the children, their way of relating to each other, their individual way of researching. Working like this, everything becomes more adventurous and changes the way you see the children. Furthermore, it makes you reflect on the role of the work of teachers [see Figures 8.2 and 8.3].

Lella: *Barbara, can you speak to us about your formation?*

Barbara: I arrived here to be an *atelierista* after having desired to be here for years. I have a background in painting. I attended the Fine Arts Academy, and so I come from a visual, spatial formation. My work has always focused on installations, and my work with the children reflects this.

The first thing I decided when I began as an *atelierista* was to get to know the children. From the outset, I felt an empathetic closeness to the children, I think because I could choose to express myself using languages other than words. Knowing how to make the hands speak helped me. They are a great channel of communication.

Lella: *What are you working on today?*

Barbara: Some time ago, we worked on the Burri project [see Chapter 6]. We studied the work of Alberto Burri, not to understand the visual models, but to gather the conceptual and cultural references within which this artist moved and explore them with the children. The project involved several schools working together. Nine schools of different grades were involved, with the participation of children and adolescents between a few months and 18 years of age. This opening toward the larger systems of schools is one of the internal innovations of the activity of the *atelier*.

Lella: *Working with adolescents and children of different ages forces one to be prepared to organize experiences differently according to age groups.*

Isabella: Good organization supports a flexible way of working when you have to start a variety of different projects. In this work with children of different ages, you have to reinterpret what you do daily, as if an accelerated metronome makes you follow the waves of the school. We must be rigorous when we research. Rigor goes hand in hand with creativity; it can help to express it.

In this work, you have to reelaborate and reinterpret the things that you do, and you have to do so in a timely manner. Otherwise, it isn't of use to the project; it isn't of use to anyone. The challenge is exactly this: to keep the high level of quality while maintaining the contact between the larger theories and the daily reality. I was impressed by a story that Vea tells about Malaguzzi: When Malaguzzi came to the school, the first thing that he did was go to the bathroom to see whether there was toilet paper (and Malaguzzi was an intellectual). The point is that when you have a strong sense of attachment to a school, you don't make priorities; everything is important. At the center of your work are the children, the culture, and the place where you live. You give yourself time frames and an organization that reflects everyone's predispositions. Diversity is the strong point in this line of work.

Lella: *Documentation is one of the key elements of the project of the schools of Reggio Emilia. Documentation requires collaboration and working in a group.*

Isabella: Group work is not easy. Documentation gives you a way to understand your errors as well as your mental process. I work with people who have 20 years of experience behind them. The nice thing is that they see things in me that were missing in the group before I came. They brought attention to these qualities, and these have become my strong points. Discussion is the main ingredient in our way of working. Our communications are not personal, but public. The most extraordinary thing happens when you are able to change your point of view and find that you have been enriched.

Lella: *What are the strategies that you have put to use that have helped you to work in groups in a positive way?*

Isabella: Teachers need to be given autonomy, to conduct small projects in their own way, where they themselves are the protagonists. Then they need to tell about these projects and illustrate them. It is a path that leads to the narration of one's lived experience.

Barbara: Working in groups requires a lot of listening to and observing the abilities and passions of individuals. Some time ago, a new teacher who was 21 years old arrived at our school. Sometimes for those who join us, the school can present itself as a train in motion. The thing that I felt like telling this young woman was that it is important for someone entering the school to bring her passion with her and to infuse it into her daily work with the children.

Lella: *Did this happen to you at the beginning?*

Barbara: Yes. When you arrive in a place, you need to try to own it; you need to live it with what you find significant. I did this through my love for space and for the environment. I used the things that were closest to me, most familiar, and at that moment it was painting and installation. Living in the place with the children, I found the space to be able to express myself.

Lella: *Let's go back to documentation—to register, reinterpret, and share with others. It is an instrument that has been created through time.*

Barbara: I entered into something that was established, and today that way of working is indispensable for me. For me, documenting is like modeling clay. Currently, our ways of documenting are evolving; the documentation is evolving. We are trying to make our work visible beyond the school.

Isabella: Since I arrived at the Diana School, I have always searched for new forms of communication. A single project could be documented in a thousand ways: in a book, an invitation to parents, a research edition of a project, a 10-page synthesis for the parents. This brought us to return continually to elaborating the same documents—hence, changing ideas and developing ideas for new projects.

Lella: *If people from outside were to ask for advice to begin to use this method of working, what suggestions would you give?*

Barbara: The first thing that I would say to an aspiring *atelierista* is to be conscious of the fact that there are many things to learn. This is precisely the nature of our work. Today, we are asked to practice a greater variety of languages, from that of the body to that of sound and of technology. These languages are used expressively and not technically. These are the areas of research, and you, the "poor *atelierista*," are asked to confront many different things. This is the difficult aspect, but it is also a great fortune, because each day you learn something new; you learn with the children. I can give you as an example my involvement with the Unexpected City Project [see Chapter 6] with Mara Davoli and the other teachers as we saw the children's transformation of Vicolo Trivelli. I discovered not only complex and truly unexpected creative ability in the children and in my colleagues, but also more resources in our own city [see Figures 8.4 and 8.5].

Another suggestion I would give is not to close yourself within the school. Have dialogues with people other than the teachers, people who come from the world of design or graphics or anyone who can give you a contemporary key through which to read the world in which we, the parents, and the children live.

Isabella: I would suggest beginning by working on small things that then become larger projects. It is important to listen to people, to know how to understand their desires and the potential of what each one of us can do. Another thing was suggested to me by the son of Bruno Munari, a researcher who came to visit our school some time ago for a discussion about art and cognition: "When you do something, think about how you could have done it in another way."

CLOSING REFLECTIONS

Mara Davoli returned to us at the beginning of this chapter with her reflections on how young women's greater range of employment choices affects the rate of turnover of teachers in Reggio Emilia. She described the successful strategies that she designed with her colleagues, in the spirit of collaboration that always sustains the fiber of the school, to help the new teachers and minimize the disorientation affecting the school. Mara then analyzed the developments in the profession of *atelierista*, highlighting the many rich elements that change can bring inside the *atelier* and inside the school. She concluded by suggesting that the positive presence of multiple types of *atelieristi* is needed and that the next step should be for individual *atelieristi* to be connected to several institutions rather than with just one school.

After her interview came the voices of Isabella Mennino and Barbara Quinti, two new *atelieriste*. They spoke about the learning process of becoming an *atelierista*—in particular, dealing with the complex relationships of teachers and children. Isabella and Barbara come from different backgrounds and have different interests; consequently, each has used a different strategy to negotiate her learning. But they both rely on their minds and hands and the guidance of expert teachers to grow. In this endeavor, they recognize the solid contribution of documentation, with the possibility to discuss differing points of view.

These interviews prepare us to be part, in the next chapter, of an extraordinary conversation among four art educators in North America who have embraced and explored the connections with the philosophy of Reggio Emilia

Figure 8.4. The Unexpected City Project: at Vicolo Trivelli, a handbag shop window set up by children and their teachers.

Figure 8.5. Detail from the handbag shop window: *Coccodrillo Borsari* (crocodile handbag).

and the *atelier* from varied perspectives. Pauline Baker tells about the transformation of the environment of two classrooms in a public preschool to give it a studio space and a thoughtfully composed, beautiful identity "to support productive, happy living" for children and teachers. Patricia Hunter-McGrath describes a four-month project in her preschool that involved dramatic explorations and inventions by young children, participation by their families, and carefully considered choices by the teachers. Cathy Topal tells of her use of found natural materials to introduce children to a sense of design, building their skills along with the joy of discovery. And Lauren Monaco presents her deep engagement in the professional development of a large group of preschool teachers through a six-month collective exploration of painting, which led the teachers to reflect that "the paintings from our study group have become metaphors for our work together." The experience of teachers and children encountering this medium brings us a new perspective on the power of a collegial experience in the *atelier*.

Credits: *Figure 8.1:* Photograph from Pablo Neruda School, 2004, unpublished. *Figures 8.2 and 8.3:* Photographs from Diana School, 2004, unpublished. *Figures 8.4 and 8.5:* Photographs by Barbara Quinti, from Bruno Ciari School, Unexpected City project, 2002, unpublished documentation. All © Municipality of Reggio Emilia—Infant-Toddler Centers and Preschools.

Voices from the Studio

Stories of Transformation

Pauline M. Baker,
Patricia Hunter-McGrath,
Cathy Weisman Topal, and
Lauren Monaco

The following are four stories of very different studio teachers from diverse locations in the United States. As you read these stories, you will see that each of our roles has been shaped by our situation, circumstances, and relationships. Our common bond is our strong belief in and commitment to the principles of the Reggio Emilia approach. Each story highlights a different aspect of our work and the uniqueness of our context. Although each story focuses on a different topic, all of the stories are connected by a shared vision that the entire school is a place to explore the hundred languages.

Telling our stories to each other has strengthened and empowered us in our work together. Our collaboration and our shared inquiry have helped us to think together and to learn from each other. Now we offer our stories as a way for others to consider the possibilities of expression and learning that can occur when an *atelier* is introduced in a setting for children, teachers, and families. Embedded within this chapter are the following experiences:

1. "The Transformation of Space into Place: A Story of Beginning in Tucson, Arizona," by Pauline M. Baker
2. "Traditional Materials: Unconventional Experiences," by Patricia Hunter-McGrath
3. "Bringing the Spirit of the Studio into the Classroom," by Cathy Weisman Topal
4. "Teachers, Materials, and the Studio," by Lauren Monaco

THE TRANSFORMATION OF SPACE INTO PLACE: A STORY OF BEGINNING IN TUCSON, ARIZONA

Pauline M. Baker

We value space because of its power to organize, promote pleasant relationships between people of different ages, create a handsome environment, provide changes, promote choices and activity, and its potential for sparking all kinds of social, affective, and cognitive learning. All of this contributes to a sense of well-being and security in children. We also think that the space has to be a sort of aquarium which mirrors the ideas, values, attitudes, and cultures of the people who live within it. (Loris Malaguzzi, in Gandini, 1998, p. 177)

My Context

I serve as a studio and resource teacher in the Tucson Unified School District's Early Learning programs, where I collaborate with and support teachers who have chosen to study and interpret the Reggio Emilia Approach to early childhood education. The district's early education programs serve low-income children, and all the children meet the federal eligibility requirements for free lunch. Eighty percent of these children are of Hispanic origin; many are also English-language learners. During the time of this story, I was the studio teacher in the state-funded Van Buskirk Preschool Program.

My Story

This story offers a glimpse of our effort in the summer of 1998 to transform two state-funded preschool classrooms located in Van Buskirk Elementary School in Tucson, Arizona, into places that would support the Reggio Emilia Approach. We had taken on a tremendous responsibility. We weren't sure what we were doing. There were many frustrations and challenges, but we had glimpsed something so profound and inspiring that there was no going back.

The preschool teachers, Carolyn Marsden and Ann Sanchez, had just attended the St. Louis–Reggio Collaborative's Delegation Days and had come back to Tucson with a powerful inspiration and plan to think in greater depth about their environment.

Ann and Carolyn wanted me to join them as a studio teacher. I had been teaching early education courses for several years, although I was certified to teach K–12 art. When I attended the National Association for the Education of Young Children conference in 1993, I first heard of the municipal schools of Reggio Emilia. From that moment, I began to study everything I could find about these remarkable schools, and in 1997 I attended my first Reggio Emilia study tour in Italy. When Carolyn called me in the spring of 1998 to ask whether I would be interested in becoming the studio teacher in their program, I felt humbled and amazed at the incredible way things happen when you most need them. To move forward with their plan, Carolyn and Ann had gained the support of Eleanor Droegemeier, coordinator of the state-funded preschool program in the Tucson Unified School District, and of Marcia Wolf, principal of Van Buskirk Elementary School. We are so appreciative of their support. Without their belief in our efforts, this story could not be told.

Christopher Day (1990) talks about transformation of space into place. He speaks of how giving identity, connection, personality, and aesthetic nourishment to an environment can change its feel and its potential to support productive, happy living. We hoped to accomplish something similar in these very ordinary classrooms.

Day also speaks of "design as a listening process," listening to what has come before and weaving in what might come in the future (pp. 98–99). Indeed, the process of transforming the Van Buskirk environment arose out of the conversations we had as we worked. We had a growing commitment to listen carefully to each other. We wanted the rooms to be beautiful, to be thoughtfully composed and inspiring to all who entered them. We cared very much about children's creativity and finding ways to support and develop it. In our decades of teaching, we had seen too many generic, cluttered, over-stimulating, and, in many ways, oppressive classrooms for young children. We wanted something different for our children. We wanted to create a place where dreams and passions could still ignite and fuel the learning process, and we wanted this to happen in many diverse and meaningful ways for the children, families, and teachers who would be working together.

We envisioned these classroom spaces as places that would be open in beautiful ways to the creativity, curiosity, and inquiry of children; communicate the philosophy, curriculum, and focus of our program; extend and communicate a constant invitation to participate in and celebrate learning together; provide studios for supporting the development of the "hundred languages" of children; and, most of all, reflect Loris Malaguzzi's belief (as he remarked many times in his speeches to teachers visiting Reggio for the first time) that a child's world should be the world of the possible (personal communication, 1994).

We began to transform these two public preschool classrooms by reinventing some spaces to bring more harmony, beauty, and practicality to them. Meaningful furnishings were added from our homes and from thrift shops. The warm and inviting rooms that resulted began to reflect value and respect for the culture and community of our school. We thought of Anita Olds' words: "Our thoughts, as reflected in our designs, in turn shape children's beliefs about themselves and life" (2000, pp. 12–13).

A child-size pigskin chair and table set (see Figure 9.1) was purchased in Nogales, Mexico, for the Casita (House Center). Many of our children and

Figure 9.1. Child-size pigskin table and two chairs.

families have come to Tucson from Mexico. We saw placing this handmade furniture in a favorite play area as a way to offer respect and visibility to the culture of many of our children and families, as well as to communicate our appreciation for this unique Mexican craft.

A feature of one of the classrooms was a strong line of the massive but beautiful windows, which we decided to soften with long pieces of transparent cheesecloth that I had purchased many years before at a garage sale. We hoped that this simple draping of fabric would enhance the message of welcome and feeling of home, and would help to lessen the institutional feeling of the rooms (see Figure 9.2).

A large table and shelves seemed important to create an attractive, well-equipped, and accessible studio, but no light-colored, large pieces of furniture were available in the school district's warehouse. During my visit to the schools in Reggio Emilia, I had observed the many beautiful ways that block platforms were used in the classrooms. I saw that the platforms facilitated building and construction and offered greater visibility for children's work. A message center was also a prominent feature in the classrooms in Reggio Emilia, promoting a high value placed on developing relationships and the desire to communicate in a hundred languages. These furnishings seemed essential within our own context, as well, so we decided to have several items made by a carpenter. Eventually, we were able to include a block platform, a studio table, and sets of shelves, and beautiful materials graced each piece of the new furnishings (see Figures 9.3 and 9.4).

Figure 9.2. Window with draped fabric along the top and studio table in front.

Figure 9.3. Studio shelf
with paper and materials.

Figure 9.4. Studio table
with groupings of colored
paper arranged for parent
workshop.

A new organization of space and materials allowed us to open larger and more enriched areas for investigation and play between the two rooms. All the art materials from two rooms and many years of teaching experience were offered to me for the studio. Organizing materials to be accessible and offer beauty, inspiration, and an invitation to learn became my challenge and a source of continuous learning. We purchased Mexican laundry baskets with handles to store recycled materials. Using recycled materials was an important part of the provocation and potential we wanted the studio to offer. These baskets were soon filled with boxes, tubes, cardboard, plastic, and a large and eclectic assortment of objects and materials gathered, cleaned, and placed for easy access right under the studio table.

To give interest, variety, and uniqueness to the studio room, we draped a simple canopy from the wall. We gave it a magical touch with strings of clear lights. It created an inviting little space within the bigger area of the classroom (see Figure 9.5). We also added a painted piece of wooden lattice over the block platforms in the block room. The lattice gave a cozy feeling to this area within the high-ceilinged room and offered a place to hang mobiles.

We placed intriguing pieces of pottery, photographs, and textile work around the room to invite study, provoke interest, and enhance the quality of the space. The majority of display space was reserved for the children's work and the documentation panels and pages that we slowly learned to create.

Figure 9.5. Canopy with matchstick curtain on wall in studio room.

Photographs of the children and their families, a statement of welcome, and a description of our philosophy joined the poem "The Hundred Languages of Children" on the bulletin boards in each room. We hoped that these would invite and encourage the development of lasting learning relationships with our children and families and provide a clear statement of our values and commitment. Thin white notebooks, with the name of each child clearly visible on the book spine, were placed in the built-in bookcase at the far corner of the studio room. These notebooks held a collection of writing samples, drawings, learning journals, evidence of district standards met, photographs, and other types of documentation. Slowly, the identity of the children, teachers, families, and administrators became a visible part of our space.

We had several hundred visitors to our classrooms that first year (1998–1999). People were amazed and provoked by what they saw and felt, and many new collaborations began between educators throughout the city, across the state, and around the nation.

On April 18, 2000, during the second year of our project, Lella Gandini from Reggio Children came to visit us in our Van Buskirk classrooms. She spoke at a dinner for 100 people from government, education, and community programs, and presented to a group of more than 300 early educators a talk titled "Reggio Emilia, Italy: A City Committed to Children." Lella Gandini's visit was a tremendous inspiration to us and to our colleagues and brought people from all over the state of Arizona together to learn more about Reggio Emilia's renowned schools.

Finally, our Tucson conversation had started with the transformation of "space into place." The study of Reggio Emilia began to inspire people to work in new ways within their particular contexts by creating places of identity and connection. We looked for the stories of the past and gained new appreciation for living in the present. We sought to see the future and give hope to the possibility and potential of children, families, and teachers listening and learning together in a state that is rated 47th in the country for the care and well-being of young children.

TRADITIONAL MATERIALS, UNCONVENTIONAL EXPERIENCES

Patricia Hunter-McGrath

The materials we choose to bring into our classrooms reveal the choices we have made about knowledge and what we think is important to know. How children are invited to use the materials indicates the role they shall have in their learning. Materials are the text of early childhood classrooms. Unlike books filled with facts and printed with words, materials are more like outlines. They offer openings and pathways by and through which children may enter the world of knowledge. Materials become the tools with which children give form to and express their understanding of the world and the meanings they have constructed. (Cuffaro, 1995, p. 33)

My Context

Payne's gray, rich terracotta red, cerulean blue—these are the colors of my childhood in Scotland. Surrounded by beauty, I spent long summer days creating microcosm worlds from ferns, willows, stones, clay, sticks, and whatever natural materials I discovered. Amid the bracken and heather a lifelong passion for materials was born. After graduating from Stevenson College in Edinburgh, I came to California to work in the field of early childhood education. I have been working as an early childhood education teacher for more than 17 years; for the past seven years I have been the *atelierista* at Evergreen Community School in Santa Monica. Evergreen is a small, nonprofit school that currently serves 60 children, primarily from the Santa Monica community. The school began in the fall of 1983 when All Saints' Episcopal Church of Beverly Hills founded a preschool to serve its parishioners and the local community. It opened its doors with four children enrolled and one teacher, Alise Shafer, as a blank canvas with a palette of possibilities. A social constructivist approach was adopted as a theoretical framework, influenced by the work of Piaget and Vygotsky, among others. As awareness of the school's program spread through the community, the student population expanded and diversified.

In 1996, having outgrown its church setting, the school transformed to an independent nonprofit status, and the entity of the Evergreen Community School was born at our current Santa Monica location. This new, fully updated facility gave us the freedom to further refine our practice, unencumbered by the constraints of shared and limited space. These freedoms enabled us to explore more deeply our constructivist roots and the approach of the municipal schools of Reggio Emilia.

During this time, my role has undergone many changes. It has evolved from set appointments with teachers and children in the *atelier* to open-ended invitations to use the *atelier* and supporting teachers' exploration of materials as an extension of the classroom. Today I work with the teachers and children in the *atelier* as well as in the classrooms. We have come to believe that the whole school is a studio. Wonderful ideas and theories are explored throughout the school and are no longer restricted to the *atelier*. Teachers, children, materials, and ideas flow from the classroom to the *atelier* and back again.

In recent years, our focus has been on exploring how materials can be used in short- and long-term explorations to uncover, support, deepen, and make visible children's learning. We have come to realize that how one introduces art materials to children can either limit or expand the children's future use of the materials. Through careful observations of children interacting with the materials, the teachers at Evergreen have moved toward using materials in nontraditional, unconventional ways. In response, the children have revealed the materials' unique characteristics and uncovered multiple open-ended possibilities. When the teachers choose a material to introduce to the children, they do so carefully. They ask themselves:

- Will the material be used in many ways, or does it dictate a particular use?
- Will the material be used by many children?
- Does it lend itself to a variety of explorations?
- What affordances does it offer?
- How might the material be best introduced to the children?

With these questions in mind, in September 2003 the teachers chose to set up a four-month exploration of paper for the toddlers and the 2- and 3-year-olds in the youngest class.

My Story

When the children came to school one Monday morning, a surprise awaited them: a room full of paper. At first, the children were unsure what to do with this new provocation, so the teacher offered an invitation to play. The invitation was too interesting to pass up. Two children who were new to the school began to form relationships with the paper (see Figure 9.6).

The children's initial experiences were delicate ones. The children needed lots of time to approach the new material. Teachers observed closely as the

Figure 9.6. Paper, an invitation to form relationships with the material, the teacher, and each other.

Figure 9.7. Spenser and Murphy move slowly, discovering the sounds of the paper.

Figure 9.8. Paper, a material that can be wrapped around you like a favorite blanket.

Figure 9.9. Paper hides and reveals.

Figure 9.10. "Can you hear it? Maybe it's a monster? I can hear it coming! I'd better take a peek."

children encountered the paper for the first time, exploring its sounds and textures (see Figure 9.7).

Children interpreted the sounds in their own ways and discovered that paper might sound like "a lion," "a dragon," "a train," and "drums." Very soon the children discovered many of the paradoxes of paper: It can be easily torn, but you can also pull it with all your might without tearing it. Paper can be strong enough to support one child's weight. You can even use it to drag two children around the room. Paper cushions you when you fall (see Figure 9.8).

The open-ended nature of paper did not dictate a particular use but, instead, allowed the children to interpret its use in any way they chose. The paper can become a blank slate and offer a surprise to the children as they create different types of interactions, experiences, and games. The children played variations of a hiding game again and again during the four months. They hid in boxes, wrapped themselves in paper, burrowed underneath mounds of paper, and hid behind large pieces of hanging paper (see Figure 9.9).

Sometimes the parents in our toddler class also became part of this game. One day, Ian slowly and carefully covered his mother with paper. Suddenly, his mother burst out from behind the paper, much to Ian's delight. Ian did not tire of this game, playing it over and over again. The older children invented a monster game. One child became the monster while others hid behind a large sheet of paper hanging from the ceiling. They waited and listened as the monster approached and searched for them. Laughter filled the room as the children discovered that the monster was really a new friend (see Figure 9.10).

Paper can provoke games and spark the imagination. A box can become a bear cave, a secret place, a car for one, a house for two or three, a boat for four or five in shark-infested waters (see Figure 9.11). After two or three months, we were still observing the children as they delighted in the hiding game and then decided to add another element. The children were enchanted when the paper room was darkened by the dimming of the lights. When the classroom was dark, flashlights were introduced to support their play and to add a

Figure 9.11. A boat for four or five in shark-infested waters.

dramatic element to the paper environment. The children burrowed under the paper to create a dark cave. The flashlights cast strange shadows on the cave walls, and light bounced off the paper and created new provocations.

Grandparents watched as the children played with the paper, and a few of the braver grandparents ventured into the paper room to play with their grandchildren. Later, a grandmother told us that for most of her life she had always found great pleasure in writing handwritten notes and letters to her family and friends, but after her experience in the paper room that morning, she would never write another letter without feeling the paper's texture and observing the way the ink seeps into its fibers. Her experience with the children had taught her (as it had taught us, as well) to appreciate the small, beautiful things in life.

The teachers held one regular monthly meeting in the paper room. Suddenly, one teacher threw a ball of paper across the room. Laughter filled the air, and paper began to fly all around. Some teachers burrowed underneath the paper; others wrapped it around themselves as they joyfully explored together. Afterward, the mood turned reflective as we discussed our behavior and concluded that it is not only children who need these rich experiences. Adults should also find moments to joyfully experience materials and each other.

Reflections on Paper

During the four-month exploration, paper served many purposes. It taught the children to use their imaginations, to find the extraordinary in the ordinary, and to slow down and play. By carefully and thoughtfully introducing the children to paper, changing the environment, and adding appropriate materials as the need arose, the teachers revealed paper's multidimensional possibilities. As the paper was released from the tabletop, it released the children's imaginations. A large piece of paper became a cave. The ripping sound of paper became the crash of a thunderstorm. A box became a cave for one or a boat for two. Paper became the conduit for new relationships, exciting explorations, and deep understandings. It opened new worlds of possibilities, and all who participated were changed by the experience.

> Paper waiting on the table,
> A quiet but eager recipient of color, line or collage?
> Maybe, maybe not.
> What would happen if we liberated it from the tabletop creating a room
>   full of mountains, streamers, and enclosures?
>   (A. Shafer, personal communication, 2000)

BRINGING THE SPIRIT OF THE STUDIO INTO THE CLASSROOM
Cathy Weisman Topal

One story of challenge and intrigue occurred when an unusual material found its way into the preschool classroom where I work. This material turned out to be one of great potential. I think that it illustrated what it means to bring the spirit of the studio into a school.

My Context

I visit the three preschool classes at the Center for Early Childhood Education at Smith College in Northampton, Massachusetts, one morning a week. The classes are mixed-age groups of 19 children from 3 to 5 years of age. I am also the studio art teacher for kindergarten children at the Smith College Campus School and teach visual arts education in the Department of Education and Child Study at Smith College.

Despite a strong desire over many years on the part of the director and teachers at our early childhood center, we still do not have a studio space. Our center has undergone dramatic growth, with many changes every year, and classrooms continue to occupy every available space. My story is about how I worked to bring "the spirit of the studio" into the classroom when a studio does not exist.

I began to ask myself an important question: What does it mean to bring the spirit of the studio into the classroom, and what is the nature of this spirit?

As I continued to reflect and work within the school, I realized that more than anything else this "spirit" is an attitude of openness to new ways of seeing and using materials. When children know that a studio teacher is coming to their classroom, they anticipate being involved in an adventure that will engage their hands and minds and spirits. At some level, children know that they will be challenged, and they look forward to that challenge. They expect to grapple with problems and enjoy the process of discovering solutions.

My Story

We began the year in all the classrooms by focusing on the most basic of all the art elements: line. The children had been exploring the many different kinds of marks that they could make with crayons, markers, and paintbrushes. We went on line hunts, looking for different kinds of lines in both the natural and the built environment. We had also been looking through our collections of found materials for "lines" to use in collages.

An Exploration That Develops from a Problem. This story began when the preschool teachers were discussing strategies and cues to use to support children's natural interest in cutting. Their request for materials became a provocation for me to look for materials that would be firm to hold, interesting to handle, and easy to cut. I brought strips that I had cut from discarded oak tag file folders, pieces of Styrofoam, a few different kinds of packing materials, and sheets of foam into the classrooms. Children enjoyed cutting these materials and were going through them very quickly.

Because it was fall, children in all of the classrooms were collecting the leaves, sticks, seed pods, and bark that are plentiful in New England at this time of year. While raking leaves and cleaning up my own yard, I noticed a big pile of dried stalks that I had pulled from the day lilies that grow in my garden. I was cutting them into smaller sizes so they would fit into the leaf bags. Suddenly I realized I'd found a new material—a new linear material!

I brought some of the lily stalks into one of the classrooms and then had a conversation with the children about this unusual medium. During the course of our discussion, I asked the children whether they would be willing to cut the stalks for use in our portable studio. Even children who had typically avoided cutting were very motivated to try cutting the lily stalks. It was while preparing these materials for use in the classroom that children discovered their unique properties. As they began cutting, the children found that small pieces pop when cut, and that they can travel—fly!—long distances.

Once they became more skillful with the very satisfying experience of cutting this natural material, the children began to discover other unique characteristics of the stalks. They found the stalks to be hollow, strong materials for building and that the stalks could stand if you cut them even on the end and if they were short enough. The children became very familiar with the

Figure 9.12. Stalks of dried day lily plants can become strong linear building materials for many studio projects.

Figure 9.13. As 4-year-old Ava arranged her lily stalks and experimented with making the lines touch, she noticed that she was creating squares and rectangles—a floor plan.

possibilities inherent in this new material. They began to arrange their cuttings and to experiment with ways to use them (see Figure 9.12).

Suddenly we had many bins of this wonderful linear material. Children began to arrange and build with the stalks as they were cutting. As a challenge, I asked them to consider arranging the stalks so that some of them touched. Children learned that when the lines touched, they made shapes (see Figure 9.13). Combining shapes led the children to form many unusual constructions. Some children worked flat, while others worked three-dimensionally. Stories and structures began to emerge.

This time of experimentation—of arranging and rearranging—is so important. Even though the children were asking for glue, I delayed in making adhesive available. I have found that this idea of testing possibilities is where the richness of an experience with materials lies. It is the time when children build relationships with the materials and try out a multitude of ideas. If I had made the glue available too quickly, rich opportunities would have been lost. So I waited. Usually, this causes children to look again at their arrangements and perhaps to add to them to make them more complex. This pause encourages children to enjoy the textures, sizes, placement, and orientation of the stalks.

While working with the stalks, the children began to talk about wooden fences, ladders, log cabins, and the framework of new houses. Ideas and stories grew more complex as children played with possibilities. I realized that knowing when to offer a material or to make a material available requires sensitivity to children's ways of working and to the time they need. It also requires that I work as a keen and engaged observer.

When I noticed that the arrangements were so complex that the stalks were starting to roll, I offered squeeze bottles of glue. The children reminded each other of their previous knowledge of this adhesive:

"Touch the bottle to the paper."
"Listen for the air so you know that the glue is working."
"Draw a very thin line with the glue and put the stick on top."
"You can move the sticks around while the glue is still wet."

Often, the arrangements that the children glued looked different from their original plan. Sometimes whole new scenarios emerged.

Enriching the Activity: Adding More Natural Materials. It was clear that the children were taking pleasure in cutting and handling this intriguing natural material. They weren't ready to stop. We also had an array of other natu-

Figure 9.14.
A portable *atelier* of natural materials, beautifully arranged, becomes a new provocation.

Figure 9.15.
Children take great pleasure in selecting items from the display of natural materials to add to their work.

ral materials available in the classrooms. There were the seeds and kernels that the children had been extracting from sunflowers and ears of corn using tweezers. There were small, flat, smooth pebbles that had been collected on the beach. Small sticks from our walks, dried flowers, and pieces of mica were added. With a new ability to look for materials in unusual places, teachers, children, and parents continued to find interesting natural treasures and brought them to school with excitement (see Figure 9.14). I believe that giving adults and children a way to extend and build on what happens during an experience is one of my most important roles.

Lella Gandini once spoke about the importance of presenting natural materials, or any materials, with "a gesture of offering something precious" (personal communication, 1990). The handling and choosing of these materials was pure pleasure for adults and children alike. We all grew to appreciate the high aesthetic quality of these materials that are free for the gathering.

Organizing small collections of a variety of natural materials allowed us to notice their subtle colors, shapes, sizes, and textures. We left little cups for the children to use as receptacles to hold their selections (see Figure 9.15). In this way we brought a portable *atelier* into the classroom, which the teacher could move around and use as she wished. These materials were then added to the shelves of materials in the ministudio areas within each classroom.

Some children selected only a few materials that they especially liked to add to their arrangements of lily stalks. Other children included a sampling of all the materials. We discovered that additional materials also generated new ways for children to elaborate on and enrich their stories and theories (see Figure 9.16).

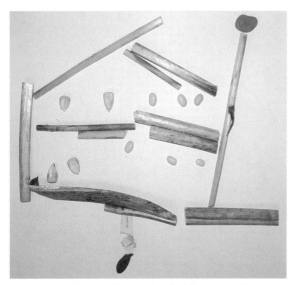

Figure 9.16. "A House for Spiderman," by Jonathan, age 5.

Reflecting on the evolution of this exploration has taught me that big adventures can grow from very simple beginnings. The provocation for this adventure grew from the desire to find new, inexpensive, and available materials to cut. Bringing an unusual material into the classroom is an intriguing way to pose questions about its origin, characteristics, qualities, and possible uses. It also became a powerful way to bring the investigative spirit and creative potential of the studio experience into the classroom.

When children and adults take time to engage in and celebrate moments of expression and discovery together, and they use those moments to spark new adventures, a spirit of wonder and trust is born. Adults can keep this spirit alive and renew it by recognizing additional discoveries as they occur, asking children to share them, and brainstorming strategies for how a discovery or additional material might be used for further exploration. In this way, the spirit of the studio is continually rekindled and continues to flourish and grow in the classroom.

TEACHERS, MATERIALS, AND THE STUDIO

Lauren Monaco

> The artist is not a special kind of man, but every man is a special kind of artist.
> (Meister Eckhart, 1260–1328)

Many educators in my school have had an image of themselves as lacking in creative understanding or ability. All too often I have heard: "I'm not creative" or "I can't even draw a straight line" or "You're the artist; you tell me." This attitude became the impetus for my work as an *atelierista*.

My Context

In 2000, shortly after I graduated with a fine arts degree from Kent State University, I took the job of studio teacher at the World Bank Children Center (WBCC). This event was a major transition in my life. I would be moving from fine artist to educator and moving away from my friends and family in Ohio to a new life in an unknown city. My understanding of the role of studio teacher was limited, but even my beginning understandings helped me to sense that I had found my life's work. I looked forward to discovering what it might mean to be a studio teacher and what this role would mean for me.

Little did I know that this new chapter in my life would become synonymous with change. I found myself moving into a community that was in the process of transformation. The WBCC had recently moved from operating as a parent co-op to a corporate managed center and had expanded from a five-classroom parent cooperative to a three-site center that would eventually hold 12 classrooms for children age 3 months to 5 years. When I arrived, the center had just expanded, and many of the classrooms were not yet staffed. Now the WBCC operates year-round and includes staff and families from all over the world. The center has more than 30 teachers, three studios, and one studio teacher.

The decision to move from a parent co-op to a corporate center was based on the need for expansion. A board of parents, teachers, and other WBCC representatives wanted to continue the strong presence of parents in this new arrangement and chose to support a center that was inspired by the infant/toddler centers and preschools of Reggio Emilia, which presented a strong image of parents' involvement. This was also one of my passions and desires for our newly reformed school.

I entered to find a mix of teachers new to the center and teachers new to the ideas of Reggio Emilia. The role of the studio teacher was another concept that had not yet been defined within the school. I was fortunate enough to be mentored by Jennifer Azzariti, an experienced studio teacher who worked as a consultant for our center (see Chapter 4). Her experience and stories helped expand my image of what it might mean to be a studio teacher. I was also blessed to have Patti Cruickshank-Schott as a major collaborator who stretched my thinking and expanded my ideas. My understanding of the role and how it could be lived out at our center grew as I read, visited other schools, had conversations with other studio teachers, and reflected on my own practice. Our center was continually changing and growing, and so was I.

As more and more teachers were hired, new classrooms were opened. My work and time had to shift with each new addition. The complex challenges inherent in this position included organizing my time to have meaningful relationships with an increasing number of classrooms; making connections between the three sites; supporting and expanding teachers' images of their own role with materials; and trying to ensure that my role as studio teacher was evolving in a positive way.

My Story

One of the things I noticed while working with teachers was that they seemed genuinely interested in the prospect of having a resident "expert" of materials. Their excitement was coupled with a deep apprehension about working with materials themselves. Many of the teachers did not seem to envision working with materials as an important part of their jobs and, perhaps, hoped that I would do this work. The teachers' image of the studio was that of a special, but separate, space. And although they valued my presence, I felt that their perception of my role was that of the sole provider of materials. In spite of ongoing meetings together and a continual attempt to make connections within classrooms, there was a real separation between the classrooms and the studio. I began to feel a great need to help teachers understand their own creativity, to see themselves as nurturers of creativity in children, and to cultivate a new image of the whole school as a studio.

Creating a New Way of Working Together. At the end of my second year, the directors and I began to think together about the coming year's professional development opportunities. We shared our observations and reflections of the previous year, made connections to the year before, and together considered ways to support the center and our current needs and hopes. We asked ourselves many questions, including:

- What does it mean—here and now at the WBCC—to be inspired by the work of the educators in Reggio Emilia?
- How do we move from working as isolated teachers to a climate that encourages staff to work and collaborate in teams, where people become confident and excited about working and learning together?
- How are we listening, observing, and documenting to support children's learning, reflective thinking, and creativity?
- What are the connections between our image of the studio teacher and our image of work with materials?
- What are we learning about how children use materials to communicate?

These questions inspired our group to look carefully at our time and to create a space for educators to come together in learning groups. We intended to give teachers the opportunity to explore a material for themselves. I remembered the comment of one teacher: "There are few times in my life when I can sit down and experiment." Our dream was that, given the time for exploration, teachers would fall in love with materials and share that enthusiasm with their colleagues and with the children in their classrooms.

After spending time considering how we might provide teacher coverage for classrooms, as well as individual teachers' needs and professional development plans, we constructed two groups of six teachers to form material research groups. Based on our observations and teachers' comments, we chose to focus on paint. Teachers would research this familiar classroom material in great depth. Our ideas were expanded when we found inspiration from fellow author Cathy Topal's book *Children and Painting* (Topal, 1992). To help make connections between children of different age groups and build relationships between sites, we consciously included two infant teachers, two toddler teachers, and two preschool teachers in each group. Our hope was that we could create an opportunity for learning groups to form by keeping the groups consistent and by making a commitment to create time for the group to come together regularly (twice a month over a period of six months). We decided that each group should be allotted two-and-a-half-hour blocks of time during the regular school day for their research in the studio. We wanted to ensure that teachers had an adequate amount of time to work together and explore the materials fully. Each session would include time to:

- Explore materials in new ways;
- Discuss ideas and struggles;
- Share observations and documentation;
- Examine hypotheses and theories; and
- Reflect on our experience as a group.

At the end of each session, we planned to ask teachers to consider the most helpful aspect from our work together. We wanted to know what had been confusing and what had been inspiring. In this way, we could design each session *with* the teachers based on the intentions of the group, their observations, and their hopes and needs. Patti Cruickshank-Schott, the preschool education director, and I, worked closely together to plan, reflect, and organize these experiences. We also intended to make the work of the group visible through documentation during the six-month experience.

Figure 9.17. Beautiful colors seem to invite participation.

The Adventure Begins. We were very excited about this new professional development opportunity; we wanted to create an atmosphere of exploration and collegiality from the very start. And so we planned to use a palette of gorgeous materials as an irresistible invitation to begin an exploration of paint. As the teachers entered the studio, they saw that it had been prepared with a huge range of colored tempera, a variety of brush sizes, and richly textured paper (see Figure 9.17).

The teachers were invited to use the materials in their own ways. Some teachers talked with their colleagues and others seemed to investigate the materials with quiet focus. Group conversations finally emerged, and we began to share our childhood experiences with paint. Some shared joyful memories of painting, while others recalled feelings of frustration, judgment, and time limitations. After the painting experience was over, we used reflective writing and drawing to express our thoughts and feelings.

Considering the Perspective of Children. Throughout the paint series, teachers were given opportunities to explore in a variety of ways. They tried watercolor painting, painting at an easel, painting on a horizontal surface, painting in combination with drawing materials, and cutting up old paintings for collages. From these encounters with materials, teachers began to consider what children might be experiencing during similar situations. We believed that when adults consider the perspective of the children, they are more prepared to support them in the classroom. These hands-on experiences went beyond providing "practical" information about a material (see Figure 9.18).

For example, when one teacher was painting at the easel for the first time, her brush dripped paint onto her work. Her frustration gave us the opportunity to discuss ways and techniques for controlling amounts of paint on the brush as well as incorporating marks into a composition.

The teachers' experiences with paint led us to think more deeply about ways to support children's explorations. So next, we mixed a beautiful range of colorful jars of paint as gifts to each classroom. Some teachers began to consider the many ways to present a variety of brush sizes to her toddlers and inspired others to do the same. Another colleague was so enthusiastic about this experience that she began to research toddlers' investigations of different sizes and types of brushes. I also found myself making more conscious and intentional choices of brushes in the studio.

The teachers commented that after exploring the material several times in different ways, they felt more competent and skilled as observers. A child's frustration or leaps of thought were more easily noted and became a foundation for further investigations (see Figure 9.19).

Thinking in Many Languages. As the paint series progressed, we noticed that the groups had gone beyond exploring materials and started to use materials to express ideas. As we approached the end of this chapter of our work together, we asked the teachers to reflect on the experiences and to translate their thinking and learning into another medium. During the first of the last three sessions, we asked teachers to write, sketch, paint, and share their reflections of the past few months. To help support their reflections, the director and I displayed the documentation panels of the paint series in the studio. We made a beautiful arrangement of the teachers' paintings near the studio window. We provided books and other resources for inspiration and shared transcriptions of our conversations and other artifacts from our work together. We were literally surrounded with our work.

Figure 9.18. "I had no idea. It's nice to watch—as a child would—the joy of mixing two different colors that will be something brand new."

Figure 9.19. Educators discussing observations.

Developing Shared Understandings

"We didn't know how beautiful it was going to be. It was exciting that it wasn't just your work; it was everybody's."

"It made me think about small-group work with children differently."

As a final tribute to the experience that we had shared, we challenged the teachers to create a collaborative design that would represent their *combined* experiences and thinking from the six-month investigation of paint. We were excited, and perhaps a bit nervous, to challenge each group to venture into this type of project, which would require collaborative thinking. We hoped this situation would inspire the same spirit and thoughtfulness that we had seen in previous encounters.

It was interesting to watch how differently the two groups worked together. One group struggled to make their ideas heard and to actively listen to one another. Using this technique, the group opted to give each member a space on the canvas for his or her unique perspective and included each person's donation to the mural (see Figure 9.20).

The second group made a list of its members' thinking first, thought about the properties of the material, and then created a new work that represented

Figure 9.20. The two groups created collaborative visual representations of their experience. Group one's offering.

Figure 9.21. Another depiction of the paint series by group two.

the group. The group chose to represent properties of the medium. There were many examples of their understandings: warm and cool colors; the drips, flow, and movement of paint; and the styles of brushes. One of the group members who felt connected to her native language, Mandarin Chinese, focused on the strokes of the brush. Her addition to the group's work was the Chinese character for "wood." When the symbol is multiplied, it builds and creates other words and concepts, such as "tree" and "forest" (see Figure 9.21).

As this experience evolved and began to come to a close, I realized that my concept of a studio teacher had been transformed. I felt more grounded. The teachers' attitudes about materials and about themselves as creators had changed. They became more comfortable with materials and excited about using them in their classrooms.

Through this six-month experience we created new shared systems of organization that connected the *atelier* to the classrooms, and vice versa. We had also found fresh sources of imagination that could travel among us and our spaces.

Meanwhile, the paintings from our study group have become metaphors for our work together. They seem to capture our identity as individuals as well as our experience as we became a group with shared understandings—like trees who have discovered they are part of a forest.

CONCLUSION

In telling our stories and reflecting on them together, we found common threads. In each of the four stories in this chapter, we recognized the importance of beauty and order in the lives of children—and in all of our lives. Beauty inspires us to maintain order. Beauty inspires us to arrange and rearrange materials and spaces. Beauty inspires us to refine our ideas and our environments. Beauty inspires us to look more closely.

Studios were inspirational learning spaces for all of us. We also recognized that as we worked to effect change in our various settings, we were also transformed both as individuals and as a group.

As we told our stories and reflected on them, we realized that our four smaller stories had become one greater story. It is the story of learning to listen and challenge one another, to respect one another's work, and to be willing to learn together; finally it is a story of "being and belonging" (Galardini & Giovannini, 2001). We found a sense of shared understanding and collaboration that each of us had longed to find with teachers on the same journey.

REFERENCES

Cuffaro, H. K. (1995). *Experimenting with the world* (p. 33). New York: Teachers College Press.

Day, C. (1990). *Places of the soul: Architecture and environmental design as a healing art.* London and San Francisco, CA: Thorsons.

Galardini, A., & Giovannini, D. (2001). Pistoia: Creating a dynamic, open system to serve children, families and community. In L. Gandini & C. Edwards (Eds.), *Bambini: The Italian approach to infant/toddler care* (pp. 89–105). New York: Teachers College Press.

Gandini, L. (1998). Educational and caring spaces. In C. Edwards, L. Gandini, & G. Forman (Eds.), *The hundred languages of children: The Reggio Approach—Advanced reflections* (2nd ed.; pp. 161–177). Westport, CT: Ablex.

Olds, A. (2000). *Child care design guide.* New York: McGraw-Hill.

Topal, C. (1992). *Children and painting.* Worchester, MA: Davis Publications, Inc.

The Evolution of the *Atelier*

Conversations from Reggio Emilia

Lella Gandini

The following interviews are part of continuous reflections recorded here through a series of connected conversations. They highlight research with new languages and tools that sheds new light on the determinant role of documentation as well as the expansion of connected learning that includes families and the culture around the schools in the city of Reggio Emilia.

We will read a new conversation with Giovanni Piazza, *atelierista* of La Villetta School. To conclude this chapter, Vea Vecchi, the *atelierista* who worked side by side with Loris Malaguzzi for many years, will give her particular interpretation of the potential of the *atelier* and her hopes for its future.

THE USE OF DIGITAL LANGUAGES AND THE *ATELIER*: INTERVIEW WITH GIOVANNI PIAZZA

The two interviews with Giovanni Piazza, one from 1997 (see Chapter 2) and the other from June 2003, although distant in time, should be seen as an essential dialogue that illustrates what is at the heart of the *atelier* and the way it continues to evolve.

Lella: *At the outset, I would like to take note of your comments expressed in our interview in 1997. Your views about the complexity of the encounter between children, materials, and languages continue to be useful to teachers. At times, educators think just giving materials to children is enough. They expect expressive languages to develop spontaneously.*

Giovanni: This is still an idea that is relatively commonplace, not only in the United States. After many years of work with children, it seems to me that if these encounters are fortuitous and the contact with materials casual, they rarely generate expressivity. Even though six years have passed since that earlier interview, this remains one of our fundamental considerations. An expressive language is rarely formed solely from a relationship between a child and materials. How do we familiarize the child with different materials? What deep contact can we sustain in order to allow children to become aware of their ability to plan the next step with materials? How can we sustain their creative imagery and creative action?

To succeed as schools, as *atelieristi*, and as teachers, it is important to review the path that bridges the gap between children and a deep knowledge of materials. We need to raise the sensitivity to this relationship among materials, tools, children, and, above all, the thoughts (and ideas) that children bring with them when they approach various situations.

I think that this is the crux of the matter. It is only when the children have a sufficient level of familiarity that they discover how each material has internal alphabetic qualities. Later they discover that this internal alphabet shares qualities with other materials and it is contaminated by them.

When we speak about a **rich normality**, we refer to daily encounters with materials that are not necessarily part of a specific project. Rather, they respond to children's desire to work with a variety of materials. At the same time, we need to observe the child's journey of understanding with each material.

Lella: *How is observation organized? Through what kind of documentation?*

Giovanni: Above all, we must construct structures and tools that allow a strong and durable visibility. During the past five years, we have focused much more on the construction of a portfolio for each child. We have realized how we can review a child's experience with the materials alongside the child and rediscover together new possibilities and new interpretative keys. The portfolios represent a progressive collection that the teacher and the child make over the course of the three years in the school.

Lella: *Are you talking about a binder of photographs, drawings, and other things?*

Giovanni: There are actually two levels. One is a collection of materials, accompanied by observations and evidence of the tools used, as well as images, photographs, and three-dimensional constructions [see Figure 10.1]. This portfolio offers a sort of mini-story that allows the child to see himself or herself from the inside, following not only his or her relationship and development with the materials, but also the learning structures of a group of children.

The second is the digital portfolio that has become so important for us. Here, all of the materials that have been scanned and saved on the computer, by the children, and by the adults become new images that can be worked on with specific software and then inserted into the children's digital portfolio. The digital narration—stories and experiences lived and constructed by the children—uses the new integrated languages of the computer: sound, movement, and, animation. It thus allows new ways of telling about one's own experience at school.

Lella: *The most difficult aspect of the portfolio is to try not to focus too much on the individual.*

Figure 10.1. One aspect of the *atelier* at La Villetta School: The construction of a city of paper by 5-year-old children.

Giovanni: This can be one of the potential risks; it is not easy to talk about an individual and, at the same time, see him or her in relation to the group he or she is part of. We try to maintain these two tracks, searching to give significance to the actions of the individual and those of the group. The construction and the sharing of the mini-stories with friends can give new meaning in different ways.

Lella: *The idea of a portfolio that has stories to tell seems constructive.*

Giovanni: Yes, I think that this has evolved from the boxes that we used to store the children's three-dimensional materials, drawings, stories, narrative voices. They were organized by the children and teachers together, but they were not always so easy to review or read.

In the research on new ideas, we maintained that the new containers would gather the narrative of the children's experiences through concrete materials and, now, also through a digital portfolio. When we review this material, both in concrete and digital form, to look for new meaning, the child realizes immediately that the use of more than one language can offer new and powerful forms of narrative for one's own story as well as the experience shared with friends.

Lella: *This is like a beautiful assemblage.*

Giovanni: This is a very important assemblage because it allows the children to construct a strong metacognitive structure and then to take hold of their own understanding and rearrange it, giving it a narrative. This is extremely important in the layers of quality of the experience. You will see then that the experience of each child within the group can immediately be made available through digital technology to the parents and to other teachers.

These experiences can be also made available to another institution, such as the elementary school, where the child will go to construct the next part of his or her educational experience. We see the child as a rich carrier of experience—experience not only of constructing, but also of elaborating, meaning in relationship with materials, experience that shows what the child has come to know, what he or she has learned, and what he or she thinks.

Lella: *That can open various possibilities of interpretation.*

Giovanni: Exactly. We started last year to construct a portfolio with experiences that begin [with entry to preschool] at 3 years of age, with a progressive selection of materials, projects, conversations, and images that are most representative of each child, in relation with the other children, through their journey in the school.

Lella: *You prepare an individual portfolio for each child. Does this come about as a collaboration between the classroom teacher and the* atelierista?

Giovanni: The planning happens with the *atelierista* and the teacher and among the teachers of the three sections that carry out the work together. The parents participate, as well.

Lella: *Certainly, the children participate in decision making?*

Giovanni: The children participate in the selection. The teachers use some observational tools to collect the criteria the children use in order to understand the process of self-evaluation that accompanies and motivates the children's choices. At the same time, the teachers share the emerging processes with the parents and transfer various parts into a digital format, preparing a digital archive that the children can consult.

Lella: *You keep two possibilities of documentation open: the one that you used in the past and the digital one?*

Giovanni: We always keep all of the possibilities open, because we think that it is important to keep all of the channels of our communication open. We think of collecting memory as dynamic rather than memory as placed in storage. I think that children understand this. Both children and adults are in the process of exploring and constructing knowledge, and we do not know what will happen next. The digital portfolio offers us all the opportunity to move to a new level of shared understanding about these processes within a dynamic situation. We are trying to maintain our strong cultural tradition of construction with materials with this new, more widely shareable, digital process of construction [see Figure 10.2].

Lella: *Thinking about a new* atelierista, *how important is it—especially for someone in the United States who is familiar with the Reggio Approach and wants to begin interpreting the work of the* atelier—*to begin from the beginning of experiencing materials and languages? That is, to begin with exploration of materials, observation, and documentation, before using digital technology to follow processes?*

Giovanni: We must always consider that inside every individual there is a biological development that requires one to construct experiences to one's maximum capacity. For this reason, we believe in the importance of giving the new *atelieristi* and new teachers the time to learn through experiences with materials. Taking the time to learn does not simply mean exploring the materials as an adult, although this remains as a valid possibility. Rather, it means observing with the children the things that they construct and produce, as well as the qualities of the relationships the children build with their hands and minds. This should be the foundation of the daily work with the children. By revisiting this course of action with the children, the teachers and *atelieristi* construct an understanding, and this is the wealth of our profession.

Figure 10.2. Digital *atelier* set up with computers and video projectors with 5-year-old children at La Villetta School.

This approach, I would say, continues to be a fundamental component of our work in Reggio Emilia. You cannot think of bringing in technological structures if you don't have, on the other side, an elaborative, constructive life flow. We understand that when materials accompany you, they bring you closer to what you want to do, and they become an expressive structure. This is a powerful enrichment. Now we can use digital technology to follow children's constructions and gather images that we can use to communicate children's growth.

We have tried to give new *atelieristi* their own time, so that they build an experience that is not only one of material offerings, but also one of experience and vision. Only in the moment in which one is able to perceive the nuances within the relationship between children, materials, and ideas will he or she be able to offer something consistently rich. Throughout the course of our history, in the professional development of teachers and *atelieristi*, we have formed a sort of large workshop where all that is being worked on, all that is being constructed, is immediately put into interpretive circulation. Without this circulatory system, it is difficult to construct experiences and understandings. With this approach, one can discover the beauty of children's competence and thoughts and, on the other side, one's personal limitations.

AESTHETIC THOUGHT AND ESPRESSIVITY: INTERVIEW WITH VEA VECCHI

It was through the support of Vea Vecchi that I was able in June 2003 to accomplish my mission of interviewing the teachers and *atelieristi* who have contributed their multifaceted reflections on creative learning and teaching in Reggio Emilia to this book. It was Vea who helped me reflect on the complexity of the development of the *atelier* in and out of the schools for young children, through the city, and in connection with many artistic and cultural events surrounding our contemporary world. She was especially attentive to the aesthetic awareness that is not only becoming strong among teachers, but also that has helped each institution, be it an infant/toddler center or a school, to find its identity.

Lella: *Let's talk about the evolution of the* atelier.

Vea: As the years passed, the aesthetic thought that characterizes our work extended to the teachers in the preschools. Lately, we have witnessed a great growth among the infant/toddler teachers; they have gained a much stronger identity.

Lella: *How did this growth come about?*

Vea: Through observation and documentation—these are the tools that permit the teachers to observe, to reflect on the identity of small children, on their way of relating to things. We started to be more daring with the children, which does not mean pushing them to be precocious; rather, it means aspiring to be more refined listeners to the possibilities children offer.

Lella: *Tell me how you define aesthetic thought.*

Vea: Aesthetic thought is transversal to various languages and disciplines. It uses expressivity to bring a language of relationships into the activities that take place. Aesthetic thought holds relational aspects and expressive aspects of life together. I like the phrase that Gregory Bateson [1980] uses when he speaks about aesthetics as an instrument of connection. Bateson speaks of a language that connects, a language that links together different parts; that highlights relationships, not only differences. Expressivity is a process that places things in relationships. Unfortunately, often in schools, in our culture, expressivity is not considered important. On the contrary, I think that increasing one's own knowledge, learning different languages, continuing to give a voice to one's own expressivity means keeping a high level of relational attention. Relation is the opposite of violence, and if expressivity is accompanied by ethic, it is, in my view, the antibody against violence.

Lella: *Let's go back to the discussion about documentation that all the* atelieristi *and teachers interviewed consider an essential part of their work.*

Vea: Documentation has been a fundamental element of our evolution. It is a tool that nourishes our own research, our attention, and our desire to discover. Observing and documenting the strategies of understanding and discovering, ways of reasoning, and the processes of learning of the individual and of children in small groups, are all extremely rich aspects of learning. In this regard, there are scholars, such as Edgar Morin [1999], who contend that even if we are aware that all of the processes of understanding cannot be foreseen, the only way to begin reflecting on them is to make these processes visible. It is a paradox that we must be willing to accept.

Lella: *Can you talk about the help that you offered to the elementary school teachers with regard to documentation?*

Vea: We began collaboration with the elementary school with some projects. We know that some of our teachers are now particularly competent to set the children up for documentation. In fact, some of them are experimenting with supporting the children doing documentation by themselves. This does not change the fact that the path is still long.

The environment in which one lives has great influence on our way of working. If one works in the elementary school, the context does not help to nurture the process of observation. In general, in the elementary school context, documentation refers to a chronicle of what has happened. Listening to and observing processes is a different thing. It requires a longer period of preparation for the teachers and for the children to understand. It could be a very important change if we could help it to come about. In the elementary schools, it would require creating a small revolution in learning—the attention would need to pass from the final product to the observation of the process. In this way, documentation would transform itself; it would be a chronicle no longer of the phases but, instead, of the processes. To observe processes would bring with it a notable growth for the teachers, all teachers.

But it is important to find the specific contexts in which this kind of work can begin. In one recent project of collaboration, a few *atelieristi* went into the elementary schools. They intervened in a delicate moment of formal learning, as the children were learning how to write. In this moment of learning a formal code, we asked ourselves how we could keep the internal magic of this code alive—for example, if we could work on the letters of the alphabet as images. We asked ourselves whether the notebook page could become a sort of theater scene in which the sentences, the words, and the letters each acquire an expressive force. Would the children be confused, or would they find a way to keep their learning more full of life? The material that the *atelieristi* collected in the elementary school classes showed us the enormous metaphorical and symbolic capacity on the part of the children with marks (signs), with colors, and with the materiality of the paper. Therefore, as always, when we give the children and teachers support to open up their own potentials, we start to see interesting results.

The other aspect we must work on in the elementary schools is how to approach contemporary art exhibits. The elementary schools take advantage of such exhibits only to take the children out to see them, but often the teachers do not use these occasions in a very knowledgeable way. These visits always begin with the artist and end with the child. All of this is the opposite of the creative process that requires that the child be the protagonist. We should be nourishing the children with words and projects that can be of interest for them.

We are trying to promote strategies that start with the child and end with the artist. To accomplish that, teachers and *atelieristi* need to understand the language of contemporary art and the language of the child and put them together, intertwine them, as we did in our project in which we connected children's creative potential with the art of Alberto Burri [see Figure 10.3]. Here, as well, it is necessary to follow the path of understanding and listening to both the works of art and the children. This is a path that in some way reproduces what we have always followed in the Reggio Emilia schools, but we could also do this work in didactic laboratories in museums.

Our attempt is to create intentional connections between different places in the city: museums, didactic laboratories, infant/toddler centers, preschools, and elementary schools.

Lella: *In this way, the* atelier *expands throughout the whole city.*

Vea: It is a gamble. In our infant/toddler centers and preschools there is one context, a daily routine that allows us to work as we had said. In the museums, however, there is not enough time; we would need to create a different way of understanding these visits as part of extended projects where schools and museums would work in relationship.

Figure 10.3. Forms of iron and clay. Poster for the exhibit of work realized with children. From the project The Expressive Languages of Children: The Artistic Language of Alberto Burri.

Something else that is new and characterizes the last few years of our activity is the professional development of the *atelieristi*. I am working on a new training course for them as we look for ways to give new *atelieristi* the possibility of creating connections among several different expressive languages. Other languages have always contaminated the visual language of the *atelier*; now we would like to make this connection explicit. In the same way, the connection between pedagogy and the expressive, artistic languages should be made even more explicit. This vital connection should be spelled out more clearly, more didactically.

The other thing that we are working on is placing together more than one professional in the same *atelier*—a musician and a professional expert in the visual languages, for example. We have been able to do that in Stockholm and at Sant'Ilario, in the province of Reggio Emilia. Our colleagues in Stockholm are doing a project on natural science using an *atelier* in which visual and musical languages are used contemporaneously.

The fundamental points in the evolution of our *atelier* can be summed up as follows: expansion toward the city [see Figure 10.4]; collaboration with elementary schools; and consulting activities for key public and private schools, with an intent to enrich the knowledge and quality of environments for young children.

Figure 10.4. Curtain for the municipal theater designed by the 5-year-old children of Diana School.

My great dream is the extraordinary adventure of understanding, of documenting, the microprocesses of learning. I intend to document them live and then to interpret them and discuss them with others. The final product will not be abandoned, but each child and teacher will be given a way to reflect on the processes of understanding. Observation and documentation are the elements that keep the attention, a high reflective tension in the schools with regard to the work that we do. Teaching is life, after all. Edgar Morin [1999] once spoke about having received the transcript of a discussion by a group of intellectuals and being asked to express his opinion on the discussion. He said that he could not respond because he had not heard the tones of voice of those who had participated in the discussion. With this thought in mind, I want to emphasize the importance of the tools that we choose to document with. We have tried many. We discovered that the most valid one is one that looks like a short script. The pauses, the eye movements, a smiling mouth become elements of these little scripts. Those who read these documents enter into the script itself.

To conclude, I would like to say something about the *atelier* in general. Expressivity is a structure that is intrinsic to the individual. Therefore, the cognitive and the imaginative inevitably go together. The *atelier* within the school places expressivity inside the process of understanding, giving life to a structure that is more complete, more human.

CLOSING REFLECTIONS

In this chapter, Giovanni Piazza focuses on what has become his great passion and expertise: the development of digital language in the children's expression and design of digital documentation. He and his colleagues have realized that, while they should continue to broaden experimentation with different languages, they should also work to construct digital documentation. This type of documentation has structures that allow for a wide and durable visibility using "the new integrated languages of the computer: sound, movement, and animation." The children participate in constructing the stories of their life at the school with the teachers. Parents can contribute digitally to their children's portfolio, as well. That documentation can then be shared widely.

Giovanni insists that the most important discovery for teachers and *atelieristi* is still the complex relationships among materials, tools, and above all, the thoughts of children. This is relevant especially in view of the links among the alphabetical qualities of different materials and media. These thoughts resonate in the next chapter, in which Louise Cadwell, Lori Geismar Ryan, and Charles Schwall analyze what the children were learning through experiences of light and reflection. In similar ways, we see the connection with the next chapter in the descriptions of school as a system, considering that Giovanni refers to his colleagues in different schools and centers in Reggio as if they were all in one large workshop, where all that is being worked on is immediately put into interpretive circulation. This is in fact a basic tenet in the philosophy of the Reggio Emilia schools.

Vea Vecchi's reflections on documentation that "nourishes our own research" and on the collaboration with teachers in elementary schools concerning the teaching of "academic" subjects through expressive languages prepares us for the complex analyses offered in the next chapter. We will see the influence of the aesthetic principles of Vea and her emphasis on the importance of documentation. The sense of continuity between these chapters will be clear and constructive to readers.

REFERENCES

Bateson, G. (1980). *Mind and nature: A necessary unity.* New York: Bantam Books.
Morin, E. (1999). *La tête bien faite.* Paris: Editions du Seuil.

Credits: *Figures 10.1 and 10.2:* Photographs from La Villetta School, 2004, unpublished. *Figure 10.3:* Poster exhibit, Alberto Burri, 2004, *Children, Arts, and Artists,* Ed. V. Vecchi & C. Giudici, p. 103. *Figure 10.4:* Curtain of municipal theater, 2002, V. Vecchi, *Sipario (Curtain),* p. 119. All © Municipality of Reggio Emilia—Infant-Toddler Centers and Preschools.

The *Atelier*

A System of Physical and
Conceptual Spaces

**Louise Cadwell, Lori Geismar Ryan,
and Charles Schwall**

When we think about how we work in
our schools in St. Louis, how school is
lived, and how teachers and children
learn, we think of banks of clouds forming and changing as weather patterns
unfold. We think of natural, organic forms
and of beauty and balance emerging in
tiny happenings as well as in big events.
These are not the usual images of school;
they come from other sources. They come
from nature, from the new physical science, from systems thinking, and from our
growing understanding that this is the
way the world works and this is the way
that learning evolves.

In the world of science, a living system is one where the parts are in constant
flux in relationship to other parts, in relationship to the whole to which they
all belong, and in relationship to other living systems. For a long time, schools
have functioned as nonliving systems where there is little evolution of parts in
relationship; rather ideas are fixed, teachers teach them, and children are sup-
posed to learn them.

The educators in the schools of the St. Louis–Reggio Collaborative are a part
of a revolution in thinking about schools that is taking place in many ways and
in many locations across the country and the around the world. The three of
us—Chuck, *atelierista* at the St. Michael School; Louise, curriculum researcher
at the College School of Webster Groves; and Lori, director of Clayton Schools'
Family Center—are all members of the St. Louis–Reggio Collaborative. We
chose to co-author this chapter because we have studied together as a small
group of three within our larger group of colleagues for 12 years, focusing on
systems theory and how it supports our work. Our study of systems is inspired
by the work of the schools in Reggio Emilia and by other sources of reform and
innovation in education as well as in other fields.

A NEW PARADIGM OF SCHOOL

In our schools, we align ourselves with a way of thinking that is generative.
As teachers, we aspire to bring all that we are to school fully present, knowing that if we do so, something new is likely to come from our being together

and that we will be changed. This is a big idea—that we teachers will be, and in fact want to be, changed by, with, and through each other and with the children every day.

Children live this way. They live as if they were conduits of energy and ideas rather than empty vessels seeking knowledge. We long to catch their comfort with living on the edge of the unexpected. We see ourselves also as conduits of energy and ideas rather than as full, complete vessels imparting what we know to the empty ones. Fortunately, for many educators, the empty-vessel idea is old and obsolete. It is a view of school as a nonliving system.

The ways that we are learning to think together in our schools excites us. We are thrilled by the anticipation of what we might create together that in turn will be a container for the unfolding of meaning and ideas among the children. We seek to create the most exciting, fertile, safe, irresistible context in which children will take off and clamor to bump their ideas up against each other in thoughts; gestures; words, spoken and written; numbers; drawings; clay; and paint. At the center of our work, the *atelier* is at once the physical hub and the conceptual space that is catalyst and container for our meaning making. It is a dance of meaning that is made in relation to others and to experience. There is no fixed outcome. The outcome, we hope, will be beyond our wildest dreams. We know we are shooting for the stars.

Systems Theory

There are key concepts that influence our thinking—indeed, that have changed our thinking, our behavior, our expectations, and our school cultures—so that when we are truly aligned, we live together inside a new paradigm of school. In the last several years, a group of us has read and discussed the work of a number of authors, including Du Four and Eacker (1998); Fullan (2001); Lambert (2003); Senge, Cambron-McCabe, Lucas, Smith, Dutton, and Kleiner (2000); and Wheatley (1999), who embrace systems theory as a way to think about school reform and organizational change and growth. It is through Wheatley's work in particular that we are gaining a clearer understanding of both the roots and the nature of our practice in school. These authors are part of yet a larger group, which includes Alexander (1979), Bateson (1980), Bohm (1996), Capra (1996), and Maturana and Varela (1980), from multiple fields— psychology, physics, biology, physiology, religion, architecture, business. They are captivated by the scientific discoveries of the twentieth century that began with physical science.

In *Leadership and the New Science: Discovering Order in a Chaotic World* (1999), Margaret Wheatley reflects on how systems theory that grew out of quantum physics can transform the way that we have traditionally thought about and managed organizations and institutions, including schools. Rather than a closed system managed from the top down—like a factory that, instead of products, produces students—schools have been an alive system of alive individuals seeking to be liberated to reach our full potential together. Wheatley reminds us that the opposite is true in closed systems that are governed by the Second Law of Thermodynamics: such systems wear down and lose energy that can never be retrieved. "Life goes on, but it is all downhill," she laments (p. 76).

The characteristics of open systems are many. Open systems seek disequilibrium. They exchange with the world openly and use what they encounter for their growth and evolution. They thrive on participation of all the parts in healthy, dynamic, ongoing relationship. They connect the parts through multiple locations and occasions for exchange; exchange is the most important means to promote the system's growth and health. They seek and find order out of apparent chaos. In an open system, order is not a structure but, rather, a "dynamic organizing energy." In an open system, information flows freely. Meaning takes on the qualities of energy, travels, and becomes a force of change. Meaning leads each and all the parts of the living system to center on and circle around deeper purpose and lasting value (Wheatley, 1999).

Frameworks

Over the years we have developed frameworks, forms, cycles, and actions that allow us to live school as an open living system. Some have to do with time and some with place; some revolve around the size of groups and numbers of people; some focus on the way that we trust each other and treat each other; and some involve ways of recording, keeping track of, and tracing our ideas and children's ideas as they unfold. All of these forms and frameworks are interrelated and interconnected; they move together in synchrony as we move with them.

Time frames are agreed-upon meeting times when we consider ideas and experiences and enter into dialogue with materials, with each other, with the world, with shared experience. These are appointments for interchange and exchange among all the players in the unfolding drama of our living system. One example of a time frame is the morning meeting with all the children in a class. Another is morning work in small groups within a complex, richly developed, and well-cared-for classroom or *atelier* environment. Another is the regularly scheduled teachers' meeting for reflection on and projection of ideas growing out of the work as it evolves. Yet another time frame is regularly scheduled meetings, exchanges, and communication with parents.

Some of the frameworks are space frames. Different spaces and places are permeable containers that generate curiosity, ideas, and exchange. These space frames are multiple and diverse and encourage interaction with the familiar and the unfamiliar. For example, we organize and reorganize big classrooms for a large group of children to include small, intimate nooks for small groups to organize themselves. We claim and rename small rooms and alcoves also for small groups. We have carved *ateliers* and *miniateliers* out of existing classrooms and protected them with glass walls. We have reclaimed neglected parts of playgrounds and imagined and constructed outdoor rooms. We have ventured out into places in the community that become more and more familiar as they extend our classrooms into the neighborhood, the zoo, the riverfront, the weather, the seasons, the community garden, and families' homes.

Other frameworks revolve around the size and nature of groupings: from random to organized; from whole to part; from large to small; from individual, to pair, to group; from teacher and child, child to child, child to teacher, teacher to teacher, teacher to parent, child to parent, and back again. Information, ideas, experience, thoughts, wonderings, longings, friendship, and love travel in and among these groups in constant ebb and flow. These are the connections among the "building blocks of matter" that really matter.

Relationships

Wheatley writes, "Matter doesn't matter" (p. 153). The relationships matter. This is the theory that the Reggio Emilia educators, influenced by Bateson, Maturana and Varela, and others, have put into practice in their schools so exquisitely. As we've studied the Reggio Approach since 1992, this practice continues to present us with the daily challenge of noticing and valuing the "in between," and this requires a figure/ground shift. We want to seek out the places, spaces, times, attitudes, and practices that cultivate the birth of ideas, that nurture them and set them off in endless cycles. This way of learning is rarely linear. There are not fixed ideas that are consumed and then owned by one child or one adult. Ideas are in constant circulation, like the air, like oxygen, like food, like clouds, like the weather. Everything is influenced by everything, and that is what we are after. This is a way of working that cultivates creative thinking everywhere in the school.

As we place more and more emphasis on the experiences that surround us, the ideas that grow among us, and the context that encompasses us, we become intimately aware of our need for each other and our interdependence. We become aware that we are on a journey into the unknown. We depend on one another to travel well, to take care of each other, to discover what is important and vital, and to make a difference in the world.

Over time, through careful attention to the processes of documentation used in the schools of Reggio Emilia and through trial and error, we are learning to make meaning of unfolding, evolving ideas. We keep track of fragments of ideas and continue to examine them together as teachers and students until they begin to take shape and to make sense. We do this on pieces of paper, on a computer screen, on audiotape, on videotape, and on film. We might record children's and teachers' ideas in a notebook at morning meeting, tape record and transcribe small-group conversations in which we explore ideas together, or follow and note one child's thinking as she imagines and draws a theory or builds a structure. We need a record, a trail that traces where we have come from as history, as foundation, as backdrop, and as framework for where we are going. We move forward as we build a context, a history, and a culture.

Wheatley (1999) uses many metaphors to describe the way it feels to work together within this new paradigm of a living system. We found this one particularly helpful:

> Those who have used music metaphors to describe working together, especially jazz metaphors, are sensing the nature of this quantum world. This world demands that we be present together, and be willing to improvise. We agree on the melody, tempo, key, and then we play. We listen carefully, we communicate constantly, and suddenly, there is music, possibilities beyond anything we imagined. The music comes from somewhere else, from a unified whole we have accessed among ourselves, a relationship that transcends our false sense of separateness. When the music appears, we can't help but be amazed and grateful. (p. 45)

THE SCHOOL AS A LIVING SYSTEM

We are amazed and grateful for the following story that is a part of our history. In many ways, it reveals the qualities of daily life of children and adults conversing, thinking, reflecting, writing, drawing, painting, and finding pleasure in being together in school. One central aspect of this story is how the concept of the *atelier* expands the interconnections of places and events into the entire community of school. Though it begins with the leading event that sparked a project and an overview of how that project developed, the heart of the story that follows is the studied documentation of one day, May 15, 2003, and the project. We were challenged by a friend and colleague from Reggio Emilia, Vea Vecchi, *atelierista* for 30 years at the Diana School, to follow one day in careful detail to see how the context of that day specifically and concretely illustrated the systems that support our work. We accepted.

Now, travel with us toward the search for light and the miracle of everyday life in the basement classrooms of the 4- and 5-year-old children at the St. Michael School. From the perspective of school as a living system, let us consider the unfolding of the following project and the day embedded within it.

An Unexpected Event in the Classroom

On the morning of September 12, 2002, as the children were sitting down for the classroom morning meeting, a few children noticed a circle of light reflecting onto the ceiling. The reflection was very animated; it jumped around the room from the ceiling to the walls, then to the floor. As more children began to arrive, they noticed this phenomenon, and a groundswell of excitement began to consume the class. At this time, Chuck, the *atelierista*, was sitting on the steps in the classroom making notes in his notebook. The reflection on the ceiling was caused by sunlight as it came in through a small basement window and bounced off the crystal of his wristwatch. As Chuck changed the position of his arm, the circle of light jumped around the room, quickly moving from the ceiling to the walls or the floor, then back to the ceiling again. He hardly noticed the reflection, but the children greeted it with shrieks of delight. They were thrilled with this remarkable new encounter, and it caused sheer joy and fascination among all of them.

The teachers, Karen Schneider and Melissa Guerra, sat down with the children to discuss this surprising event. Karen asked them, "What is it?" The children offered many ideas. Some called it "the flying thing"; others said it was "Tinkerbell" or "Peter Pan." One girl said, "It's a reflection"; another boy proclaimed, "It's the sun!" (see Figure 11.1).

Everything in the school environment is filled with potential for children's learning. At the same time, each part of the environment is not always given attention and value. The St. Michael School preschool is located in the basement of a church building. This location has presented the staff with many barriers. As teachers, they have tried to view these barriers not as deterrents that

Figure 11.1. The children are thrilled with the remarkable new encounter.

prevent them from trying but, rather, as catalysts that can produce solutions that are new, unexpected, and innovative (see also Chapter 3).

St. Michael School preschool classrooms have few windows with little or no natural light. The only windows are small rectangular ones located just under the ceiling. Sunlight falls into the basement for only a short period of time each day. It would be easy to think that these windows offer the children no connection to the outdoor environment and that they therefore cannot enrich children's learning experiences. The event that occurred in the classroom for 4- and 5-year-olds at the St. Michael School on September 12, 2002, reminded us that devalued elements of the environment can become powerful characters in children's learning.

This unexpected occurrence, when light danced through the basement classroom and the children responded to it, was an opportunity filled with potential for learning, investigation, and continued study. Following this exciting morning, the teachers began to hypothesize what this experience might mean for the children and for their learning. Teachers shared ideas, exchanged some initial questions, and wondered, "Will the children's excitement about the light continue for more than one day?" The teachers were hopeful that the energy they felt during one of the first morning meetings of the year could support something bigger.

There were practices in place that served as frameworks to support the unfolding work of the children and the teachers. One such practice was regularly scheduled conversation and dialogue between children and teachers, as well as among the teachers. Another was the practice of recording conversation, revisiting ideas, and reflecting on some of the most provocative ideas together.

Ongoing Relationships and Sustained Conversations

At the St. Michael School, the preprimary teachers follow the children for a three-year cycle, beginning when the children are 3 years old and culminating when the children finish kindergarten. When the reflected-sunlight event occurred, the children and the teachers were beginning their second year together as a class. The teachers knew the children and the specific qualities and characteristics they brought to their learning.

At the beginning of each year, the teachers share their observations with one another and use them to develop intentions. Karen and Melissa had observed an emerging richness in the morning large-group meetings during the previous year and had written specific intentions about supporting this richness in the new school year:

> Last year we began to notice that as the year progressed the group time conversations grew richer and richer. There was a pleasant collaborative spirit in the classroom. Children began to have bonds born of conversation and collaborative talk. Though they may also be a springboard or a seed for future experiences, the act of conversing is an experience in

itself. This sense of purpose in the social environment permeates the morning group meeting, as well as the entire day at school. This year, one teacher will take notes during each morning meeting to document the ideas expressed so that we can trace the children's conversations and ideas as they develop over time.

To ensure that this intention became a reality, the teachers created a notebook that they called the Morning Meeting Journal. This journal was designed to capture children's dialogue about many important topics that occur every day. One teacher would facilitate the meeting with the children while the other would take notes. The teachers played both roles in a way that included the children as active participants. After the meeting, these notes were then placed in the journal. The Morning Meeting Journal was a key container of information that allowed the Sunlight and Reflection Project to take shape. The teachers recorded the children's thoughts and ideas in the journal and used them as a catalyst to organize and support new experiences (see Figure 11.2).

At the beginning of the project, collaborative talk at morning meeting was the main vehicle the children used to introduce and shape their ideas. The initial encounter with the light had been a collective experience shared by everyone in the class. Because of this, when one child offered an idea, others contributed or responded to it. Ideas began to emerge within the context of the group, and as this happened the engagement of the class evolved and grew.

Figure 11.2. Recording the children's thoughts and ideas in the Morning Meeting Journal.

In the middle of one such conversation after the reflected-sunlight event, Chuck asked the children,"How did the circle of light get on the ceiling?" The children had many explanations to offer. Some children immediately made connections between the light and Chuck's watch, while others had different theories. The teachers carefully listened to all of the children's ideas.

John began, "The watch makes it go up on the ceiling."

Elaborating on this idea, Jamie said, "The light is reflecting through the hole, reflecting onto the watch, and reflecting onto the ceiling."

Catherine added, "Maybe it climbed up there."

"Maybe one of the cameras is doing it," Steven commented as he noticed the lens of Chuck's camera.

Ian said in a very confident voice, "It's a reflection. It goes from the window to the wall."

Jamie pondered for a minute and remarked, "I think a reflection is something that shines on you."

John John speculated, "How can we make reflections?"

Questions like John John's were embraced by the teachers as opportunities to fulfill their intentions. The children inspired the teachers to proceed into uncertain but fertile territory. When the light entered the classroom on these early days in September, the commitment to collaborative, purposeful talk became stronger. Knowing one another well and knowing that they had another entire school year before them connected the past not only with the present, but also with the future. In the weeks and months to come, the children and the teachers had many new ideas born out of their interest in the reflection on the ceiling, their strong relationship and knowledge of each other, and their established practices as a learning community.

An Overview of the Sunlight and Reflection Project

The following is a synthesis of how the experiences with sunlight and reflection evolved and transformed into a long-term project during the course of the school year. This survey of events is meant to provide a vantage point from which to view the whole project. It is presented here as an abbreviated sequence of events in order to ground the project in time and space. The experiences discussed later in this chapter can be examined and appreciated more fully once this larger context is understood. Embedded in this survey you will recognize the systems frameworks that were introduced at the beginning of the chapter. For example, time frames, space frames, size and nature of groupings, and records of thoughts and ideas in words and in media are examined, culled, and carried forward toward ever more layered and deeply shared experience and learning.

- During the first weeks of school in September, the children noticed a reflection of sunlight on the ceiling in the classroom. They responded with enormous excitement and curiosity.

Figure 11.3. Children observed objects and noticed reflections they made at different times of the day.

- Teachers had already organized themselves to document children's dialogue at the morning large group meeting. Because sunlight came into the classroom mainly in the morning, the large group meeting was the central forum where children talked about light and reflection.
- Teachers informed the parents about the children's interest in light and reflection at an evening meeting in October. Children's conversations were shared with the parents using an overhead projector. Together they discussed the children's curiosity and enthusiasm and the potential that these qualities offered for learning during the school year.
- The teachers invited Louise Cadwell to meet with them to promote the development of the experiences with sunlight. She agreed to visit the classroom periodically and offer her observations, thoughts, and questions as the project developed.
- In an effort to involve the families in the research, a letter was sent home asking parents to help their children think about objects that would make a reflection. The children brought these objects to school. They included shiny stickers, small mirrors, pinwheels, jewelry, and mini disco balls. The children tested their objects in the sunlight to find out which ones might make a reflection (see Figure 11.3). These objects were

then placed in a basket on the floor in the classroom where the children could use them throughout the day.

- The children observed the objects and noticed the reflections they made at different times of the day. The children and the teachers created a mobile of the reflective objects brought from home and hung it from the ceiling near a window in the classroom.
- Children wondered and discussed how the sunlight entered the class-room at various times of the day. The four windows of the classroom were labeled with numbers so children could easily identify them.
- Pairs of children took turns observing the morning sky to predict whether the sun would shine that day. The children reported the weather conditions to the class, and teachers documented the findings in a small journal.
- At an evening family event in January, the children and parents created mobiles of reflective objects to take home (see Figure 11.4).
- Teachers reviewed the transcripts of the children's conversations from the morning meetings and made lists of the children's interests. Teachers

Figure 11.4. At an evening family event, the children and the parents created mobiles of reflective objects to take home.

grouped the children's interests and ideas into categories. Then the children worked in small groups to investigate some of these topics:

- *Light and colors.* The idea that colors come out of sunlight came up when one child brought in a CD. When the CD was placed in the sunlight, it created a beautiful rainbow. The children experimented with glass prisms and transparent materials and drew their ideas about reflection. They also used wire and transparent paper to make a rainbow that represented their ideas of how rainbows are formed.
- *Theories about the sun and the moon.* As children discovered that sunlight came in through different windows at different times of the day, they began to discuss and explore ideas related to time change. This led to conversations about the movement of the sun, moon, planets, and solar systems. Groups of children collaborated on inventive stories about the sun and moon that were illustrated using markers and watercolor.
- *Where does the sun go when it's not sunny?* Sometimes there was no sunlight in the classroom because it was cloudy outside. The children's question, "Where does the sun go when we can't see it?" prompted investigations about clouds and, ultimately, rain clouds. Children expressed their ideas about how rain clouds function using drawing and later made clouds with wire, beads, and fabric.
- *Combining dramatic play and light.* The teachers observed children using the reflective objects in dramatic play. The children painted large murals with acrylic paint on transparent plastic depicting the daytime and nighttime sky. The murals were hung in the classroom and used in combination with dramatic play episodes.

- Teachers presented the sunlight and reflection experiences to the parents at the end of the school year. Books of children's work about these experiences were presented to the families as gifts.

A Culture of Thinking Together

As we have written, the practice of dialogue is critical to our work. Regularly practiced dialogue can support and sustain a culture and community that thinks together. Thinking together is one of the bonds that connects the *atelier* to the classroom, the spaces within the classroom to one another, each classroom to the overall school, and, in our case, the St. Michael School to other schools in the St. Louis–Reggio Collaborative. Different types of meetings are arranged, and informal exchanges take place at various times of the day, the week, the month, and the year. Planned and unplanned conversations are essential to the evolution of the work. It is within the context of these encounters that we reflect on children's learning, exchange ideas, create new understandings, and organize for new experiences. Collaborative thinking, where multiple perspectives are shared, is essential to the individual and collective growth of teachers who view the school environment as a learning organization. These conversations become catalysts for new ways of approaching children's learning, for forming connections, and for creating something together that we otherwise could not imagine on our own. Rooted in the idea of the *atelier* as conceptual space, these practices occur in many places throughout the school and among various members of the community.

The teachers at the St. Michael School meet with the *atelierista*, Chuck, approximately once per week throughout the year to discuss initiatives in the classroom and the studio. During the evolution of the light project, Louise periodically joined these meetings. This was an agreed-upon time frame that supported the development of the work. As teachers in the St. Louis–Reggio Collaborative, we continue to learn to play the roles of peer coach, questioner, analyst, provocateur, and co-teacher for one another. Over the years, many of us have had the opportunity to work not only in our own schools but also in each other's schools. We offer the views of colleagues who live and breathe similar systems and practices but who, at the same time, may see the work from a different perspective.

From time to time we tape or video record a teachers' meeting or a parents' meeting primarily to share our work with other educators. As a matter of course, individual teachers keep their own notes at these meetings, and sometimes minutes are taken by a designated scribe. We tape recorded the meeting of May 14, 2003, because it was to be the "official" beginning of the day we had decided to document in detail to respond to Vea's challenge, as mentioned earlier. Our documented day continued through the morning of May 15.

The quality worth noting in this meeting is its normality. It offers one example of our way of thinking about what to do next with various information and ideas. It is a real meeting about real teachers making daily decisions. Yet the decisions are based on our trust in the process of dialogue and our hope that new, wonderful, and sound ideas will come out of our encounter with one another, our individual experience and perspectives, and our shared intentions.

Karen, Melissa, Chuck, and Louise sat down together in the *atelier* late in the afternoon with a sense of openness and expectation as they prepared to discuss and organize for the upcoming last days of school (see Figure 11.5). Soon after the meeting began, Karen shared some of her recent observations about the children's dramatic play:

Karen: The children's dramatic play has sometimes, not always, been dictated by the reflections that were created by the objects we had in the classroom. When the sun came in through the window, it would hit the disco balls, and the children would place them in different areas of the room. And they would say, "It's the stars" or "under the water." We probably didn't document it well or value it as much as we could have.

Figure 11.5. The meeting on May 14 to organize for future work.

What could we do to have some new experiences that build on this idea of light as a character?

Louise: I've never heard of that before. I've never heard of reflected light becoming a character.

Chuck: The children use dramatics continually, but we don't always choose to support it as a language. Also, I think that the most powerful dramatic play episodes take place when several different elements come together.

Louise: What if you harnessed this idea of the "character" of light. There is mystery involved. When will it appear? What will it do? What will the children do with it? Dance? Move? Pretend?

Karen: They love to dance to the light, and they ask for it.

Louise: Maybe they could watch for the light and then have a dramatic response to it. We could just see what they do.

Karen: I think the children would be pretty excited about doing that.

Louise: What if you asked them, "What kind of things do you think you might do?" and "Are you going to use dress-ups? What else do you need if you are going to be a character with the light?" Also, it would help if they could have a cleared out space and, ideally, a small group.

Melissa: The light is always on the small block platform. That area always gets the light. Maybe we could say, "Do you remember when you pretended that the lights were the sky and the stars?" Maybe they would pretend they are on the moon and they are waiting for the light to come.

Louise: Maybe the lights are something else—maybe not stars or a rocket ship.

Melissa: Oh, so a better question might just be, "What could it be?"

Louise: I think that kind of question leaves it more open to the new interpretations that the children might come up with. Also, I wonder if sound could be part of it. If the group is set to wait for the light, you could ask them, "If the light had a sound, what would it be?"

Melissa: Oh, light and sound together!

Louise: Maybe one child could be responsible for giving the light a sound. Then another child waits for the next light and gives it a sound. I don't know how to structurally organize this.

Melissa: Definitely a small group. I'm thinking: move the small block platform to give them room; set up some instruments in that space; and talk with them before the light comes.

Karen: But we don't want the instruments too close to the block platform, because Chuck probably will have a group in the mini-studio. They will hear that noise.

Chuck: But won't it just be little bells and things?

Louise: I have some bells! That's the sort of thing I was thinking. Tinkling sounds. Like Tinkerbell.

Melissa: Remember, at the beginning of the project last September the children said the light was like Tinkerbell!

Chuck: That was one of the very first ideas. It's in the very first conversation.

Louise: If it's a sunny day and this happens, it might be a good idea to be ready to video tape.

Chuck: We can do that.

This meeting deepened our thinking about the children's work and helped us to imagine new connections that could be made among past experiences and present possibilities. Karen's and Melissa's descriptions of how children used reflective objects with their dramatic play was a key element. This generative, collective thinking led to the organization of an open-ended provocation where the children would wait for the sunlight and respond with voice, instruments, movement, and imagination.

The teachers hypothesized that this small-group experience would expand the children's understanding of and relationship with reflected light. Moreover, it could push the role materials play individually and collectively as they expand the possibilities for the children's learning.

This idea of finding new ways to combine light, its reflection, musical instruments, movement, dance, and drama was exciting to the teachers, and they began to prepare. The teachers agreed that Melissa would facilitate a small-group experience involving sunlight, dramatics, and sound. Together they drafted questions for Melissa to ask the children. They brainstormed an inventory of types of bells and other musical instruments that Melissa would offer the children the following morning. Preparation also included how the classroom space would be used for this small group and the other two groups of children, who would be working with Karen in the *atelier* and Chuck in the classroom.

Projections in Action: The Next Day Unfolds

The morning after the teachers' meeting was a busy one in the 4- and 5-year-olds' classroom. The teachers were eager to begin the day, anticipating the three small-group experiences they had organized for the morning. Some children would work in the *atelier* with Karen to discuss and draw ideas about rain clouds; Chuck would be in the classroom *miniatelier* with children mixing colors for a new mural; and Melissa would facilitate the sunlight, sound, and dramatic play group.

Before beginning small-group work, Chuck arrived at morning meeting with a large painting representing the daytime sky made by several children earlier in the week. The painting was inspired by one boy who had suggested making murals of the sky to use as backdrops in the dramatic-play area. All of the children liked his idea, which was to have two large paintings of the sky—one for the daytime and the other for nighttime. On this morning, a group of children would begin mixing colors with Chuck for the nighttime sky mural.

The children who had created the daytime sky painting explained to the rest of the class how it was made. They shared the reasons for their color choices and that they drew with pencils before they worked with paint.

While looking at the painting, one boy asked out loud, "Did you know there are always clouds at nighttime?" This led to a lively discussion about the nighttime sky. The children wondered together, "Are there clouds in the sky at night? How could you see the stars and the moon if there are clouds at night?" Many children had strong opinions, and not everyone agreed. As the conversation played out, Melissa recorded the children's ideas for future reference. After some discussion about the logistics of the day, the morning meeting concluded, and the children dispersed into their small groups.

Rain Cloud Theories. Karen and a group of children moved into the *atelier* to discuss rain clouds. This group had already made two large clouds using wire, beads, and fabric, and they had many ideas to share with one another. As the children walked to the *atelier*, Emma told the others, "When clouds turn gray, that means they're getting full of water."

The children sat down at the table, and Karen turned on her tape recorder (see Figure 11.6). After several minutes of dialogue, the conversation centered

Figure 11.6.
The children and
Karen engage in
conversations
about rain cloud
theories.

Figure 11.7. Angela's representation
of the cycle of evaporation.

on how water might fall from a cloud during a rainstorm, and that it would somehow get back inside again.

Angela said, "My dad told me this about rain. First, there is water in lakes and rivers, and rain goes up to the clouds and then keeps going back and forth. Up and down." "So it's a cycle?" Karen asked. "Yeah, like when we said it's daytime and nighttime. Back and forth," Angela answered, referring to a conversation that had taken place with the large group.

Emma joined in, "I need to tell you something. The water from the rivers evaporates. It goes up to the clouds. Then it comes down." "How do you see it go up?" wondered Renee. "You can't see it go up," Angela replied. Renee thought out loud, "It turns invisible? I think you can see water when it goes up." Angela clarified her idea, "You cannot see water when it goes up. The water drops are so tiny."

"I thought you were saying it goes up like a waterfall. Like as fast as a waterfall. That's what I thought you were saying!" said Renee, noticing the difference between her idea and Angela's.

The conversation continued, and the children discussed what it might look like to be inside a rain cloud. After the conversation, Karen asked the children to draw their ideas. Each child made several drawings based on the ideas discussed (see Figure 11.7).

Colors of the Night Sky. Back in the classroom, Chuck had prepared the *miniatelier* by placing bottles of paint, empty jars, and spoons for mixing on the table. The purpose of the experience on this morning was to mix colors that would later be used to paint the mural. Earlier in the week, he had asked the children, "What colors would you need to paint a nighttime sky?" The children specified that they would need blue, gray, and black paint. These colors, along with many others, were ready for the children to use.

Each child began with three jars of paint, one of each color, which were filled about halfway. Other empty jars were available for the children to pour paint into. The children began mixing the paint from their full jars into the empty ones (see Figure 11.8). They used large spoons to transfer paint from one jar to another. Within a few moments, brilliant new tones of each color appeared in the jars. When the children were satisfied with the newly mixed colors, these jars were removed from the table and saved for use on the mural.

Chuck documented each child's ideas as he or she worked, writing notes in a journal and taking photos with a camera (see Figure 11.9). As the children worked, they talked about the stars and informed Chuck that they needed yellow and silver paint, too. The experience was a symphony of children's voices and the sounds of pouring, mixing, and stirring.

Figure 11.8. Children mixed and selected colors for the mural of the night-time sky.

Figure 11.9. Colors for the nighttime sky.

Sunlight, Sound, and Dramatic Play. Outside the school building, the morning clouds had broken apart, and patches of sky were beginning to show through. In the classroom, Melissa had prepared an area of the classroom near the windows for the small group. There she had placed two baskets on the floor, one containing reflective objects and the other small musical instruments. She sat with four children on the floor, and they talked while they waited for the sunlight to peek through the windows.

John John immediately observed the overcast conditions and said, "There is a faint sunlight today."

A spot of bright sunlight appeared, and Ellie exclaimed, "The light!"

"It's not faint anymore!" cried Melissa.

John John added, "We could make reflections and shadows, too!"

Melissa had the Morning Meeting Journal with her, which contained the children's previous conversations. She reminded the children of the time they first noticed the reflection in September. She asked, "Remember when we first saw the reflection of Chuck's watch on the ceiling?" The children responded that they did.

Then she read to them from the journal, "We asked everyone, at that time, 'What is it?' People said that it was a flying thing, a space ship, or maybe the tooth fairy. Well, if the lights that we see today had a sound, what do you think they would sound like?"

Catherine said, "Tinkerbell."

Ellie agreed and added, "A bell."

"I have a basket of bells and other instruments, and I thought maybe you could choose some and try to make a sound that you think the light might make." The children chose the ones they wanted to try first.

Melissa continued, "If it's a strong light today, and the disco ball makes reflections, what kind of sound would the reflections make?"

Catherine exclaimed, "One big noise!"

John John, captivated by this idea, added, "Yeah, we could do that at once! It could go, *shwoosh*! We can count to two, and then we will ring it!"

Ellie suggested a different idea, "Maybe it could be one soft noise."

John said, "Or a lot of little noises."

John John continued with the big-sound idea, "If you do it a lot, it might scare the light away!" "

"And then we couldn't do it," Jamie concluded.

The children took turns placing reflective objects where they thought the light would shine. Suddenly, the sunlight arrived, and reflections appeared around the room. The children immediately made many sounds with the bells, all at the same time. After a minute, the sunlight faded, and the children exchanged instruments. This cycle of trading instruments and experimenting with sounds to the light was repeated several times.

Melissa suggested that the children take turns individually. Jamie decided that he wanted to make one soft noise and carefully rang his bell one time for the light. John John announced that he wanted to do "a bunch of little noises" and hit his triangle many times when the reflections emerged. Catherine noticed light reflected on the ceiling and said, "I want to lie down." She lay on her back and rang a bell while she looked at the reflections on the ceiling. "It's quiet and loud," she said.

Suddenly, the children noticed that the reflections were shining on their bodies. Jamie shouted, "It's on you! It's on your mouth! It's on your cheek!"

Melissa said, "Look! It's on John John's leg!" Everyone broke into laughter.

"It's on my foot, or it used to be," John John said as he watched the reflections move across the floor.

"It's on your neck!" declared Jamie.

John John pointed with his finger and exclaimed, "It's on your hair!"

When Jamie noticed the beads and sparkles on Catherine's shoes, he announced a new idea: "I know what can shine. Catherine's shoes!" Everyone agreed, and the shoes were placed in the sunlight. Instantly, tiny reflections covered the floor (see Figures 11.10 and 11.11).

At this point, the children could no longer contain themselves. Jamie asked Melissa, "Can we dance to it?" All of the other children echoed his desire. Melissa agreed, and the children got up and danced around the room with great enthusiasm.

"We're dancing! We're dancing!" they exclaimed as they moved.

The room was entirely transformed. Reflections from the disco ball and Catherine's shoes sprinkled across the walls and the floor. Melissa played the bells as the children danced through the sunlight and reflection.

Figure 11.10. Reflections from the disco ball and Catherine's shoes sprinkle across the walls and floor.

Figure 11.11. Experimenting with sound and light.

What Are the Children Learning?

We have used a close-up lens to examine the systems inside one day as well as the particular story of that day. As teachers looking back on this day, what meaning do we make of it? How can it inform us about the whole project and, further, about our way of working within a systemic context? What the children are learning during the course of this, or any, project is of critical concern. From a systemic perspective, our questions become:

- What did we all learn, children and adults, because of the way we immersed ourselves in the processes, depth and breadth, and relational qualities of our experience?
- If we place value on relationships above all, what has changed in our understanding of light and other elements of our world because of the course of this project and all that evolved out of it?
- What have the time frames, space frames, various groupings, dialogues, recordings, and reflections in words and in media enabled us to learn?

We started out with the intention of learning with breadth and depth, all of us, in a way that was expansive, cross-disciplinary, and relational. The knowledge, skills, attitudes, and behaviors that come from this way of learning are greater than the sum of the parts. There was a wholeness that grew out of our learning journey that is manifest in the whole as well as in the single day we follow here. The children reached high levels of scientific skill not because we taught them, but because their discoveries unfolded in meaningful and significant ways. Parts of their learning connected to other parts and together manifested in something bigger than discrete, narrowly defined bits of information. The children became experts in the study of light and, more important, skillful and competent scientific thinkers with research questions to pursue and solve. In her provocative book, *Talking Their Way into Science*, Karen Gallas (1995) writes:

> I wish that every child would desire to know about the world in a boundless and wondering way, and that every child would believe that he or she could engage in conversations and investigations about the world *with pride*, rather than hesitation. I believe that if that could happen for every child, we would discover that many children have the ability to study science with intelligence and skill. That shift alone would change the face of science as it is conceptualized and practiced. It would become a discipline where our understanding of the world would come to include the viewpoints of many cultures and races, and both genders. (p. 99)

During the documented day and throughout this project we've observed evidence of learning within high-quality environments for young children, as written about by members of the Education Development Center supported by a National Science Foundation grant. Worth and Grollman (2003) describe characteristics of environments that reflect scientific learning. Such environments

- Build on children's prior experiences, backgrounds, and early theories.
- Draw on children's curiosity and encourage children to pursue their own questions and develop their own ideas.
- Engage children in in-depth exploration of a topic over time in a carefully prepared environment.
- Encourage children to reflect on, represent, and document their experiences and share and discuss their ideas with others.
- Embed learning in children's daily work and play and are integrated with other domains.
- Provide access to science experiences for all children.

Moreover, Worth and Grollman suggest that earth and space science is perhaps the most complex of the sciences.

> To understand the structure of the earth and its history, climate, and meteorology, the solar system, and the universe requires understanding of many concepts of life and physical sciences. In addition, studying the ideas of earth and space science means thinking about long time scales, unseen forces, and faraway places. (p. 143)

Although these complicated ideas were not fully understood by the children in this project, they were explored and pondered and theorized.

When we consulted a rubric for a K–6 report card in Grant Wiggins's well-respected and influential *Educative assessment* (1998), we were intrigued to discover that most of the children would have attained the fourth level out of eight in science understanding and communication skills, as shown by their engagement in inquiry, observation, representation, and communication of their learning.

Beyond this sampling of science and communicative knowledge and skills, we reviewed *Habits of mind: A developmental series* (Costa & Kallick, 2000). The authors describe 16 observable characteristics of intellectual growth. Based on the work of key researchers on intelligence and creativity, these characteristics occur again and again among people in all walks of life who have developed their thinking abilities:

1. Persistence
2. Managing impulsivity
3. Listening to others with understanding and empathy
4. Thinking flexibly
5. Thinking about thinking (metacognition)
6. Striving for accuracy

   7. Questioning and posing problems
   8. Applying past knowledge to new situations
   9. Thinking and communicating with clarity and precision
 10. Gathering data through all senses
 11. Creating, imagining, innovating
 12. Responding with wonderment and awe
 13. Taking responsible risks
 14. Finding humor
 15. Thinking interdependently
 16. Remaining open to continuous learning

Evidence of developing intellectual behaviors can be seen in both children and adults in the Morning Meeting Journal; teachers' notes; a file of digital photographs; video documentaries; teachers' and parents' observations of children's developing interest, knowledge, and skill over time; and children's questions, observations, and work in media collected over time and sequenced. But beyond even these ways of assessing knowledge, skills, attitudes, and behaviors, what is the gestalt of the whole? How do we all feel now about this story in our lives and about what we experienced and discovered together?

EMBRACING THE COMPLEXITY

As teachers we search to make sense of our experiences, of the moments in our lives in school, and of the bigger picture and possible consequences of our actions. Systems thinking has taught us that sense-making is not a simple process of looking at life's events in a linear, cause-and-effect way. The temptation to see teaching as a string of events where "a leads to b" and then "b leads to c" is difficult to reject. Most of us have interpreted our lives this way forever. It seems this view is no longer possible in schools where light shines through a basement classroom window, connects myriad events, processes, and structures, and then sparks, ripples, and reflects the complexity of the lives of a group of children and their teachers.

These experiences, and others like them, coax us to avoid the appeal and convenience of educating children in a linear fashion. They force us to see teaching and learning in a more circular way. The complexity can be compelling. It can push us to look beyond our influence on the children, to notice and embrace their profound effect on us. During this project, Karen reminded us of this when she spoke about these experiences as "a gift from the children."

Complexity leads us away from planning a lesson for what we will teach and toward searching for systems that organize and prepare us to think together. In this project, the children expanded their understanding of reflected light not in isolation or in a simple way. They learned about reflected light in connection with a multitude of other elements—reflected light and music, reflected light and movement, reflected light and dance and drama, reflected light and color and prisms, and the sun, moon, and sky. At times, it seemed that these combinations and connections occurred all at once. At other times, they fragmented and disconnected, only to come back together as a whole that made sense in yet a new way.

When we work this way, we discover a renewed sense of ourselves as teachers. The children, the parents, and the ever changing experiences inside and outside the school become part of this complex mix of events and part of our reality. We all become meaning makers within the spirit of the conceptual *atelier*. And perhaps most important, as lifelong learners ourselves, we venture into new places where the light draws us—places we have never really been before.

REFERENCES

Alexander, C. (1979). *A timeless way of building*. New York: Oxford University Press.

Bateson, G. (1979). *Mind and nature: A necessary unity*. New York: Bantam Books.

Bohm, D. (1996). *On dialogue*. London and New York: Routledge.

Capra, F. (1996). *The web of life*. New York: Anchor Books.

Costa, A. L., & Kallick, B. (2000). *Discovering and exploring habits of mind*. Alexandria, VA: Association for Supervision and Curriculum Development.

Du Four, R., & Eacker, R. (1998). *Professional learning communities at work: Best practices for enhancing student achievement*. Reston, VA: Association for Supervision and Curriculum Development.

Fullan, M. G. (2001). *Leading in a culture of change*. Hoboken, NJ: John Wiley.

Gallas, K. (1995). *Talking their way into science: Hearing children's questions and theories, responding with curricula*. New York: Teachers College Press.

Lambert, L. (2003). *Leadership capacity for lasting school improvement*. Reston, VA: Association for Supervision and Curriculum Development.

Maturana, H., & Varela, F. (1987). *The tree of knowledge*. Boston: Shambala.

Senge, P., Cambron-McCabe, N., Lucas, T., Smith, B., Dutton, J., & Kleiner, A. (2000). *Schools that learn*. New York: Century.

Wheatley, M. J. (1999). *Leadership and the new science: Discovering order in a chaotic world* (pp. 45, 76). San Francisco, CA: Berrett-Koehler.

Wiggins, G. (1998). *Educative assessment: Designing assessments to inform and improve student performances*. San Francisco, CA: John Wiley.

Worth, K., & Grollman, S. (2003). *Worms, shadows, and whirlpools: Science in the early childhood classroom* (p. 143). Portsmouth, NH: Heinemann.

The Whole School as an *Atelier*

Reflections by Carla Rinaldi

EDITED BY
Lella Gandini

Carla Rinaldi was the first pedagogical coordinator (*pedagogista*) to work with Loris Malaguzzi in developing the preschools and the infant/toddler centers of Reggio Emilia. Carla is a reflective writer who has been an attentive researcher and contributor to the continuous evolution of the thought and work developing in the schools of Reggio Emilia. Through her writing she continues to present the many connections and layers of complexity within the philosophy of the Reggio Emilia Approach. Here, in an excerpt from a conversation with Ettore Borghi, are her reflections about the evolution of the Reggio Emilia schools as published in 2001.

Ettore Borghi: *It was in the [1970s]. Your universe becomes richer: an* atelierista, *two co-teachers together, and interaction of more adult educators. . . .*

Carla Rinaldi: First, I want to highlight the very innovative element of the presence of two co-teachers per classrooms. The presence of the two co-teachers, although they have analogous professional profiles, was completely focused on their differences. I think this choice was steeped in the idea of having two different points of view, considering dialogue and exchange as essential qualities of education and of the educator. Here the deep meaning of group work and, in an anticipatory way, a systemic interpretation of the relativity of the child emerges. We can see that the value of diversity is introduced through the presence of the two co-teachers and clears the way for the other presence, the one of the *atelierista*. This presence brings diversity into the school that is deliberately chosen and counted on, where the metaphor of the hundred languages is represented in the professional formation in the visual arts.

While the *atelier* was already in the schools in 1963, it was in the [1970s] that the theory of the hundred languages developed. It was then that the *atelier* was declared as the place for the hundred languages: drawing, painting, sculpture, math, poetry—languages that dialogue with the different disciplines and different cultural worlds. The *atelier* brought another difference into the school and pushed the idea of diversity to the utmost, encouraging a new pedagogy that would highlight the subjectivity [and interconnectivity] of the child. Considering the *atelier* as a metaphor, I like to say (and I am not the only one) that the whole school has to be a large *atelier*, where children and adults find their voices in a school that is transformed into a great laboratory of research and reflection. (Borghi, 2001, p. 138)

CREATIVITY AS A QUALITY OF THOUGHT

We continue with part of a lecture Carla delivered to educators in the city of Pistoia in the spring of 2003, offering her thoughts on creativity, an interpretation of this basic ingredient, which is not always discussed in the workings of the *atelier*.

What is extraordinary in the human mind is not only our capacity to move from one language to another, from one "intelligence" to another; we are also capable of reciprocal listening, which makes communication and dialogue possible. Children are the most extraordinary listeners of all. They encode and decode, interpreting data with incredible creativity. Children "listen" to life in all its facets, listen to others with generosity, and quickly perceive how the act of listening is an essential act of communication. Children are biologically predisposed to communicate and establish relationships. This is why we must always give them plentiful opportunities to represent their mental images and share them with others.

Moving from one language to another, from one field of experience to another, children can grow in the idea that others are indispensable for their own identity and existence. Through the act of sharing, we realize not only that the other becomes indispensable for our identity, for our understanding, for communication and listening, but also that learning together generates pleasure in the group, that the group becomes the place of learning. This is a fundamental value, which we can choose to adopt or not. We thus create what we call a "competent audience," subjects capable of listening reciprocally and becoming sensitive to the ideas of others to enrich their own ideas and to generate group ideas.

This, then, is the revolution that we have to put into place: to develop children's natural sensitivity toward appreciating and developing and sharing the ideas of other children. This is why we consider the learning process to be a creative process. By "creativity," I mean the ability to construct new connections between thoughts and objects that bring about innovation and change, taking known elements and creating new connections.

Here is an example: A 3-year-old child is playing with a piece of wire. First he makes a bracelet; then, on the back of the chair, the wire becomes a horseman riding his steed. Finally, the wire is transformed into the horse's ear [see Figure 12.1a, b, c].

As we know, human beings are equipped with two forms of thinking: convergent thinking, which tends toward repetition, and divergent thinking,

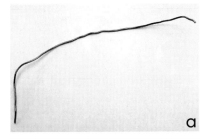

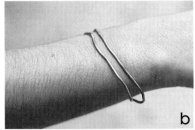

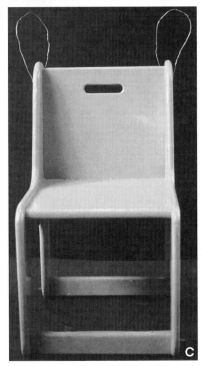

Figure 12.1

a. The child takes a piece of wire.

b. The child makes a bracelet with it.

c. The child places ears of wire on the chair and says, "Horse."

which tends toward the reorganization of elements. Divergent thinking is the type we see in the previous example. It is the combination of unusual elements that young children put into place very easily because they do not have a particular theoretical background or established connections among objects and facts.

Why is it so hard for adults to use divergent thinking? Primarily because convergent thinking is convenient, but also because changing your mind often represents a loss of power. Children, on the other hand, search for power *by* changing their minds, in the honesty that they have toward ideas and toward others, in the honesty of their listening. But (unfortunately) they quickly understand that having ideas that diverge from those of their teachers or their parents, and expressing them at the wrong moment, is not considered a positive thing. So it is not creative thinking that dies but the legitimization of the creativity of thinking.

Creative thinking can also lead to solitude. Creativity is in principle relational; it needs to be approved in order to become a shared wealth. Too often, however, we are afraid of this creativity, even our own, because it makes us "different." In play, as Piaget noted, children take reality in hand in order to take possession of it. They freely decompose and recompose it, consolidating this quality of convergent and divergent thinking. Through play, children confront reality and accept it, develop creative thinking, and escape from a reality that is too often oppressive. It is here that some of our most serious mistakes take root. The dimension of play (with words, pretending, and so on) is thus an essential element of the human being. If we take this dimension away from children and adults, we remove a possibility for learning. We break up the dual play–learning relationship. The creative process needs to be recognized and legitimated by others.

Creativity is not just the quality of thinking of each individual; it is also an interactive, relational, and social project. It requires a context that allows it to exist, to be expressed, to become visible. In schools, creativity should have the opportunity to be expressed in every place and in every moment. What we hope for is creative learning and creative teachers, not simply a "creativity hour." This is why the *atelier* must support and ensure all the creative processes that can take place anywhere in the school, at home, and in the society. We should remember that there is no creativity in the child if there is no creativity in the adult. The competent and creative child exists if there is a competent and creative adult.

Think of our relationship with art. Art has too often been separated from life and, like creativity, it has not been recognized as an everyday right, as a quality of life. The disciplinary development of the sciences has provided many benefits but has also led to problems such as the over-specialization and compartmentalization of knowledge. In general, our social system adheres to this logic of separation and fragmentation of the levels of power. We are too often taught to separate that which is connected, to divide rather than bring together the disciplines, to eliminate all that could lead to disorder. For this reason, it is absolutely indispensable to reconsider our relationship with art as an essential dimension of human thinking. The art of daily life and the creativity of daily life should be the right of all. Art, then, is a part of our lives, of our efforts to learn and to know [see Figure 12.2].

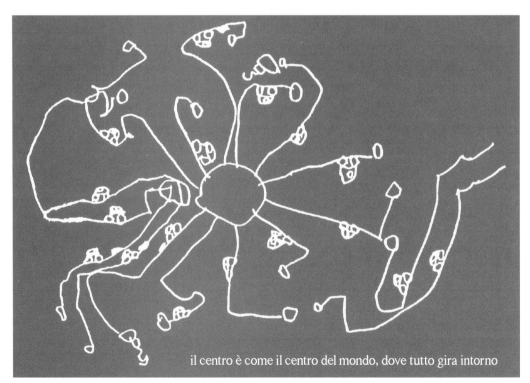

il centro è come il centro del mondo, dove tutto gira intorno

Figure 12.2. The center (of Reggio) is like the center of the world, where everything goes around it.

CLOSING REFLECTIONS

In her conversation with Ettore Borghi about the evolution of the schools in Reggio Emilia, Carla Rinaldi immediately pointed out that we cannot separate the powerful effect of the *atelier* from the important innovations that paved the way for its establishment. In particular, she highlighted the introduction of the roles of two co-teachers, which was focused completely on contributing different points of view and "the value of diversity" to group work. Once again, we see a system at work to create positive effects in learning and teaching.

Next we read Carla's reflections on the connections among dialogue, communication, relationship, and reciprocal listening toward the formation of quality of thinking and, as a consequence, of creativity. After the many rich contributions of the conversations in this book among the educators of Reggio Emilia and those from various places in the United States, it is especially fitting to have Carla's excellent thoughts about creativity as we approach the final chapter of this volume. She invites us to reflect on how the context of the schools, with the support of the *atelier*, must enable creative processes to take place everywhere, and to consider that creativity and art have to be recognized as everyday rights as a quality of life. She says, "The competent and creative child exists if there is a competent and creative adult."

In the next chapter, Ashley Cadwell will take us through the systemic transformation of the context and the content of the St. Michael School in St. Louis, Missouri. From architecture to schedules, from parents' participation to quality of light, Ashley considers patterns and networks. This follows naturally from the Reggio philosophy, which sees the school as a system of relationships, highlighted here by Carla. Ashley restates this, echoing the Italian philosopher Aldo Masullo: "Schools need to be environments that cultivate creativity and collaboration, invention and innovation and inquiry."

REFERENCE

Borghi, E. (2001). L'organizzazione, il metodo (Organization and method). In *Una storia presente: L'esperienza delle scuole comunali dell'infanzia di Reggio Emilia* (A present history: The experience of the municipal schools of Reggio Emilia). Reggio Emilia, Italy: Associazione Internazionale Amici di Reggio Children & Reggio Children S.r.l., Edizioni RS Libri.

FURTHER RELEVANT SOURCES

Bruner, J. S. (1990). *Acts of meaning*. Cambridge, MA: Harvard University Press.
Bruner, J. S. (1996). *The culture of education*. Cambridge, MA: Harvard University Press.
Ceruti, M. (1989). *La danza che crea*. Milan, Italy: Feltrinelli.
Fabbri, D. (1990). *La memoria della regina*. Milan, Italy: Guerini e Associati.

Levy, P. (1994). *L'intelligence collective. Pour une anthropologie du cyberspace.* Paris: Découverte.

Malaguzzi, L. (1996). *I cento linguaggi dei bambini/The hundred languages of children* (exhibit catalogue). Reggio Emilia, Italy: Reggio Children S.r.l.

Morin, E. (1999). *La tête bien faite.* Paris: Editions du Seuil.

Pontecorvo, C. (Ed.). (1993). *La condivisione della conoscenza.* Florence, Italy: La Nuova Italia.

Project Zero, Harvard Graduate School of Education, and Reggio Children S.r.l. (2001). *Making learning visible: Children as individual and group learners.* Reggio Emilia, Italy: Reggio Children S.r.l.

Rinaldi, C. (1999). *L'ascolto visibile.* Reggio Emilia, Italy: Comune di Reggio Emilia.

Pedagogical Patterns

Ashley Cadwell

As a child, I loved the sandbox behind the house, next to the calf pasture in a barnyard on a 250-acre dairy farm in the middle of Vermont. My earliest memories are of constructing roads and villages with my neighborhood buddies. While we fabricated entire civilizations out of sand and sticks and straw, the calves grazed and blatted in the background. When we weren't outside, we were inside the house "making": trains of chairs for long cross-country trips to California; dens of blankets over stools and chairs for secret societies; stage productions born out of chests full of grandparents' and parents' old clothes and shoes; grand banquets served from cauldrons (old tin pots) on fine china and silver (recycled dented plates and bent tin flatware). We even had a studio of sorts. My mother is an architect and loved to sketch. I used to watch her drawing at her drafting table as I played with blocks on the floor at her feet. In our home, it seemed as if the possibilities for invention were endless.

In a way, during the past 12 years at the St. Michael School, my colleagues and I have created a school with similar endless possibilities. The endless possibilities are manifest in the pedagogy of the preprimary–kindergarten *atelier* and the elementary school "hub" (a version of the *atelier* with both a studio and a laboratory). Personally, the desire to develop such a school was driven by many factors, including past experiences in teaching third and fourth grade, starting and heading a secondary sports academy for world-class ski racers, designing and building homes and a village in Vermont, living for a year in Reggio Emilia, and harboring nagging memories of my own elementary school experience.

FIRST SCHOOL MEMORIES

In the beginning, first grade was a great adventure: in the village, a whole mile from my house; new friends; a nice, big room with hardwood floors and 10-foot ceilings and tall, south-facing windows; a dear woman somewhere between my mother and grandmother in age. But gradually, the constant, diminutive drill began to kill all that. I came to enjoy most the bus ride to school with my buddies, recess, lunch, and the long walk home—especially the walk home, which was always an adventure. We took different routes along the sidewalks of the village and terrifying diversions through three-foot-diameter culverts under U.S. Route 7 or shortcuts through backyards and into the fields and woods and valleys, over the streams and creeks, and up into old-growth maple climbing trees.

School got worse. By fourth grade, I was a behavior problem. Notes began to go home. I hated to disappoint my mother, but I was bored. I tried to explain it to her: "I mean, how many times do I have to do a worksheet about something that I already know? Why can't I talk with my friends? Why can't we figure it out together? Why can't we do something interesting, like explore the creek out back of the school. I wonder . . ." Mother always listened. I don't remember her ever getting really mad, except when she thought I'd been disrespectful, which I was at times. She always redirected me to the positive things, especially to my friends. And she firmly reminded me that there was no alternative. Someday, I thought, I'll make sure there is an alternative—a much better alternative.

PATTERNS

My answer to the alternative has become the St. Michael School and is most clearly manifest in the pedagogy of the preprimary–kindergarten *atelier* and the elementary school hub. In the *atelier* and the hub I see children doing all of the things I naively yearned for when I was in school. To create these places, to develop the organization, to come to a new understanding of how children learn, my colleagues and I have discovered a complex intersection of patterns in architecture, organizational systems, and educational philosophy. I say "patterns" because over the years of developing the St. Michael School program, we have found that this approach to education does not reduce itself to neat "how tos" or methodologies. Why should it when our very human nature is evolution and change? Rather, we have discerned that these patterns take on different forms depending on the space, the situation, and our thinking.

My original association with the idea of patterns came from my personal background in architecture and considerable research I have done in the new urban development schemes of architects, especially Christopher Alexander. His tome on architecture, *A Pattern Language* (1977), profoundly influenced my home-design strategies and a village-development plan. In *A Pattern Language*, Alexander outlines and elucidates 253 critical patterns essential to successful community design. Ranging from macro to micro in scope, his architectural and planning "patterns" include (taken from his chapter titles):

> identifiable neighborhood, network of learning, sacred sites, old people everywhere, local town hall, green streets, network of paths and cars,

children everywhere, quiet backs, small public squares (piazzas), dancing in the streets, still water, adventure playground, teenage society, corner grocery, beer hall, pedestrian street, main entrance, hierarchy of open space, indoor sunlight, entrance room, staircase as a stage, sleeping in the east, small meeting rooms, outdoor room, garden seat, cooking layout, bed alcove, half-open wall, interior windows, child caves, secret place, windows which open wide.

The pattern language of design became an integral part of my thinking and has been a lens through which I have focused on different contexts: education, the Reggio Emilia Approach, and the St. Michael School. I identified a correlation between Alexander's thinking in design and Reggio Emilia's approach to education. Both take a wide-angle view, macro and micro in scope, and while doing so also incorporate ideas from every discipline of thought. The breadth and specificity of Alexander's patterns are illustrated above. In education, the patterns proceed from macro philosophical ideas such as the image of the child, down to micro issues such as the organization of materials on shelves. In our most recent experience, the greatest inspiration for thinking in these educational patterns has come from Reggio Emilia.

A YEAR IN REGGIO EMILIA

In the summer of 1991, our family (Alden, 11; Chris, 8; my wife, Louise; and I) had a rare opportunity to move to Reggio Emilia for a school year (see Figure 13.1). There Louise studied the municipal preprimary schools, which were fast

Figure 13.1. My sons and I in Italy.

Figure 13.2. From the door of the Diana School: the piazza and the *atelier*.

becoming world renowned. One day in late August, after my sons had biked across that old Roman town to school, I walked from our two-bedroom apartment across Piazza Valdisnieri and then across the Giardini Publici (Public Gardens) to meet Louise at the Diana School, where she had begun her internship. As I entered through the plain, white-framed, front-window doorway and into the understated entryway, I stopped (see Figure 13.2). From that single vantage point at the inside of the front entry, I was on the edge of a large, open common area with a 16-foot ceiling, and I could see directly into the dining room to my left, into the two interior courtyards diagonally to my left and right, and into the *atelier* straight ahead. I could also see indirectly into two of the three classrooms to the left and right of the *atelier*.

From the very first moment I was in the school, I was completely oriented in the physical space. Present activity and the artifacts of past activity were everywhere. Children and teachers moved around with purpose and pleasure. Somehow, I intuitively felt completely aware of everything going on in the space. In the much referenced phrase of Loris Malaguzzi, the father of the Reggio Emilia Approach, "nothing without joy" was palpable and—to my childhood deprived, then adult design-acute, psyche—overwhelming. Everything that I knew about childhood, education, architecture, and community was manifest before me. I was weak in the knees.

I have heard responses similar to my own from numerous visitors to the St. Michael School who have also visited Reggio. Somehow, our cumulative knowledge of what a school could look like, how a program could be organized, what experiences children could have, the role a teacher could have, and the consequent growth in each child that would occur in such conditions, are all manifest in the highest imaginable order in the Reggio Emilia schools. Though sight and understanding of the Reggio system are overwhelming in their evolved genius, they are also empowering. In the act of creating the schools and the systems behind them, Reggio Emilia educators have affirmed that such high-level educational alternatives are possible elsewhere. That's what I believed with all my heart when I saw those alternatives. Little did I know that just about one year later, I would have the opportunity to act on what I felt.

THE ST. MICHAEL SCHOOL FROM THE BEGINNING: CHANGE

In the late summer of 1992, our family moved back from Reggio Emilia to St. Louis, Missouri. Louise began a new job as *atelierista* at the College School and, through a grant from the Danforth Foundation, a consultant to schools in St. Louis interested in the Reggio Emilia Approach. I had one eye on applying for different jobs in education and real-estate development, and one eye on our boys, our home, and several golf courses. As fate would have it, the day after Labor Day, I was offered a position as headmaster of the St. Michael School (see Figure 13.3).

Figure 13.3. A sketch of the St. Michael School by Ashley Cadwell.

From the beginning, I was charged by the Board of Trustees to study whether the school should continue. As an independent school, the business was a mess, with an accumulated deficit of more than a third of the annual operating budget. Economically, the school was on precarious ground. Furthermore, the school program was fragmented. Really, it was two different schools under one roof—and in an 80-year-old Gothic church, at that. There was an apparently successful preschool in the basement-level rooms (90 or so children age 2.5 to 5 attending in various combinations of mornings and afternoons; half days and full days; and two, three, or five days). Then there was an elementary school in the second-floor rooms, with about 50 students in grades 1–6, operating with a very traditional organization of self-contained classrooms and part-time pullout specialists in art, physical education, music, science, and Spanish. Except for my one-year experience in Reggio Emilia, preprimary education was entirely new to me. The St. Michael School elementary school was a familiar version of my own, unfortunate, childhood elementary school experience.

By January 1993, I had completed my "study" for the Board of Trustees. I outlined the possibilities for them:

1. Close the school (and thereby require the church to cover the considerable financial shortfall to finish the year).
2. Hire someone else to take over as head and continue the school on the same dubious path.
3. Hire me as head to change the school almost completely, based on my experience and what I had seen in Reggio Emilia.

"Reggie who?" they asked. I explained:

Right now you have a nice day-care center and a mediocre-to-boring elementary school, each separate from the other. In fact, the teachers hardly talk with one another.

The educational program and systems of support need revision. The three-floor facility is a fascinating maze of a variety of rooms, which could be reorganized and interconnected in ways that would physically support a new program. For instance, with new window doors and window walls between classrooms, visual connections could be made that would link the spaces and the activities and thereby facilitate teacher partnerships and collaboration. A fundamental beginning point for this step will be the building and organization of a preprimary *atelier* and an elementary hub.

There are several fine teachers who could work together to create a truly integrated, dynamic, and effective educational program. We could create a preprimary and elementary school that would come together around simple yet profound philosophical points of view: children are protagonists; teachers are researchers; the school classroom environment is a third teacher; parents are partners; and all four parts are dynamically interconnected.

This simple assertion will be quite complex to fully understand and a lot of work to realize, but if we do, it will be amazing. It could become "nothing without joy."

To my astonishment, the trustees chose to take the greatest risk: They chose number 3. Just when I thought I would be invited to retreat to the domain of the healthily unemployed, the golf course, I was captured by idealism—and my own bravado. I was ready in more ways than I knew (or, certainly, than the board knew). I was ready to "go for it," as my sports-academy ski-racing students would holler at each other as they launched themselves out the starting gate and down a mile-long vertical drop during which they would career around 45-degree corners and reach speeds of 70 miles per hour. The next dozen years would be my downhill run; a test of life experiences, skills, conviction, endurance, courage, understanding, invention, and, above all, collaboration.

THE PATTERNS OF CHANGE DEVELOP

The following brief history is a complex mosaic of experiences, conflicts, resolutions, and continuing evolutions. As with a mosaic, when viewed up close it looks like individual pieces, and it doesn't make much sense. Yet when viewed from a distance, patterns emerge from the pieces of the mosaic: forms take shape; a picture is composed. So it is with our work at the St. Michael School. The preprimary *atelier* and elementary hub are crucial developments: Architectural patterns emerge in changes to the environment; organizational patterns emerge in changes to the systems of support; and pedagogical patterns emerge from changes in our thinking about how children learn. In the end, a picture of a highly functioning school is composed, and a meaningful educational project continues to evolve.

The work really began in the two months following the Board of Trustees' January 1993 decision. With the extraordinary collaborative help of several key teachers and parents, we redesigned the education program and shared it with the parents for re-enrollment for the following year. In both the preprimary and elementary programs, significant changes occurred in the organization of space and in the job descriptions of the teachers. The reorganization of the physical space was motivated by the ideal of creating an environment that could be a resource, like an extra teacher, for experiences of provocative and sustained value to the children. The redefinition of the role of the teachers was motivated by the ideal of creating systems that would support optimal experiences— for initiation, preparation, observation, reflection, and composition (each fundamental element of the learning cycle explained more completely later). All of the reorganization was determined by a new understanding of the hundred languages of children and of how children learn.

Architectural Patterns and Changes to the Environment

Extensive physical work went into the reorganization of the classroom spaces and their contents (some projects took several years to complete, while some continue to evolve). Each change fit an architectural and program design pattern and was inspired primarily by the schools of Reggio Emilia and the work of Christopher Alexander, as well as myriad other sources. There were many changes that fit many patterns, too numerous to outline in detail here. Several major examples, however, are mentioned later, and I have highlighted each pattern by putting it in italics the first time it appears. With help from my partners, I have enumerated a growing comprehensive outline of patterns ranging from macro (pedagogical) to micro (architectural) in scale. Each pattern is a short chapter unto itself in a book in progress, *Pedagogical Patterns*.

We built *a studio in the middle*, an *atelier*, in the preprimary–kindergarten and elementary school. These are spaces in which the hundred languages of children are actively explored, clearly organized, and represented. In the pre-

Figure 13.4. The *atelier* looking through the interior greenhouse to the 3- and 4-year-olds' classroom.

Figure 13.5. The hub from the meeting room to the laboratory and studio.

primary space, we transformed an interior room that had been used for storage and a teacher's lounge. The major transformation of the *atelier* occurred using the pattern of *interior light*, so that an interior greenhouse was created using recessed ceiling grow lights in a new window wall between the *atelier* and the classroom for the 3- and 4-year-olds (see Figure 13.4). The elementary *atelier*, the hub, encompassed three contiguous rooms: an art studio, a science laboratory, and a meeting room and library. In the hub, the connecting architectural pattern was *transparency*, with windows from four feet to the ceiling between rooms (see Figure 13.5).

Using the same pattern of transparency, we created connections between two preprimary classrooms and five elementary classrooms by replacing solid classroom doors with clear window doors and with window walls and window doors between rooms. Paying attention to interior light, we installed skylights in the ceiling of the interior kindergarten room. In an effort to create more *natural light* throughout the school, we replaced all of the blue–white fluorescent lighting with solar-frequency fluorescent lighting, and we placed many sources of incandescent lighting throughout the rooms, including floor and table lamps with shades.

To make the children's and teachers' work visible—that is, to better show the students' artifacts and teachers' documentation—we repainted the walls

Figure 13.6. Incandescent lights and walls as galleries.

and shelves in *neutral colors*. We also installed as much tackboard on the walls as possible (not modular, framed bulletin boards but entire walls of bulletin-board material), and we built and installed shelves to display three-dimensional works of children. We transformed the *halls as galleries* for displays of learning experiences and new understandings of learning processes. To do so, we installed tackboard on all hallway walls and eliminated the ceiling fluorescent lighting wherever possible, replacing it with track flood and spot lighting on the ceiling that washed the walls of documentation and shelves of children's artifacts with good viewing light (see Figure 13.6).

We reorganized each classroom. We thought of *classroom routes as streets and paths* and therefore arranged a traffic flow in each room to allow free and easy movement. We also arranged the areas of activity so that they were easily discerned from the entry of the room. We created a *piazza, small central squares*, and *meeting spots* by locating a central area in each room for class group meetings and a central area in the preprimary and elementary school for large group meetings. We designated a central area for whole school meetings and family events.

We considered each classroom in terms of *gradation of space*, with areas dedicated to experiences such as blocks, reading, writing, drama and movement, studio arts, science laboratory, mathematics and manipulatives, computers, and so forth. Each was defined by using combinations of furniture and shelves; each was furnished appropriately for small-group work and supplied with well-organized materials in ways that are attractive and available to the children (see Figure 13.7). We realized that *less is more* (for inspiration, we read about *feng shui*), and we weeded out everything: cluttered shelves, forgotten drawers, packed file cabinets, overstuffed closets. (I should note that most of the changes listed here came from volunteer effort and donated materials. On many Saturdays, several parents and I turned the gym into a woodshop. The window wall in the *atelier*, window doors, tackboards, and other items were part of the ongoing physical-plant-improvement budget and were installed over four years.)

Organizational Patterns and Changes to the Systems

Intertwined with the architectural patterns and commensurate physical changes came the challenging mental and emotional work of the redefinition of the role of the teacher. As the fundamental changes and agreements in this work developed, many patterns emerged, each thematically recognizable and manifested in many details, again too numerous to detail here. However, here are a few critical changes, with the correlating pattern highlighted in italics.

Figure 13.7. A "gradation of space" in a preschool classroom.

First of all, we reconsidered the typically isolated and self-contained-classroom teacher and decided to change to *teacher partnerships* so that teachers worked in teams and agreed on equal and complementary partners. We established working patterns and schedules that supported this collaboration. We rethought the use of part-time specialist teachers and created a new full-time position for the *atelierista* and new full-time positions for the hub teachers. We made the *atelierista* and hub team *classroom partners*, with a balanced interrelationship among classroom teachers and between the *atelierista* or the hub teachers. We also created a *flexible schedule* in support of interaction between the *atelier* or the hub and the different small groups of students and classroom teachers.

We realized the importance of *large group meetings as a daily affair*, and we set up regular times for classroom meetings, and whole K–elementary meetings (15-minute morning ecumenical chapel for K–6; see Figure 13.8). We discovered that *small groups* were the essential unit of most effective teaching and collaboration, so we organized the flow of each day around a pattern of small-group work (see Figure 13.9).

To *make children's learning visible*, we scheduled regular times for teacher teams and groups of teacher teams to collaborate on planning, reflect on experiences, and compose documentation. The constant documentation of our work with children and the children's learning was crucial to assessing our progress

Figure 13.8. Kindergarten class group meeting.

Figure 13.9. A small group in the hub.

and to demonstrating the effectiveness of our program to parents. Yet after about five years of work, we realized that we needed to articulate in one document a succinct and simple outline of our educational program. We composed it in a graphically clear and attractive *education map* for both present and prospective parents.

To further support *parent partnerships*, we established media for communication with parents, including daily journals outside each classroom and a weekly newsletter to be sent home. (These are now regularly posted on our website.) The journals and the newsletter improved substantially over the years as we became more sophisticated with our digital cameras and Macintosh-based graphic-arts programs (see Figure 13.10). We also established Parent–Teacher Partnership Committees, which, among other things, helped host special events to feature and celebrate children's learning accomplishments and teachers' research (see Figure 13.11).

To support *teachers as researchers*, we scheduled weekly small-group meetings for reflection on observations of experiences and hypotheses about future provocations. We also scheduled biweekly faculty meetings whose agenda included reflection on the larger scope of projects unfolding in the classrooms.

Figure 13.10. The daily journal.

Figure 13.11. A special event organized by a Parent–Teacher Partnership Committee.

We organized outside support for professional development in the Reggio Emilia Approach by retaining consultants from Reggio Emilia to visit our school each year. We created new professional development contexts in educational areas, including learning-style differences and brain development. We connected with other schools, such as the Boulder Journey School in Colorado, and locally we joined in establishing the St. Louis–Reggio Collaborative with the College School of Webster Groves, Clayton Schools' Family Center, and Webster University (see Figure 13.12). Together with our partners, we hosted Delegation Days for visiting educators highlighted by tours and observations of the schools and presentations by our teachers of their research. We encouraged our teachers to be consultants to other educators in schools around the country that were interested in our research.

Pedagogical Patterns and Changes in Our Thinking: The Learning Cycle

None of the changes listed here would have made any sense, taken on any real meaning, or had any real effect on the children without a fundamental shift from a traditional view of how children learn. We worked long and hard to

Figure 13.12. A meeting of the St. Louis–Reggio Collaborative at the exhibition *The Hundred Languages of Children*, St. Louis, 2001.

develop a collective understanding among our faculty and parents that derived from our personal histories in education. (Again, my own story related at the outset resonates only as an example of the myriad stories represented by my colleagues.) Collective understanding also derived from our new experiences with the Reggio Emilia Approach and from shared reading and professional development focused on specific areas such as brain research, literacy development, and learning styles.

Basically, our understanding falls within a constructivist theory of how children learn. A fundamental premise is that children have an innate desire to understand their world and to master ways of interacting in it. Children make sense of the world by acting on the physical and social world. Through their actions they construct knowledge and character. They are not empty vessels waiting to be filled with the body of knowledge. Rather, they are vessels that are already full—full of questions and theories. When children can act on their questions and theories, they develop knowledge and, most essentially, the ability to think deeply and make meaning.

At the St. Michael School, we found evidence for our shared understanding. Immersed in the materials available in, and provoked by, the essential experiences emanating from the *atelier* and the hub, children were learning through a pattern of inquiry and invention: cycles of hypothesis, experiment, and conclusion or cycles of experience, reflection, and expression. The cycle of inquiry is often referred to as the scientific process. The cycle of invention is often referred to as the creative process.

In any learning experience, both inquiry and invention intermingle to such degrees that, at the St. Michael School, we find it most useful to refer simply to the learning cycle. The cycle can begin and move in all directions, often seemingly at once. In the beginning, the *atelier* and the hub became the centers in the school for inquiry and invention, the central sources of experience. The experiences in the *atelier* and the hub spilled into the whole school, and eventually a natural ebb and flow of vital experiences evolved within the whole school.

Seeing the processes of learning displayed graphically in Figure 13.13 gives one a picture for understanding the development of thoughts:

- The circles represent the actions of learning.
- The intersections of the circles represent the roles of the teachers and *atelieristi*.
- The center intersection represents the ideal: "flow."

Note that the movement of learning, moving from one circle to the next, is represented as counter-clockwise dotted lines and arrows for invention (evoking the intuitive nature of process) and clockwise dotted lines and arrows for inquiry (implying the logical nature of the process). Again, the dynamic of these twin processes crosses and interweaves, just as does the complex reality of any child's thought process at any given moment.

The Learning Cycle

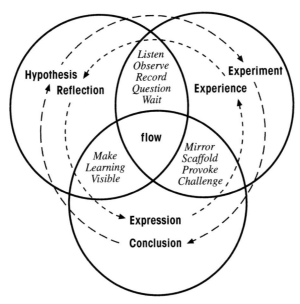

Figure 13.13. The learning cycle.

The implications of the learning cycle are complex and pervasive. All of the patterns of architecture and systems of support evolve from an understanding of the learning cycle. To use the metaphor of the chemical reaction: to supply catalytic experiences, then to convert reaction to energy, then to channel the energy, and then to enhance the composition of the final chemical, one must create an environment, architectural and organizational, that supports this pattern of learning.

SOCIAL-POLITICAL-CULTURAL CHANGE

Collaborative research in the learning cycle goes beyond its pedagogical implications, organizational systems, and architectural manifestations at the St. Michael School. Our actions, catalyzed by the *atelier* and the hub, are an attempt to respond to the present pervasive malaise in education and society. At the end of a typical Delegation Day at the St. Michael School, a visitor will almost inevitably ask, "This is all so much, so much work. Where do you find the time? Where do you find the energy?" Our thinking and work has been spurred by an almost visceral drive to create for our children something better than we had. We were also motivated by an understanding of the problems that we see all around us—an inertia in the educational, social, and political systems.

Our work reverberates among wide circles and deep thinking. In February 2004, I sat in the middle of the floor level in an opera house built in the 1700s, refurbished to its gilded glory in the 1980s, with five levels of box seating rising in a circle around the periphery. I was surrounded by 1,200 educators from 50 different nations and all seven continents. We were there to celebrate Loris Malaguzzi, who had died ten years earlier at age 74, and who had teamed with many parents and teachers from the 1940s forward in the city of Reggio Emilia to evolve a truly exemplary approach to education. The celebration took the form of a four-day conference during which we listened to 15 different speakers from 12 different countries, each with the pointed reference of progressive education but coming from a wide range of perspectives, including philosophy, economics, politics, architecture and design, and art.

This was a highly political conference, charged by the wide range of challenges present in our world, especially in child care and education. As Sergio Spaggiari, director of the Instituzione Scuole e Nidi d'Infanzia (the Reggio schools), starkly stated: "We are approaching a school-less world." Knowing the situation in the United States and listening to descriptions from Africa, Nepal, India, and Albania, we understood what he meant.

Aldo Masullo (2004), a philosopher at the University of Naples, framed the context of our present, contradictory world: "In our society, the key value is to produce more, but our essential existence is dependent on our expressive self. . . . In addition, we have moved from an industrial society to an industrial community." An industrial society is a culture driven by production in which a few people, each with a good idea, set up industry systems in which many people produced the product. Now, however, we have clearly entered an age of industrial community, in which our culture is driven by the creation of many new ideas, by many people, through networks of small and medium-size companies that are organized as highly collaborative systems.

The industrial society constructed schools in which desks were placed in rows, instruction came from one source, and the student sat alone receiving the orders and fulfilling the assigned tasks. To the extent that this is still the case, Masullo declared, schools are archaic. Clearly, an industrial community requires a different organization of schools. Schools need to be environments that cultivate creativity and collaboration, invention and innovation and inquiry, as well as fundamental skills. Ultimately, schools need to cultivate relationships. They must be essentially democratic. Masullo continued:

> Democracy is not only a legal construct or a system. It is a feeling. I am democratic if I have the feeling that the person in front of me is my brother or sister. Democracy must be nourished by our sentiments . . . just as is true of our intellect.

He then asked:

> Who are children? They are people living on the border between present and future. They are nomads who haven't found their homeland. They are on a con-

stant search for meaning in life. Therefore, school must be a place where children feel affirmed through relationships and are free to think together. This is certainly true in the schools of Reggio Emilia.

As I stood to applaud this wonderful thinker, I felt a welling up inside. Certainly, much of my emotion came from the long, hard path that my colleagues and I have traveled. There were many times when we found ourselves with initial structures in place but with minimal foundational understanding beneath them. Our best-laid plans were built on sand and washed away in the waves of events. Nevertheless, a spirit compelled us (and continues to do so) to deepen our understanding of how children learn. So at that moment, I felt a profound gratitude for our community at the St. Michael School, for I am sure that, were Aldo Masullo to visit us, he would see and feel a manifestation of just what he and we hope for.

THE PATTERNS TAKE SHAPE AND FLOW

When they all come together, the patterns outlined here create a tapestry of learning that might best be described as "flow." Mihaly Csikszentmihalyi (1990) describes this "optimal experience" as an interweaving of challenge and skills to meet that challenge. Flow occurs when a team of teachers becomes completely involved in the task, concentrating deeply and moving from one step to the next naturally, as though without thought.

In our experience at the St. Michael School, we expand this state of flow to a community level. In our whole school environment, the children have opportunities to become, in the words of our mission statement,

Thinkers who listen,
Inventors who negotiate,
Inquirers who collaborate,
Individuals who are confident in themselves.

When I was a child, I wished innocently for a school where I could think with others, be an inventor, and inquire about everything. Though my school did not fill these needs, my Vermont barnyard and parents did. When I was a young teacher, I sought to create conditions in my elementary school classroom and then in a secondary school that fostered inquiry and invention. When I ventured into architecture and village planning, I discovered, through personal inquiry and invention, ideal patterns in three-dimensional form. When I went to Reggio Emilia, I saw new versions of ideal patterns take an educational form.

At the St. Michael School, in the St. Louis–Reggio Collaborative, with our mentors at Reggio Children, and in my associations with the many educators who have visited our schools and who have invited us to their schools, I have found a network of colleagues who share aspirations to realize these ideals within education. To do so, we search for patterns. When we are at our best, our most insightful, we make brilliant connections between our past experiences and our present situations, and we discover new ways of working. In every moment of the day, in every deductive and inventive act, in every collaborative effort, in every reflective composition there is evidence of the breadth and depth of the essential action that propels our lives—learning.

REFERENCES

Alexander, C. (1977). *A pattern language*. New York: Oxford University Press.

Csikszentmihalyi, M. (1990). *Flow: The psychology of optimal experience*. New York: HarperCollins.

Masullo, A. (2004, February 25). *The rights and potentials of children and adults*. Presentation at the Crossing Boundaries conference, Reggio Emilia, Italy.

Epilogue

We end as we started, with the words of Loris Malaguzzi, as we continue to highlight his commitment to children. Here he speaks to Lella Gandini on the genesis and meaning of creativity during an interview in 1990:

> As we have chosen to work with children we can say that they are the best evaluators and the most sensitive judges of the values and usefulness of creativity. This comes about because they have the privilege of not being excessively attached to their own ideas, which they construct and reinvent continuously.

They are apt to explore, make discoveries, change their points of view, and fall in love with forms and meanings that transform themselves.

Therefore, as we do not consider creativity sacred, we do not consider it as extraordinary but rather as likely to emerge from daily experience. This view is now shared by many. We can sum up our beliefs as follows:

1. Creativity should not be considered a separate mental faculty but a characteristic of our way of thinking, knowing, and making choices.
2. Creativity seems to emerge from multiple experiences, coupled with a well-supported development of personal resources, including a sense of freedom to venture beyond the known.
3. Creativity seems to express itself through cognitive, affective, and imaginative processes. These come together and support the skills for predicting and arriving at unexpected solutions.
4. The most favorable situation for creativity seems to be interpersonal exchange, with negotiation of conflict and comparison of ideas and actions being the decisive elements.
5. Creativity seems to find its power when adults are less tied to prescriptive methods, but instead become observers and interpreters of problematic situations.
6. Creativity seems to be favored or disfavored according to the expectations of teachers, schools, families, and communities as well as society at large, according to the ways children perceive those expectations.
7. Creativity becomes more visible when adults try to be more attentive to the cognitive processes of children than to the results they achieve in various fields of doing and understanding.

Figure E.1. In the *atelier* of La Villetta School, a 5-year-old girl explores the projection of lights and color, part of a story about robots created by a group of children with the *atelierista* and their teachers.

8. The more teachers are convinced that intellectual and expressive activities have both multiplying and unifying possibilities, the more creativity favors friendly exchanges with imagination and fantasy.

9. Creativity requires that the *school of knowing* finds connections with the *school of expressing*, opening the doors (this is our slogan) to the hundred languages of children

Often when people come to us and observe our children, they ask us which magic spell we have used. We answer that their surprise equals our surprise. Creativity? It is always difficult to notice when it is dressed in everyday clothing and has the ability to appear and disappear suddenly. Our task regarding creativity is to help children climb their own mountains. No one can do more. (Malaguzzi, 1998, pp. 75–77)

REFERENCES

Malaguzzi, L. (1998). History, ideas, and basic philosophy. In C. P. Edwards, L. Gandini, & G. Forman (Eds). *The hundred languages of children: The Reggio Emilia Approach—Advanced reflections* (2nd ed.; pp. 49–97). Westport, CT: Ablex.

Glossary

Action research: A method used by qualitative researchers, often teachers, to record their own observations accurately while uncovering the meanings their subjects bring to their life experiences. Change and evolution can be the products of such collaborative efforts within a school. (See Chapter 7.)

Amiability: Derived from Loris Malaguzzi's objective for the schools in Reggio Emilia of creating an amiable environment, where children, families and teachers feel at ease. (See Chapter 7.)

Atelier: A French word referring to the kind of workspace typically used by an artist in the second half of the nineteenth century and the first half of the twentieth century. The term was chosen by Loris Malaguzzi to differentiate this space in the Reggio schools from the art room used in traditional elementary schools and to introduce a new way of working that valued children's expression, multiple materials, and the research of meaning-making processes of both the child and the adult.

Atelierista (*m & f, s.*): The person with a background in the visual arts who works in close collaboration with the teachers to supply and organize a wide variety of materials and tools in the *atelier* and around the school to provoke and observe children's creative and learning processes. The *atelierista* supports teachers in the thinking and design necessary to communicate effectively through documentation. **Atelieristi** (*m, pl.*); **atelieriste** (*f, pl.*)

Contamination/contaminated: Pointing to change through absorption of new, usually enriching elements, as in the linguistic model. As used by educators in Reggio Emilia, this term does not have a negative meaning. (See Chapter 8.)

Cycle of inquiry: The process of documentation of children's and teachers' learning, as used by Jeanne Goldhaber and her colleagues at the University of Vermont. Each step in documentation represents a process of inquiry that is based on the previous step and determines the following ones repeating itself in an outward spiral. (See Chapter 5.)

Miniatelier: A space set up in or adjacent to each classroom with the same type of or different materials and as inviting as the central *atelier*. The *miniatelier* makes it possible for small groups of children to work together with or without a teacher. (See Chapter 2.)

Pedagogista: A pedagogical coordinator who supports the work of teachers, enriches their professional development, supports their relationship with families, and facilitates the connection between teachers and the superintendent of schools. There are eight *pedagogista*s in the city of Reggio Emilia. They work as a group to support the city's 33 early childhood educational institutions, infant/toddler centers, and preschools. (See Chapter 6.)

Progettazione: Derived from the Italian verb *progettare*, meaning to design, to plan, to devise, or to project in a technical engineering sense. The noun *progettazione* is used in the educational context in opposition to *programmazione*, which implies predefined curricula, stages, and so on. The concept of *progettazione* thus implies an overarching flexible approach in which initial hypotheses are made about classroom work (as well as about staff development and relationships with parents) but are subject to modifications and changes of direction as the actual work progresses. (See Chapter 6.)

Project: Used by the educators in the Reggio Emilia schools with various meanings, depending on the context. Therefore, in translating, we have adopted the following terms:

> **Overall educational project:** When educators refer to the philosophy, organization, practice, and strategies that guide their work globally in their city. (See Chapters 2 and 6.)

> **Project-based work** or **didactic projects:** When the Reggio educators speak about their daily way of working with children in their schools. (See several chapters.)

Reggio Children: An organization designed by Loris Malaguzzi and incorporated in 1994. Reggio Children S.r.l. is supported by a majority holding of the City of Reggio Emilia plus corporate and private shareholders (including parents and teachers). The goals are to promote research and study of the philosophy of Reggio Emilia through seminars, conferences, and study tours; to document, publish, and distribute books, videos, and other media on this subject; and to maintain open channels of communication with other institutions and educators throughout the world. (See Chapter 4.)

Rich normality: A translation of the Italian phrase *una quotidianità ricca*, which describes the wealth of possibilities that should be available to children on a daily basis rather than as some exceptional opportunity. (See Chapter 10.)

Ricognizioni: An Italian word meaning "surveys" or "bird's-eye views" and used when teachers, among themselves or with a *pedagogista*, take stock of all of the aspects connected with the development of their work, or of a particular project, to make decisions about the next step to take. (See Chapter 6.)

About the Editors and Contributors

Lella Gandini holds a B.A. and M.A. in education and child study from Smith College and an Ed.D. from the University of Massachusetts, Amherst. She is an Adjunct Professor in the School of Education at the University of Massachusetts, Amherst, and a consultant in the municipality of Pistoia, Italy. She serves as liaison on behalf of Reggio Children for the dissemination of the Reggio Emilia Approach in the United States. She conducts research, lectures, consults, and writes in Italian and English on many issues in early childhood teaching, parenting, children's fears, nursery rhymes and fairy tales, bedtime rituals, and parent–teacher–child relationships. Among her many publications, she co-edited and contributed to *The Hundred Languages of Children: The Reggio Emilia Approach—Advanced Reflections* (with Carolyn Edwards and George Forman; 2nd ed., 1998), and *Bambini: The Italian Approach to Infant/Toddler Care* (with Carolyn Edwards, 2001).

Lynn Hill has worked with families and children for more than 30 years. She has been art director, social worker, child-care administrator, director of curriculum, and studio teacher. She holds a B.S., M.S., and Ph.D. from Virginia Tech, Blacksburg. She has spoken throughout the country; led student and colleague delegations to Reggio Emilia and Pistoia, Italy; and hosted international conferences at Virginia Tech. She has published articles in *Early Childhood Today* and *Innovations in Early Education: The International Reggio Exchange*. She has co-edited and written two books with colleagues Victoria Fu and Andrew Stremmel: *Teaching and Learning: Collaborative Exploration of the Reggio Emilia Approach* and *Teaching as Inquiry: Re-thinking Curriculum in Early Childhood Education*.

Louise Cadwell lives in St. Louis, Missouri, where she is Curriculum Coordinator at the College School, a private, independent school for students from preK to eighth grade. She returned to St. Louis after a one-year internship (1991–92) in the preschools of Reggio Emilia, where she worked alongside Italian educators. She holds an M.Ed. in Child Development and the Arts from Lesley University, and a Ph.D. from Union Institute. She is the author of two books: *Bringing Reggio Emilia Home: An Innovative Approach to Early Childhood Education* (Teachers College Press, 1997) and *Bringing Learning to Life: The Reggio Approach* *to Early Childhood Education* (Teachers College Press, 2003). Her work as a teacher and researcher has focused on children's development through the arts and spoken and written language, particularly as children discover their place in the natural world.

Charles Schwall is the *atelierista* at the St. Michael School in St. Louis, where he works with children and teachers in the preschool through first grade classes. He has studied the Reggio Approach since 1993, frequently presents at conferences, and works as an educational consultant in schools. His chapter, "Recognizing the Power of Materials as Languages," was included in *Next Steps Toward Teaching the Reggio Way* (J. Hendrick, editor). In addition to his role as an educator, he is also a practicing artist and holds a B.F.A. from Kansas City Art Institute and an M.F.A. from Washington University in St. Louis.

Pauline M. Baker has been an early childhood education instructor since 1992 and studio and resource teacher in the Tucson Unified School District since 1988. As a certified art teacher with a B.F.A. and an M.F.A. she consults through *Integrity Designs* for Head Start Child-Parent Centers.

Barbara Burrington teaches in the Early Childhood Pre-K–3 Teacher Education Program at the University of Vermont. She is coordinator of older toddler/preschool programs of the University of Vermont's Campus Children's Center. In collaboration with the staff and students of the Campus Children's Center, she has been engaged in the study of teaching and documentation as processes that promote inquiry and reflection among all the protagonists of a learning community. Their work has been published in early childhood education journals and as chapters in edited volumes.

Ashley Cadwell has been the headmaster of the St. Michael School in Clayton, Missouri, for 12 twelve years. He has also consulted with several schools around the United States. He was previously headmaster of the Green Mountain Valley School in Fayston, Vermont; capital gifts officer for Middlebury College in Middlebury, Vermont; and president and owner of Villages of Vermont. He holds a B.A. in American literature and an M.A. in English literature from Middlebury College and an M.A. in education administration from the University of Vermont. He is currently writing a book titled *Pedagogical Patterns*.

Lori Geismar Ryan is the director of the Clayton Schools' Family Center in St. Louis, Missouri, a public school-based early childhood and parenting education program that offers programs for families beginning in infancy. She holds a Ph.D. in early childhood education/research and evaluation from the State University of New York at Buffalo. Her current interests include cultivating constructivist teaching and learning communities for children, parents, and teachers and nurturing school change through systems-thinking approaches. She is a board member of the Association for Constructivist Teaching and the North American Reggio Emilia Alliance.

Patricia Hunter-McGrath is the *atelierista* at Evergreen Community School in Santa Monica, California, where she has developed an innovative approach to children's symbolic languages. She is an artist with more than 17 years of experience in early childhood education and has been studying the Reggio Approach for more than nine years. She also teaches an Introduction to Reggio class at Santa Monica College. She completed her first degree in human development at Stevenson College in Edinburgh, Scotland; holds a certificate in art, design and architecture from Santa Monica College; and recently completed her M.A. in Human Development with specialization in Art Education at Pacific Oaks College in Pasadena, California.

Lauren Monaco is formally trained as a fine artist and has been working in the field of early childhood since 1995. After receiving her B.F.A. from Kent State University, Kent, Ohio, she began working as the studio coordinator for the World Bank Children's Center (WBCC) in Washington, DC. She has collaborated with colleagues to host professional development initiatives for other educators in her area. She has also created and implemented a unique system of sharing skills, techniques, and multiple languages with the large staff at the World Bank.

Cathy Weisman Topal began her career as a junior high school art teacher in a public school. She is now a studio art teacher at the Center for Early Childhood Education and Smith College Campus School and is a lecturer in visual arts education in the Department of Education and Child Study at Smith College in Northampton, Massachusetts. She has written three books: *Children, Clay and Sculpture*, *Children and Painting*, and *Beautiful Stuff! Learning with Found Materials* (with Lella Gandini). She recently created the interactive CD-ROM program *Thinking with a Line*.

Index

Page numbers followed by italic letter *f* refer to photographs or drawings.

Action research, definition of, 197
Adreon, Christina, 27
Adult Day Services (ADS), Virginia Tech, 73
Aesthetic sensitivity, and materials, 67–68
Aesthetic thought, 139
Albers, Susan, 39
Alexander, Christopher, 145, 176, 182
All Saints' Episcopal Church of Beverly Hills, 114
Alphabets of materials, 13–15, 134
  definition of, 13
Amiability
  and community, 74
  definition of, 197
Anderson, Hans Christian, 28, 30
Architecture, 176–179
Art
  adults' creations
    collaborative paintings, 130–131, 130*f*, 131*f*
    mural, 79*f*
    sketch, 179*f*
  children at work
    with clay, 49*f*
    with colors, 78*f*
    with flowers, 88*f*, 89
    with lines and shapes, 120–124, 121*f*, 123*f*
    with paint, 37, 53*f*, 55*f*, 100*f*, 101*f*
    with paper, 135*f*
    with pencil and paper, 52*f*
    self-portraits, 26
  children's creations, 47–48
    in clay, 25*f*, 26*f*
    collages of natural materials, 124*f*
    displayed in hallway museum, 78–79
    of iron and clay, 141*f*
    mobiles, 154*f*
    on paper, 9*f*, 12*f*, 14*f*, 29*f*, 30*f*, 69*f*, 160*f*, 172*f*
    theater curtain, 142*f*
    with wire, 171*f*
  and creativity, 172
  as essential dimension of thought, 172
  as everyday right, 172
  painting, 159, 171*f*
Art as Experience (Dewey), 16
Atelier (studio), 146–147, 190–191
  and children of different ages, 49, 102
  and the city, 140–141
  and classroom, 74
  creativity and, 170–172
  definition of, 197
  digital, 137*f*
  establishment of, 7, 75–80
    difficulties in, 76–77, 84
  evolution of, 6, 10
  furniture in, 109–112
  greenhouse in, 182*f*, 183
  group visits to, 11
  and hundred languages theory, 71
  intergenerational, 80–90
  photographs of
    at Child Development Lab School (CDLS): first, 77*f*; second, under construction, 83*f*
    at Diana School, 100*f*, 178*f*
    at Infant/Toddler Center Bellelli, 66*f*
    at La Villetta School, 135*f*, 137*f*
    at Pablo Neruda School, 96*f*
    at St. Michael School: before, 20*f*; after, 21*f*, 31*f*, 182*f*
    at University of Vermont, 51*f*
    at Van Buskirk Elementary School, 110*f*, 111*f*, 112*f*

Atelier (studio) (*continued*)
  vs. separate "art room," 40
  simplicity and, 56–57
  student teachers in, 50
  and technology, 8, 98
  views of
    as centralized space, 10
    as complex organization, 10
    entire school as, 114, 169–170
    as laboratory for thinking, 49
    as mind-set, 59
    as separate space, 125–126
    as tool box, 99
    as workshop for children's ideas, 17
Atelierista (*atelieristi*)
  beginning, 137–138
  co-teachers and development of, 169
  definition of, 197
  evolving role of, 6
  expense of, 10
  freedom of, 10
  in infant/toddler center, 63–64
  and *pedagogista,* 68–69
  professional development of, 141
  and teachers
    complementarity of, 59, 61
    in infant/toddler centers, 64–66
Autonomy, teachers', 103
Azzariti, Jennifer, 4, 32, 34, 46, 125
  interview with, 39–46

Baker, Pauline M., 4, 105, 107, 202
  narrative by, 107–113
Bambini (magazine), 6
Barchi, Paola, 4, 61*f,* 71
  interview with, 58–63
Bateson, G., 139, 145, 147
Beautiful Stuff: Learning with Found Mate-
  rials (C. Topal & L. Gandini), 50
Beauty
  children's understanding of, 53
  importance of, 132
Bells, 159, 163
Bohm, D., 145
Boredom, and traditional schooling, 176
Borghi, Ettore, 169, 170, 173
Boulder Journey School, 189
Bulletin boards, walls as, 184
Burri, Alberto, 65, 102, 140, 141*f*
Burrington, Barbara, 4, 46, 202
  chapter by, 47–57

Cadwell, Ashley, 4, 17, 19, 173, 177*f,* 202
  chapter by, 175–194

Cadwell, Louise, 1, 4, 17, 19, 143, 153,
  156–158, 157*f,* 177–178, 201–202
  chapters coauthored by, 1–5, 144–168
Cambron-McCabe, N., 145
Campus Children's Center, University of
  Vermont, 4, 48
Capital Children's Museum, 4, 32, 39
Capra, Fritjof, 145
Carini, E., 6, 9
  interview by, 6–9
Carnegie Mellon University, 39
Castagnetti, Marina, 59*f*
CD, reflectivity of, 155
CDLS. *See* Child Development Lab School
  (CDLS)
Center for Documentation and Educational
  Research, 97
Center for Early Childhood Education,
  Smith College, 119–124
Ceramic art, 25
Change, difficulty of, 40, 74
Child(ren)
  and beauty, understanding of, 53
  creativity of, 1–2
  and exhibitions of contemporary art, 140
  image of, 7, 177
  as listeners, 170
  potential of, 1–2
  respect for, importance of, 33
  rich in resources and interests, 7
  subjectivity of, 169
  very young, 63–64
  views of
    as conduits of energy and ideas *vs.*
     empty vessels, 145, 170
    constructivist, 7, 190
    as full *vs.* empty vessels, 190
    interactionist, 7
    as nomads, 192–193
  world of, 109
Child Development Lab School (CDLS),
  Virginia Tech, 73
Children and Painting (Topal), 126
Children, Art, Artists: The Expressive Lan-
  guage of Children, the Artistic Language
  of Alberto Burri (Vecchi & Giudici), 65
Cicero, Marcus Tullius, 86
Classroom
  spatial organization of, 184–185
  at St. Michael School, photograph of, 185*f*
Clay, 24–25
Clayton Schools' Family Center, 18, 144, 189
Clouds and rain, children's theories on,
  159–160

Co-teachers
  and the *atelierista,* 169, 173
  and diversity, 169, 173
Colla, Lucia, 4, 58, 66*f,* 71–72
  interview with, 63–68
Collaboration, faculty, 33–34, 35*f,* 37, 126
  on paintings, 130–131, 130*f,* 131*f*
College School of Webster Groves, 18, 19,
  144, 179, 189
Colleges and universities. *See also* Schools
  Carnegie Mellon University, 39
  Framingham State Teachers College, 47
  Kent State University, 124
  Smith College, 39, 119
  Stevenson College (Edinburgh), 114
  University of Massachusetts, 33
  University of Naples, 192
  University of Vermont, 48
  Virginia Tech, 73
  Webster University, 18, 189
Color, and younger children, 78
Commitment, importance of, 33
Community
  characteristics of, 91
  definition of, 75
  and interdependence, 147
  intergenerational, establishment of, 85
Community Peace Mural. *See under* Ver-
  mont, University of
Compartmentalization of knowledge, 172
Competent audience, definition of, 170
Complexity, 167–168
Constructivism, 7, 190
Consultancy to Schools in the United
  States (organization), 32
Contamination/contaminated, 98, 141
  definition of, 197
Convergent thinking, 170–171
Costa, A. L., 166
Creative thinking, and solitude, 170
Creativity, 8, 195–196
  and art, 172
  and the *atelier,* 170–172
Cruickshank-Schott, Patti, 125, 127
Csikszentmihalyi, Mihaly, 193
Cuffaro, H. K., 113
Culture and everyday life, mountain
  metaphor for, 16
Cutting, children's natural interest in, 120
Cycle, learning, 190–191, 191*f*
Cycle of inquiry, 53
  definition of, 197–198
Cyert Center for Early Education (Carnegie
  Mellon), 39

Danforth Foundation, 18, 179
Davoli, Mara, 3, 4, 6, 15, 104–105
  interviews with, 10–12, 94–99
Day, Christopher, 108–109
Delegation Days, 108, 189, 191
Dellmann-Jenkins, M., 82
Democracy, 192
Design, and children's beliefs, 109
Dewey, John, 1, 16, 31
Diana School, 10, 17, 25, 58, 68, 100, 103,
  148, 178
  atelier of, 100*f,* 178*f*
  piazza of, 178*f*
Diary or journal, classroom, 97–98, 187, 188*f*
  Morning Meeting Journal, St. Michael
    School, 151, 151*f*
Didactics (teaching practice), and pedagogical theory, 58
Divergent thinking, 170–171
Diversity, and co-teachers, 169, 173
Documentation, 102, 139–140, 161, 186–187.
    See also Diary or journal, classroom;
    Portfolios
  development of, 60–61
  documentaries for parents, 97
  good *vs.* bad, 42–43
  as guide for new teachers, 95
  importance of, 60
  as instrument, not product, 37, 38*f*
  new forms of, search for, 60
  power of, 86, 87*f*
  of processes *vs.* phases, 140
  review of, by *pedagogista* and *atelierista,* 70
  as script, 142
  seminar, "Documentation on the Walls,"
    63
  and shared experience, 41
  with slides, 65–66
    vs. printed booklet, 70–71
  technology and, 60, 97
    digital portfolio, 61*f*
  types of, 103, 147–148
  videotapes and, 42–43
  visual communication and, 70
  vs. written evaluations, 63
"Documentation on the Walls" (seminar), 63
Dramatic play, 156–159
Droegemeier, Eleanor, 108
Du Four, R., 145
Dutton, J., 145

Eacker, R., 145
Easels, 24*f,* 86
Eckhardt, Meister, 124

Education Development Center, 165
Education map, 187
Educative Assessment (Wiggins), 166
Environment
  classroom, 11
  as extra teacher, 181
  for scientific learning, 166
Evergreen Community School (Santa
    Monica), 4, 113–119
  room full of paper, 115–119, 115*f*, 116*f*,
    117*f*, 118*f*
Exchange, intergenerational, 80–90, 86*f*, 87*f*,
    88*f*, 89*f*, 90*f*
  difficulties of, 85
Experiments, with light and reflection,
    164*f*
Expressive education
  and the *atelier*, 7
  vs. traditional education, 7
Expressive language(s), 10–11
  and digital technology, 12–13
*Expressive Languages of Children: The Artistic
    Language of Alberto Burri* (exhibition),
    poster for, 141*f*
Expressivity, 8
  as structure, 142

Feng shui, 185
Filippini, Tiziana, 4, 58, 65, 67, 72
  interview with, 68–71
First Presbyterian Nursery School (Santa
    Monica), 37
FISM. *See* Italian Federation of Nursery
    Schools (FISM)
Flexible schedule, 186
Floor plans and maps, 11–12
Flow, 193
  in the learning cycle, 190–191, 191*f*
Flowers, dried, 88*f*, 89, 121*f*
Forman, George, 13
Frameworks, 146–147
Framingham State Teachers College, 47
Fronzoni, A. G., 99
Fruit, D., 82
Fullan, M. G., 145
Furniture, 109–112
  block platforms, 110
  child-sized, 109–110, 109*f*

Galardini, A., 132
Gallas, Karen, 165
Gallery, hallway as, 184
  at St. Michael School, photograph of,
    184*f*

Gambetti, Amelia, 4, 18, 24, 32, 36*f*, 40, 43,
    45, 46
  interview with, 33–39
Gandini, Lella, 1, 3, 32, 49, 77, 92, 108, 169,
    195, 201
  chapter coauthored by, 1–5
  interviews by, 10–15, 32–46, 58–71,
    94–105, 133–142, 169–173
  visits Van Buskirk Elementary School, 113
Geismar Ryan, Lori, 4, 143, 202–203
  chapter coauthored by, 144–168
Geography of the imagination, 49
"Getting to Know Materials, Ourselves,
    Our World" (documentation), 52
Giovannini, D., 132
Giudici, C., 65
Grammar of materials. *See* Alphabets of
    materials
Grandparents
  role of in U.S. *vs.* Italy, 82
  and room full of paper, 118
Graphic design, 99–100
Greenhouse, in the *atelier*, 182*f*, 183
Griff, M., 82
Grollman, S., 166
Group work, photographs of, 149*f*, 186*f*, 187*f*
Groups, size and nature of, 147
Growth
  and experience, 36
  intellectual, characteristics of, 166–167
Guerra, Melissa, 149, 150, 156–163, 157*f*

Habits of Mind: A Developmental Series
    (Costa & Kallick), 166
Hawkins, David, 1
Head Start, 4
Hill, Lynn, 1, 4, 72, 74, 78, 201
  chapter by, 73–93
  chapter coauthored by, 1–5
Hub, 190, 191
  definition of, 175
  at St. Michael School, photographs of,
    183*f*, 187*f*
The Hundred Languages of Children (exhibit),
    6, 25, 39–40
The Hundred Languages of Children (poem),
    113
Hundred languages theory, 97, 169, 182,
    196. *See also* Language(s)
  and the *atelier*, 71
  in practice, 128
Hunter-McGrath, Patricia, 4, 105, 107, 113,
    203
  narrative by, 113–119

Images, importance of, 9
Imagination, geography of, 49
Industrial society *vs.* industrial community, 192
Infant/toddler centers
    atelieristi in, 63–64
    fragile identity of teachers in, 64
    increasingly strong identity of teachers in, 138–139
Infant/Toddler Center Bellelli, 58
Inquiry, cycle of, 53
    definition of, 197–198
Instituzione Scuole e Nidi d'Infanzia, 192
Interdependence, and community, 147
Intergenerational exchange, 80–90, 86*f*, 87*f*, 88*f*, 89*f*, 90*f*
    difficulties of, 85
Interior light, in the *atelier,* 183
Italian Federation of Nursery Schools (FISM), 97
Italian Women's Union, 47

Jazz, as metaphor for working together, 148
Journal, for faculty communication, 48–49
Journal or diary, classroom, 97–98, 187, 188*f*
    Morning Meeting Journal, St. Michael School, 151, 151*f*
Joy, 178, 181

Kallick, B., 166
Kent State University, 124
Kleiner, A., 145
Knowledge, compartmentalization of, 172

La Villetta School, 6, 12, 17, 99, 196
Lambert, D., 82
Lambert, L., 145
Language(s). *See also* Hundred languages theory
    as communicable form of thought, 71
    contaminations between, 98
    expressive, 10–11, 60, 103, 141
        development of, 133–134
        and digital technology, 12–13
    pattern, 176–177
    representational, 53, 54
    symbolic, children's, 48
Leadership and the New Science: Discovering Order in a Chaotic World (Wheatley), 145–146
Leaf, transformation of, 69, 69*f*
Learning
    nonlinear, 147, 167
    scientific, 166

Learning cycle, 190–191, 191*f*
Lewin, A. W., 32, 34, 40
Light
    and color, studies of, 27–30, 95–97, 196*f*
    interior, in the *atelier,* 183
    natural, 183
    and reflection, 164*f*
        experiments with, 148–155, 153*f*, 154*f*, 164*f*
    and shadow, experiments with, 27
Light boxes, 43
Lines and shapes, 120–124
Listening, 45*f*, 103
    and children, 170
    design as, 109
Little, Lester, 39
Lucas, T., 145

Macintosh (computer), 187
Malaguzzi, Loris, 3, 4, 10, 15, 17, 31, 34, 60, 99, 102, 133, 178, 179, 196
    and the idea of the *atelier,* 6, 38
    interview with, 6–9
    memorial service for, 192
    quoted, 1, 54, 107–108, 109, 195–196
Maps and floor plans, 11–12
Marsden, Carolyn, 108
Martiri Di Sesso Centro Verde Preschool, 47
Masullo, Aldo, 173, 192–193
Materials
    and aesthetic sensitivity, 67–68
    in *atelier,* 111*f*
    children's first encounters with, 13, 114–115
    children's knowledge of, 14
    collections of, 21–23
        parents' contributions to, 43–44, 77
        photographs of, 22*f*, 56*f*
        as portable *atelier,* 122*f*, 123*f*
    nature of, 13, 20, 113
    organization of, 177
    sorting, categorizing, and displaying, 50
    and techniques, 11
    transformations and modifications of, 14
    types of, 21–23
        found *vs.* prefabricated, 44–45
        natural and recycled, 50, 112, 121*f*, 122*f*, 123*f*
        paints, 127*f*, 161*f*, 162*f*
        paper, room full of, 115–119
        reflective, 153–154
Matter *vs.* relationships, 147
Maturana, H., 145, 147

Meetings, 49, 59*f*
  daily, 186
  with parents, 188*f*
  of teachers, 129*f*, 157*f*
    with paint-mixing, 129*f*
    planning, 186–187
    in room full of paper, 118
    from several schools, 189*f*
  of whole classes, 186*f*
Meister Eckhardt, 124
MELC (Model Early Learning Center), 4,
    32–36, 35*f*, 36*f*, 39, 40
Mennino, Isabella, 4, 58, 94, 105
  interview with, 99–106
Microprocesses of learning, 141–142
Miniatelier (ministudio), 6, 37, 80, 95–96,
    146–147, 159
  definition of, 198
  development of, 11–12, 38
  organizational difficulties of, 63
  photographs of, at Child Development
    Lab School (CDLS), 80*f*, 81*f*
  seminar on, 62–63
Model Early Learning Center (MELC), 4,
    32–36, 35*f*, 36*f*, 39, 40
Monaco, Lauren, 4, 106, 107, 124, 203
  narrative by, 124–131
Montessori, Maria, 1
Morin, Edgar, 139
Morning Meeting Journal, St. Michael
    School, 151, 151*f*
Museums and art exhibits, as source of
    ideas, 44
Music, 44, 159, 163

National Association for the Education of
    Young Children, 108
The National Learning Center (TNLC), 32
National Science Foundation, 166
Neruda School. *See* Pablo Neruda School
Networks, 192
Newsletter, weekly, 187
Notebooks, children's, 113

Observation, value of, 33
Olds, Anita, 109
Organizational systems, 176
Over-specialization of knowledge, 172
Overhead projector, 27
Ownership, children's sense of, 15, 16

Pablo Neruda School, 6, 10–11, 94, 96*f*
Paint and painting, 23–24, 126–128, 127*f*,
    129*f*, 161, 161*f*, 162*f*

Paper, room full of, 115–119, 115*f*, 116*f*, 117*f*,
    118*f*
  teachers' meeting in, 118
Parent–Teacher Partnership Committees, 187
Parents
  documentaries for, 97
  at holiday party, 44, 44*f*
  materials provided by, 43–44, 77
  meetings with, 43–44
  role of, in building collections of mate-
    rials, 35, 50
  worries of, about reading and writing, 39
Pattern language, 176–177
A Pattern Language (Alexander), 176
Pedagogical Patterns (A. Cadwell, book in
    progress), 182
Pedagogista (pedagogical coordinator)
  and *atelierista*, 68–69
  definition of, 198
  role of, 68–72
Peter Pan, 149
Philosophy, educational, 176
Photographs, as classroom decoration, 113
Piaget, Jean, 1, 114, 171
Piazza, Giovanni, 3, 4, 6, 12, 15, 60, 62*f*, 98,
    143
  interviews with, 12–15, 133–138
Play, and creative thinking, 171
Portfolios, 134–137. *See also* Documentation
  digital, 134
  telling stories with, 135–136
Prisms, 155
Professional development, 7
Progettazione (concept)
  definition of, 198
  and *ricognizioni*, 68
Progressive movement, Italian, 1
Project, definition of, 198
Project-based work, 11
Projector, overhead, 27

Quantum physics, 145
Questions, importance of, 2, 33, 41
Quinti, Barbara, 4, 94, 105
  interview with, 99–106

Radke, Mary Beth, 33
Rain and clouds, children's theories on,
    159–160
Rainbows, symbolism of, 55
"Realizing Our Right to a Sanctuary"
    (documentation), 52
Reelaboration and reinvention, 69, 69*f*
Reggio Approach, 1, 2, 6, 12, 40, 147

Reggio Children (organization), 4, 32, 72, 193
definition of, 198
Reggio Tutta (postcard collection), 6f, 9f, 12f, 14f
Relationships *vs.* matter, 147
Respect for children, importance of, 33
Ribizzi, Laura, interview with, 58–63
Rich normality, 134
definition of, 199
Ricognizioni (surveys, bird's-eye views)
definition of, 199
and *progettazione,* 68
Rinaldi, Carla, 4, 169, 173
interview with, 169–170
lecture by, 170–172
Roland, Frances, 27
Rubizzi, Laura, 4, 59f, 71
Ruozzi, M., 67

St. Louis Art Museum, 23
St. Louis–Reggio Collaborative, 4, 18, 144, 155–156, 189, 189f, 193
Delegation Days, 108, 189, 191
St. Michael School, 3, 4, 16–31, 144, 173, 175–194, 179f
transformation of, 19–20, 179–189
organizational, 185–189
physical, 182–185
Sanchez, Ann, 108
Schafer, Alice, 114
Schedule, flexible, 186
Schneider, Karen, 149, 150, 156–159, 157f
School
as *atelier,* 114, 169–170
as living *vs.* nonliving system, 144, 148
traditional
as factory, 145
miseries of, 109, 175–176
"transparent," and contemporary culture, 60
Schools. *See also* Colleges and Universities
Center for Early Childhood Education, Smith College, 119–124
Child Development Lab School (CDLS), Virginia Tech, 73
Clayton Schools' Family Center, 18
College School of Webster Groves, 18, 19, 144, 179, 189
Cyert Center for Early Education (Carnegie Mellon), 39
Diana School, 10, 17, 100, 103, 178
atelier of, 100f, 178f
piazza of, 178f

Evergreen Community School (Santa Monica), 113–119
room full of paper, 115–119, 115f, 116f, 117f, 118f
First Presbyterian Nursery School (Santa Monica), 37
groups of
Instituzione Scuole e Nidi d'Infanzia, 192
Italian Federation of Nursery Schools (FISM), 97
St. Louis–Reggio Collaborative, 18
Infant/Toddler Center Bellelli, 58
La Villetta School, 6, 12, 17
Martiri Di Sesso Centro Verde Preschool, 47
Model Early Learning Center (MELC), 32–36, 35f, 36f, 39, 40
Pablo Neruda School, 6, 10–11, 94, 96f
St. Michael School, 16–31, 173, 175–194, 179f
transformation of, 19–20, 179–189
University of Massachusetts Laboratory School, 33
University of Vermont, Campus Children's Center, 48
Van Buskirk Elementary School (Tucson), 107–113
World Bank Children's Center, 4, 39, 124–126
Schwall, Charles, 1, 3, 4, 15, 38, 143, 148, 149, 152, 156–162, 157f, 202
chapter by, 16–31
chapters coauthored by, 1–5, 144–168
Science, theories about rainclouds, 160f
Second Law of Thermodynamics, 146
Seminars, with other schools, 62–63
Senge, P., 145
Sergiovanni, Thomas, 75, 91
Sheldon-Harsch, L., 32
Simplicity, and the *atelier*/studio, 56–57
Smith, B., 145
Smith College, 4, 39, 119
"The Snow Queen" (Anderson), 30
Solitude, and creative thinking, 170
Sound and light, experiments with, 159, 163
Space
activities in, 178–179
characteristics of, 107–108
gradations of, 184–185
transformed into place, 108, 113
Space frames, 146–147
Spaggiari, Sergio, 54, 192
Stevenson College (Edinburgh), 114

Strozzi, Paola, 59*f*
Student teachers, in the *atelier*, 50
Studio. *See Atelier* (studio)
Sun and sunlight, 154–155
Sunlight and Reflection Project, 27,
      152–155, 153*f*, 154*f*
Systems
    living *vs.* nonliving, 144, 148
    open *vs.* closed, 145–146
    organizational, 176
Systems theory, 145–146, 167–168

Tackboard walls, 184
Talking Their Way into Science (Gallas), 165
Teachers
    and *atelieristi*, in infant/toddler centers,
        64–66
    autonomy, importance of, 103
    teams and partnerships, 186
    turnover among, 73, 94–95
Teaching practice (didactics), and peda-
        gogical theory, 58
Technology
    and the *atelier*, 8, 26, 98
    digital *atelier*, 137*f*
    and documentation, 60, 97, 187
    digital portfolio, 61*f*
Territoriality, 74
Texture, and older children, 78
Thinking/thought
    aesthetic, 139
    convergent, 170–171
    creative
        in children and adults, 172
        context of, 171–172
        and play, 171
        and solitude, 171
    divergent, 170–171
    linear *vs.* nonlinear, 147, 167
    scientific, 165
Time frames, 146
Tinkerbell, 149, 162
TNLC (The National Learning Center), 32
Topal, Cathy Weisman, 4, 49, 77, 106, 107,
        119, 126, 203
    narrative by, 119–124

Treasure hunt, 89–90
Tree, decoration of, 89–90, 90*f*
Trust, reciprocal, importance of, 33–34, 37
Tucson Unified School District, 4, 108
Turnover, staff, 73, 94–95

Unexpected City (project), 67–68, 104, 105*f*
    slide presentation *vs.* booklet, 70–71
University of Massachusetts Laboratory
        School, 33
University of Naples, 192

Van Buskirk Elementary School (Tucson),
        107–113
Varela, F., 145, 147
Vecchi, Vea, ix–x, 4, 10–11, 25, 42–43, 58–59,
        65, 67, 100, 102, 133, 143, 148, 156
    interview with, 138–142
    quoted, 63–64
Vermont, University of
    Campus Children's Center, 48
    Community Peace Mural, 54–56, 55*f*, 57*f*
    Living and Learning Complex, 54–55, 55*f*
Vessels, children as, 145, 170, 190
Vicolo Trivelli, handbag display at, 104,
        105*f*
Virginia Tech
    Child Development Lab School (CDLS),
        4, 73
    Department of Human Development,
        76
Vision statement, 48
Vygotsky, Lev, 114

WBCC. *See* World Bank Children's Center
Webster University, 18, 189
Wheatley, Margaret J., 145–148
Wiggins, Grant, 166
Wolf, Marcia, 108
Wonder
    and surprise, 2, 8
    and trust, 124
Work plans, 11
World Bank Children's Center (WBCC), 4,
        39, 124–126
Worth, K., 166